Latin American History
through its
Art and Literature

Jack Child

American University

Copley Custom Textbooks

An imprint of XanEdu Custom Publishing

ISBN 13: 978-1-58152-540-3
ISBN 10: 1-58152-540-0

About the cover:

The cover was inspired by a well-known work ("The Presidential Family of Latin America") by the Colombian painter Fernando Botero. It portrays the conservative power structure that gave Latin America a long period of stable (but non-democratic) rule: the alliance of landowner-politician, army officer and priest. The "three legged stool" of representatives of economic-political, physical, and spiritual power kept the lid on for almost three centuries, but led to explosive revolutionary situations in Mexico (1910), Cuba (1959), and Nicaragua (1979). Uncle Sam is portrayed as manipulating the landowner-politician. Two students did the art work: Daniel Silver the original black-and-white drawing, and Jen White the colorizing.

Copley Custom Textbooks
An imprint of XanEdu Custom Publishing
138 Great Road
Acton, Massachusetts 01720
800-562-2147

LATIN AMERICAN HISTORY THROUGH ITS ART AND LITERATURE

By Jack Child, American University, May 2007

TABLE OF CONTENTS

Acknowledgements
1 Introduction 1
2 The Geographic Setting 3
3 The Pre-Columbian Period: Overview and the Maya 13
4 The Aztecs and the Incas 23
5 The Encounter 37
6 The Conquest of Mexico 47
7 The Conquest of Peru and Chile 57
8 The Indigenous Perspective and "The Defender of the Indians" 67
9 The Colonial Baroque 77
10 Independence and Neoclassicism 93
11 Neoclassicism - Forging the New Nations 109
12 Civilization and Barbarism 121
13 Romanticism 133
14 Costumbrismo 149
15 Positivism, Realism, Naturalism 161
16 Modernismo 171
17 The U.S. Emerges 183
18 The Mexican Revolution 193
19 20th Century Nationalism, Ethnic Relationships, Role of Women 211
20 Guatemalan Reform/Revolution 229
21 The Cuban Revolution; Che Guevara 237
22 Central America: Conflict and Peace 249
Index 261
About the author 268

Acknowledgments.

This text would not have been possible without the assistance of a great number of individuals, including the long-suffering students in earlier offerings of the course.

A number of American University administrators contributed with their encouragement and support, especially grants for the drawings which are an essential visual component of the text and course: Deans Ann S. Ferren, Ivy Broder, Kay Mussell and Haig Mardirosian. Support from Language and Foreign Studies Department chairs is also much appreciated: Professors John Schillinger, Naomi Baron, Alina Israeli Nadia Harris and Olga Rojer. Also colleagues in the Spanish and Latin American Studies Section, several of whom taught sections of the course: Ana Serra, Brenda Werth, Elena Olsen, Marlene Temes, Shelley Harshe, Esther Holtermann, Alison Marcoff, Lisa Andion, Rut Román, Claudia Caicedo, Consuelo Hernández, and Amy Oliver.

Technical assistance was provided by word processing and computer graphics specialists María M. Macarena, María M. Mactusi and María Diez. Vanessa Mueller provided ruthless (but exteremely helpful) editorial comments. Moral support came from Leslie Morginson-Eitzen, Evita Canal de Beagle, Mayo and La Perrichola.

Most of the drawings were done by students, many of whom also took earlier offerings of the course: Ferdinanda Hogroian, Kevin Kim, Daniel Neuland, Ilya Schillinger, Jen White, Jackie Fortier, and Daniel Silver.

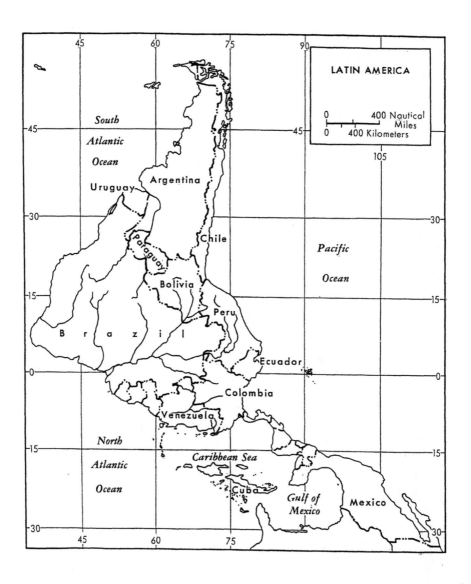

Map: a different perspective on Latin America

1: Introduction

The Text and the General Education Program.

This text has been developed for use with The American University's General Education Course LFS-210, "Latin America: History, Art, Literature". We felt it was necessary to write it because we were not able to find any text, or combination of texts, which achieved the purpose of the course. The first edition of the text, was prepared in the Summer of 1990, with several updates. This version was prepared in 2007.

The purpose of the course, as described in the syllabus, is:

This undergraduate General Education course explores the history of Latin America through the words of the writer, the brush of the painter, the pen of the cartoonist, and the lens of the photographer. It will include the Latin (Spanish/Portuguese+Islamic), the African, and the Indigenous cultural heritages in Latin American history, and will seek to show how these strands have combined to produce a unique Latin American culture. The relationship to Anglo-America, and especially the United States, will also be explored on a cross-cultural basis.

The major objective of this course is to study Latin America as a unique culture-area by using an interdisciplinary approach (history, art, and literature). History will be the basic discipline used to organize the course; art and literature will be used to illustrate and to provide windows of insight into that history with visual, plastic, and written images.

Relationship to the General Education Program.

The course must be placed in the context of the University's General Education Program. Again, quoting from the course syllabus:

Course LFS-210, "Latin America: History, Art, Literature" is a second level course in Cluster 2 (Multicultural Experience) of Curricular Area 3 (the Global and Multicultural Experience), in the University's General Education Program. This dimension of the curriculum is designed to create an informed understanding of our interdependent world and to foster greater intercultural awareness and communication. Courses in this area seek to develop an understanding of non-Western cultures and traditions. They also address both timeless and newly emergent issues of international relations, and provide students with new forms of cultural diversity and its effects on the interaction of peoples and states. In order to complete Curricular Area 3 with course LFS-210, "Latin America: History, Art, Literature", you must have previously completed one of the following foundation courses in Area 3: Anthropology-110: Culture: The Human Mirror OR Literature-150: Third World Literature OR Religion-185 Forms of the Sacred: Religions of the East OR School of International Service-140 Cross-Cultural Communications OR Sociology-110 Views from the Third World.

The rationale for linkages to each foundation course:

ANTH-110: Culture: The Human Mirror: the course examines the contribution various Latin American cultures have made to the pluralism of the contemporary world (including the US).
LIT-150 Third World Literature: the course uses Latin American literature as a key element.
RELG-185 Forms of the Sacred: Religions of the East: I cant think of any except a comparative approach.
SIS-140: Cross-cultural Communications: the course emphasizes the unique features of various Latin American cultures and how they relate to other cultures
SOCY-110 Views from the Third World: Examines those parts of Latin America that are "Third World".

Organization of the Text:

The text is organized into 22 chapters corresponding to the semester's scheduled class sessions (see the Syllabus for each day's assignment). With some exceptions, each lesson consists of a reading assignment from this text, the instructor's list of Power Point slides which will be shown in class, and a literature reading. The literature readings come from both this text as well as an anthology of short stories.

There will also be optional outside readings dealing with Latin American art, history, and current events. This text is an integrator of the outside texts, the instructor's class lectures, the slides shown in class, and other materials. The text will pull together the three basic disciplines which are the heart of the course: history, art, literature. You should use the text as your basic guide to help you do this and in the process learn more about Latin America in an interdisciplinary way.

Readers may obtain a free CD-RoM with the Power Point lectures for each chapter by contacting the Department of Language and Foreign Studies, The American University, Washington, DC, 20016.

2: The Geographic Setting

What is "Latin America"?

This is a seemingly simple question, but there is no simple or clear-cut answer. The term "Latin" suggests those nations whose basic language is derived from Roman Latin,
and in the Americas this would include Spanish, Portuguese
and French. But to speak of "Latin" America leaves out two
basic population groups: the Indigenous (Indian) one, and the
African one. Perhaps a more meaningful (but awkward) term
would be "Latin-Indo-African America", but that term would
then include areas of the United States and Canada.

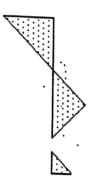

We should realize also that the term "Latin America"
was not invented by the Latin Americans. It came into popular use starting in France in the 1860's during the time the
French were intervening in Mexico, and wanted to stress the common heritage.

**2.1: Stylized
Hemisphere**

French intellectuals used the term later because many Latin American nations
looked to France for cultural and political models. "Latin Americans" sometime
resent the term because it tends to lump them all together into one single category. Although they acknowledge their cultural commonalties, they under-
standably also like to stress their individual identities, and often they prefer to
call themselves Mexicans, Argentines, Brazilians, etc.

Where does it begin and end?

We also run into problems attempting to define where Latin America begins
and ends. If we take a strictly state-oriented approach (more on this below), we
could say that Latin America begins at the US-Mexico border and ends at the tip
of South America. Let's take another look at that starting point. While politically
it may be valid, culturally there is a border area between Mexico and the U.S.
which is neither Hispanic nor Anglo alone. A similar phenomenon occurs in
southern Florida, to such a degree that a hot current political issue is whether or

not English should be declared the official language so as to protect it from further incursions by Spanish. From a cultural perspective we could say that Latin America begins on the west coast of North America somewhere between Los Angeles and San Francisco, and on the east coast a few miles north of Miami.

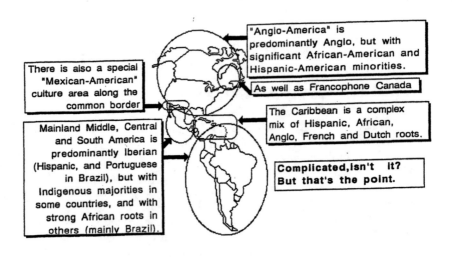

There is also a special "Mexican-American" culture area along the common border

"Anglo-America" is predominantly Anglo, but with significant African-American and Hispanic-American minorities.

As well as Francophone Canada

Mainland Middle, Central and South America is predominantly Iberian (Hispanic, and Portuguese in Brazil), but with Indigenous majorities in some countries, and with strong African roots in others (mainly Brazil).

The Caribbean is a complex mix of Hispanic, African, Anglo, French and Dutch roots.

Complicated, isn't it? But that's the point.

2.2: Culture-areas of the Western hemisphere

Defining the southern boundary of Latin America gets us into a political problem. At first glance the answer seems obvious: the tip of South America, or perhaps the large triangular-shaped island of Tierra del Fuego, or even the Island of Cape Horn, which is the last island directly linked to South America. But if we take a look at a map centered on the South Pole, we can see that there is a long and narrow peninsula which seems to reach out from Antarctica to South America. There is geological continuity (the Antarandes mountains) between the two which is interrupted by only 600 miles of ocean (the Drake Passage). And two South American nations, Argentina and Chile, claim that their national sovereignty extends as far south as one can go: the South Pole. Several other South American nations, while not claiming sovereignty in Antarctica, have a presence there and feel that the one-quarter segment of Antarctica which faces them should be considered "South American Antarctica". To add to the political sensitivity, Great Britain also has an Antarctic claim (linked to their possession of the Falklands and other South Atlantic Islands) which to a large degree overlaps the claims of Argentina and Chile.

If we choose to use the simple state-centered approach to the question of "what is Latin America", we can define "Latin America and the Caribbean" as everything south of the US. The "Latin American" portion includes all those

There is much diversity in South America. The Orinoco and Amazon River basins are hot, steamy tropical areas dominated by rivers and the thick vegetation of the rain forest and jungle. Although humans have penetrated the basins and cleared large areas (causing great ecological concern in the process), these regions are generally not suitable or comfortable for human habitation. In considerable contrast are the deserts of the Pacific coasts of southern Peru and northern Chile, some of which have never had recorded rainfall in all their history.

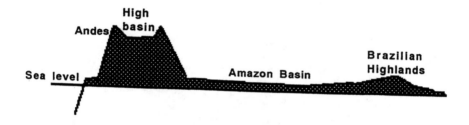

2.6: A horizontal cut across South America at the Equator

The Andean nations have the advantage of "vertical climates", which means that when you have high mountain ranges in the tropics and sub-tropics, the temperatures (and thus climate, vegetation, crops and human activity) are determined by the altitude. At sea level the climates are hot and tropical; in the peaks of the Andes there is permanent snow, even on the Equator. In between there is every possible variant. And since these are the tropics, there is little seasonal variation and no real difference between "winter" and "summer". Where the mountains branch out to create pockets that are valleys or high mountain basins, there can be very favorable conditions for human habitation.

Uruguay (the only Latin American nation outside of the tropics), and Argentina provide the climatic conditions most suitable for human activity. The grassy plains of Uruguay and the Pampas of Argentina contain some of the most fertile and productive soils on earth for grains and cattle.

The Far, Far South

The last region we will consider is the far South Atlantic and the islands which connect South America to Antarctica (Falklands/Malvinas, South Georgia, South Sandwich, South Orkneys). These may seem to be unimportant islands, but in 1982 Argentina and Great Britain fought a short but bitter war over them.

And beyond the islands lies Antarctica. In the United States we tend to think of Antarctica as a isolated continent but, as we mentioned earlier, many South Americans feel there is a geographic and geopolitical link between Antarctica and South America. And two countries (Argentina and Chile) claim that their country extends all the way to the South Pole. The Argentine and Chilean argument can be better understood from this map, which shows how close Antarctica comes to South America (about 600 miles).

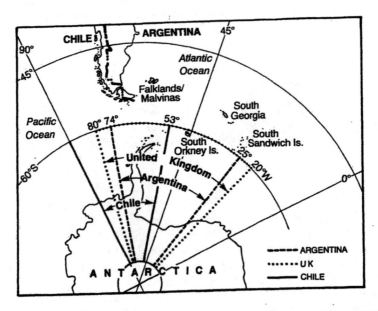

2.7: The far, far South and Antarctic claims of Chile, Argentina and U.K.

Conclusions

This concludes the overview of the major features of the physical geography of Latin America and the Caribbean. It is a large and diverse area which stretches from subtropical Mexico and tropical Central and South America, to subtropical and temperate South America and finally to the extreme cold of the Antarctic region. To compound the diversity, there are high mountains which provide further variations of temperature, climate, vegetation and possibilities for human habitation and economic activity. One way to summarize this diversity is to list the principal natural regions of the area (see map on the next page).

As we move from the physical geography to study the humans who lived and live in this area, a useful metaphor suggested by a geographer is that of a tapestry. The tapestry suggests the complex mixture of nations and peoples that lies to the south of the US. We can think of the loom that is the physical environment of the Western Hemisphere, and the various threads as representing the major currents of humanity that came to these lands (the original Indigenous current, the European, and the African).

THE 15 NATURAL REGIONS
OF LATIN AMERICA

1. The Gulf and Caribbean lowlands
2. The Antilles (West Indes)
3. Pacific coastal plains and valleys
4. Andes, Sierra Madre (and basins)
5. Orinoco River Llanos
6. Guiana highlands
7. Amazon Basin
8. Brazilian highlands
9. Coastal desert of Peru and N. Chile
10. Valley of Central Chile
11. Fiords, lakes of Southern Chile
12. Patagonia and NW Argentina
13. La Plata-Paraná River Basin
14. South Atlantic Islands
15. South American Antarctica

Source: Alfonso González in Jan Black,
Latin America: Its Problems and Promise.
Adapted by Jack Child, 1989.

2.8: The 15 natural regions of Latin America

The first description of the Americas, by Columbus.

(Extract from Christopher Columbus' letter to the Catholic Monarchs Isabel and Ferdinand, written on the return leg of his first voyage, off the Canary Islands, on 15 February 1493.)

...This island and all the others are very fertile to a limitless degree, and this island is extremely so. In it there are many harbors on the coast of the sea, beyond comparison with others which I know in Christendom, and many rivers, good and large, which is marvelous. Its lands are high, and there are in it very many sierras and very lofty mountains, beyond comparison with the island of Tenerife.

All are most beautiful, of a thousand shapes, and all are accessible and filled with trees of a thousand kinds and tall, and they seem to touch the sky. And I am told that they never lose their foliage, as I can understand, for I saw them as green and as lovely as they are in Spain in May, and some of them were flowering, some bearing fruit, and some in another stage, according to their nature. And the nightingale was singing, and other birds of a thousand kinds, in the month of November when I was there. There are six or eight kinds of palm, which are a wonder to behold on account of their beautiful variety, but so are the other trees and fruits and plants. In it are marvelous pine groves, and there are very large tracts of cultivable lands, and there is honey, and there are birds of many kinds and fruits in great diversity. In the interior are mines of metals, and the population is without number. Española is a marvel.

The sierras and mountains, the plains and arable lands and pastures, are so lovely and rich for planting and sowing, for breeding cattle of every kind, for building towns and villages. The harbors of the sea here are such as cannot be believed to exist unless they have been seen, and so with the rivers, many and great, and good waters, the majority of which contain gold. In the trees and fruits and plants, there is a great difference from those of Juana. In this island, there are many spices and great mines of gold and other minerals.

its cities were located in what is today Guatemala. The Classical Maya period can be called the golden age of pre-Columbian civilization, with extraordinary accomplishments in sculpture, architecture, astronomy calenderics, hieroglyphics, and painting.

Indeed, this period has often been described as having a parallel to the height of Greek culture in the Mediterranean. Then, for reasons that still remain a mystery (but which might be related to crop failure, disease, drought, or war), around the year 900 CE the Mayan cities were abandoned and the center of their civilization moved to the Yucatan Peninsula in Southeastern Mexico. There it flourished for a relatively brief period and then declined considerably over the next few centuries until the arrival of the Spaniards.

3.3: Maya Profile

Maya calenderics blended their refined knowledge of mathematics, astronomy, science, and art. Like many of the pre-Columbian civilizations, their notion of time was cyclical, and not linear, like the Europeans'. Thus, what had occurred in the past could happen again when the next cycle evolved. The Maya had calculated the solar year with considerable accuracy, and they built their chronology on the basic unit of time, the katun (20 years). They believed there were five major cycles of 5,200 years which the earth would go through before destruction by some cataclysm. At the time of their height they were living in the fifth of these cycles, which they calculated would come to a destructive end on 24 December of the year 2011. This idea that events that occurred at a similar point in a previous cycle could very well repeat themselves causes some confusion when reading the scattered bits of surviving Maya poetry, since it is not entirely clear (as we shall see below) whether the poet is speaking of events which have already happened or are still to come (or both).

The political organization of the Mayas has been described as one of semi-independent "city-states" under no single unifying empire, thus further strengthening the notion of a parallel to Greek civilization. This notion is reinforced by the fact that the most impressive surviving legacies of the Maya are their ruined cities and the artifacts found in them. Ironically, it seems that these cities, for all their religious, civic and ceremonial monuments, were not inhabited by many individual Maya, and remained fairly empty except for ceremonial occasions. The typical Maya focused his or her life in the villages and fields which surrounded the major cities. Here is where corn, the staple of their civilization, was grown, and where they lived out the years of their existence.

Furthermore, one of the basic purposes of the sophisticated advances in science, mathematics, religion and astronomy was to help guarantee abundant harvests of corn and other foods by making sure the moments were just right in the chronological cycle, and that the gods would be pleased by the timing of the sowing and harvesting. This need to predict and choose the correct time extended beyond agriculture to many other ritualistic activities of the Maya, from the compressing of the baby's head for cosmetic purposes, through the rituals of puberty and marriage, to the moment of death and burial.

Maya art.

Maya art was unique, and of a refinement and grace that make its Classical period comparable to that of any of the other advanced civilizations on earth. Although the monuments and sculptures were not as large as those of the civilizations of the Central Valley of Mexico, nor the stonework as precise as that of the Incas to the south, Maya art had a special quality of delicacy and humanity that gave it distinct characteristics.

The dominant art form was architecture, in the shape of the ceremonial cities which served as places of gathering and ritual. One hallmark of Maya architecture was the corbeled arch, constructed by placing stones closer and closer together until the final gap was closed by the keystone. Sculpture served to enhance architecture, and stela recorded important events and names associated with the great cities. Relatively little Maya painting has survived, but that which has, such as the Bonampak murals, serves as invaluable records of their way of life.

3.4: Corbeled arch

Maya literature

The Maya civilization had declined markedly by the time the Spanish conquistadors arrived in what is today southern Mexico and Central America, but the Quiché, a major branch of the Mayas, still existed in the area of today's Guatemala and maintained many of the oral traditions of their ancestors. They also had old book-like records, but most were destroyed by the Spaniards or had seriously deteriorated due to the tropical climate. Three of these codices or books which have been preserved apparently deal mainly with numbers, the calendar, and rites; they include many decorative elements and picture writings.

4: The Aztecs and the Incas

The Aztecs

When the Spaniards arrived in Mexico in the early 16th Century, the most powerful and advanced civilization in the Central Valley of Mexico was the Aztec. In a sense they too were relatively recent arrivals since they were originally from an area far to the north, and had settled in the Valley of Anáhuac (Central Mexico) in the early 13th Century. According to their tribal legend, they were required to keep migrating until they found a very specific sign: an eagle devouring a serpent while perched on a cactus located on an island in a lake. When they reached Anáhuac they ended their nomadic existence, and finally settled on an island in the middle of Lake Tex-

4.1: Eagle and serpent

coco, where they founded their capital city of Tenochtitlán in the year 1325. From there they gradually extended their reach to dominate other tribes in the Valley.

To a large extent the Aztec empire was based on war, coercion, and tribute. They were fierce fighters, and quickly came to intimidate and control their neighbors. One reason for going to war was religious: the Aztecs believed that their gods required frequent blood sacrifices in order to remain strong, and the most valued sacrifice was the enemy warrior who had fought bravely. And so eventually wars were waged for the sole purpose of obtaining such prisoners, who were led up the long flights of stairs of Aztec pyramids to have their hearts ripped out from their still-living bodies and be offered to the gods. Sometimes the sacrifices were by means of ritualistic combat, with the prisoner being given the possibility of freedom if he defeated four or five of the best Aztec warriors (few did). These sacrifices to the gods were euphemistically called "flowers", and the "wars of the flowers" were almost constant.

Although they made few original contributions to human knowledge or the arts, they were intelligent masters who easily adopted and adapted the ideas and creations of others. Because of this, and their high degree of political and military organization, the Aztecs have sometimes been compared to the Romans, and the Mayas likened to the Greeks for their intellectual and artistic refinement. Although this analogy is a simplistic one, it does serve to bring out some of the principal traits of both civilizations.

Aztec Art

4.2: Aztec sacrifice

The art of the Aztecs, like their warfare, was designed to impress and inspire awe. It tended to be massive and monumental, in contrast to the more delicate Maya art. The Aztecs excelled in their heavy and colossal sculptures, their immense truncated temples and pyramids, and their crown jewel, the central area of their city of Tenochtitlán.

The plumed serpent was a common theme, and was associated with the founding myth of the serpent and the eagle, as well as the teacher-ruler Quetzalcoatl, a man with fair skin and a white beard who before disappearing had promised to return one day from the east. Perhaps the best known of the Aztec sculptures is the so-called calendar stone, at 24 tons the largest of all the Aztec sculptures. It is not so much a calendar as a symbol of the Aztec notion of circular time, and a reminder of their belief that the world had been destroyed four times before the present "fifth sun" period in which they were living. The calendar stone today lies in the Mexico City's Museum of Anthropology, one of the finest in the world.

Aztec writing was limited to hieroglyphs. Most of these were pictograms in which the symbol bore a close resemblance to the physical object, such as an animal, a god, or a particular human being. This form of writing could not adequately convey abstract concepts, and for this they employed ideograms in which the symbol had some relationship to the abstract idea being presented. Words or songs, for example, were represented by a comma-shaped scroll placed near the mouth of the person speaking. Among the most frequent themes in Aztec art (and literature) were concerns over the meaning of life, what lay beyond death, and the duality of human nature and life itself (good versus bad, light versus darkness, sensuality versus spirituality, the concrete versus the abstract).

4.3: Aztec scribe and hieroglyphs

Aztec Literature

Because of this lack of an advanced form of writing, Aztec literature was passed on by the oral tradition. They were skilled at declamations of poetry in their Nahuatl language, and after the conquest the Spanish did permit the transcribing of these poems using Spanish letters. Many were later translated into Spanish. The fragments that follow show the Aztecs' concern with the themes of death and the meaning of life. They also confirm the importance of war and flowers (sometimes symbolizing human sacrifices) in their daily lives.

We do know the names of a very small number of Aztec poets, mainly those who were also rulers or of royal blood. One such poet-king was Nezahualcoyotl (1402-1472), whose mother was related to the rulers of Tenochtitlán (his father was a nobleman from the neighboring tribe of Tetzcoco, which was allied with the Aztecs). Nezahualcoyotl eventually came to be king of Tetzcoco, and was able to persuade his people to give up some of the more brutal practices of the Aztecs, including human sacrifice.

Song of Flight by Nezahualcoyotl

(Nezahualcoyotl's flight from the Lord of Azcapotzalco)
I have been born in vain
In vain I have come out
of the house of god down to earth
I need so much!
Truly I wish I had not come out,
truly I should not have come down to earth.
I do not say it, but...
what is it that I will do?
Oh princes who have come here!
Will I live facing the visages of the people?

What could it be?
Reflect!
Shall I rise up on the face of the earth?
What is my destiny?
I need so much!
my heart is heavy,
you are my only friend
here, on earth.
How does one live beside the people?
Does He who sustains and raises up mankind
work rashly?
May you live in peace!
I have submitted,
I live only with my head bowed
next to the people.
This is why I am afflicted,
I have been abandoned
next to the people on earth.
How does your heart determine it,
Giver of Life?
Let your anger come out!
Extend your compassion,
I am at your side, you are God.
Or do you wish to give me death?
Is it true that we cannot be happy
we who live on earth?
It is not true that we live
and have come to be happy on earth,
Thus we are all needy.
Destiny predicts bitterness
here, next to the people.
May my heart not anguish.
Truly, I barely
have compassion here on earth.
Bitterness has come to grow,
next to you and at your side, Giver of Life.
I only seek,
I remember my friends.
Will they perhaps come again?
Will they perhaps live again?
Alone, we perish once,
alone only once here on earth.
May hearts not suffer!
Next to the Giver of Life.

4.4: Nezahualcoyotl

goes far to explain the unifying power of the family dynasty of Inca emperors. From Cuzco successive Incas (the name applies to the ruling kings as well as to the civilization as a whole) built fortress-cities and roads from which they launched conquests of neighboring groups. But unlike the Aztecs, the defeated tribes were not taken prisoner for bloody sacrifices; instead they were given the opportunity to join the Inca Empire by accepting the Quechua language and the authority of the Inca in Cuzco.

4.11: The Inca and his sister

One strong element in the political organization of the Inca Empire was that the power of the king in Cuzco was balanced by the authority of the local community group, known as the ayllu. The ayllu owned the land in communal fashion, and decisions were taken by consensus within the group. Harvests and other riches were divided three ways: one third went to the Inca for the expenses of government and the maintenance of the court; one third went to the sun as symbol of religion and (along with the government's share) as a reserve in case of drought or disaster; the last third was kept by the community itself.

This division of income and the provisions for a state welfare program has led some observers to call the Inca system socialist or communist, but it was more a benevolent and paternalistic monarchy in which religion was closely tied to the state. In any case, the arrangement did much to keep the loyalty of the Inca's subjects and thus enabled the empire to reach its impressive geographic spread along the length of theAndes from today's Ecuador to northern Chile..

In the fields of science and learning the Incas were ahead of the Aztecs, but not at the level of the Mayas. They were, however, quite advanced in the healing arts using numerous herbs and roots which can still be bought in Andean marketplaces today. In one particular surgical technique known as trepanning the skull of a mentally or physically sick person was opened using a metal instrument known as a *tumi*. Bone regeneration in skulls proves that many of the patients survived the operation.

The Incas solved the problem of mountain agriculture by building terraces of stone which held the soil, channeled the water used for irrigation, and provided the small but fertile flat surfaces in which the potato was cultivated. In many ways this crop meant as much to the Incas as corn did to the Mayas, giving them not only their basic subsistenance, but also having a mystical and religious significance.

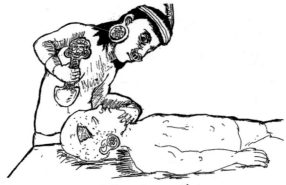

4.12: Inca trepanning

Inca Art

Like the Aztecs, the Incas built great monuments which symbolized the power and wealth of their empire. Their use of stone was especially advanced, and featured the use of massive blocks which were meticulously smoothed and finished so that it is impossible to work a knife blade into the joints between the stones. Although many of these monuments were destroyed by the Spanish conquerors, many also remain as lasting testimony to the Incas' skills as stonemasons. As an example, in the city of Cuzco a Spanish Catholic church was built on top of the foundations of a pre-Columbian Inca temple; during a severe earthquake the Catholic church was badly damaged, but the Inca stonework survived the quake. This example is sometimes cited as a metaphor for the veneer of Spanish civilization placed on top of the solid foundations of Andean indigenous culture.

The various pre-Incan cultures were also skilled in pottery and weaving, and these arts were adopted by the Incas as these civilizations were absorbed into the Empire. Since they did not have a written language, pottery was sometimes used to record historical events, scenes of daily life, and to teach medical techniques and sexual practices. Inca pottery is highly realistic, and the faces of individuals who achieved important positions, or who had distinguishing features (including physical abnormalities) have been preserved to this day in museums and collections. The lack of a written language also led to the use of knotted cords (the *quipus*) to record important data such as the inventories of food in the empire's warehouses.

4.13: Inca pottery

Inca and pre-Inca weaving is startling in its refinement and patterns. Some of the weavings use threads so fine, and are so tightly worked, that they have never been reproduced except using advanced machinery. Metallurgy was equally sophisticated, especially artwork using the abundant gold and silver of the Andes.

Inca Literature

Like other pre-Columbian civilizations, the Incas had strong oral traditions of story-telling, philosophy and poetry in the Quechua language. Some of these oral traditions glorified the Inca God-King and his Empire, but others were of a popular nature, and may even have served as a form of social protest. The principal recorder of Quechua oral traditions was a remarkable individual who symbolized the fusion of the Spanish and Inca races into the *mestizo* so typical of Latin America: Garcilaso de la Vega, known as *El Inca Garcilaso* (1539-1616). He was the son of a Spanish captain and an Inca princess, and grew up with both heritages in the old Inca capital of Cuzco.

4.14: Inca Garcilaso

He later moved to Spain, where he was influenced by the cultural currents of the Renaissance. His Royal Commentaries of the Incas, from which the following is extracted, is an invaluable record of the Inca Empire in its final days, and its conquest by the Spaniards and subsequent transformation into the Vice-Royalty of Peru.

Royal Commentaries of the Incas by El Inca Garcilaso

After having made many approaches and taken many paths to enter into an accounting of the origin and beginning of the Incas, who were the natural kings of Peru, it seemed to me that the best approach and path, which would also be the easiest and most direct, would be to tell what in my childhood I had heard so many times from my mother and her brothers and uncles, and others who were older, about this origin and beginning. This is because everything that is said on this subject in other manners, can be reduced to the same thing that we will say, and it is better that we base our knowledge on the very words of the Incas themselves, and not on those of strangers. And so it was that when my mother lived in Cuzco, her home, she would receive visits almost each week from the few relatives who had managed to escape the cruelties and tyrannies of Atahualpa (which we shall tell about in his life story). During these visits to my mother they frequently discussed the origin of their kings, of their majesty, of the greatness of their empire, of their conquests and deeds, of the government which they had in peace and war, of the laws that they ordered for the benefit and favor of their vassals. In sum, they left nothing out among all the things that had occurred to them.

From the greatness and prosperous times in the past they came to things present: they cried over their dead kings, their lost empire, their finished government, etc. The Incas and their princesses talked about these and similar topics in the discussions, and recalling the good that they had lost, always ended their talks with tears and crying, saying: we have given up our kingdom and become vassals. In these talks I, as a boy, would come and go among them many times, and it was pleasing to hear them tell these stories, in the same way that it was pleasing to hear fables.

The days, months and years passed, and I was now sixteen or seventeen years of age, and it happened one day that my relatives were engaged in a conversation regarding their kings and ancient things, and I spoke to the oldest among my relatives, who was telling of these things. I said to him: Uncle, Inca, since among you there is no writing, which is what preserves the memory of things past, what information do you have of the origin and beginnings of our kings? After all, the Spanish, and other nations which are their neighbors, have stories both divine and human which tell of the beginning of the reigns of their kings and those of others. They also tell when one empire gives way to another, even so far as knowing how many thousands of years it has been since God created heaven and earth. All this and more they know from their books. But since you have no books, what memories do you have of your ancient things? Who was the first of your Incas? What was his name? What was the origin of his lineage? In what manner did his reign begin? With what people and with what arms did he conquer this great empire? What was the origin of our deeds?

The Inca, who was pleased to have heard these questions, because he liked to tell of these things, turned to me (I had heard these things many times, but never had I paid so much attention) and said to me: nephew, I will be very pleased to tell you of these things, and it would be wise for you to hear them and keep them in your heart (this was a phrase they used to mean to memorize). You will learn that in the ancient centuries all this part of the earth which you see, consisted of great forests of brambles and thorns, and that the people in those times lived like beasts and brutal animals, without religion or law, without houses or villages, without sowing or reaping the soil, without clothing to cover their flesh, because they did not know how to grow cotton or wool to make clothing. They lived in groups of two or three, and they came together to gather in the caves or crevasses in the rocks or the caverns of the earth: like the beasts they ate the grass of the fields or the roots of the trees, and whatever fruit they could gather, and even human flesh. They covered their skin with leaves and the bark of trees, and animal skins; others went about naked. In sum, they lived like the deer and wild beasts, and their women were the same way, because they did not know how to take care of them properly.

We should not be annoyed to hear repeated so many times the words "Our Father the Sun", which was Inca language, and their way of showing veneration and respect, because they always named the sun, since they prized their belief that they were descended from the sun. And anyone who was not an Inca was not allowed to use these words, for it would be blasphemy, and he would be stoned. And so the Inca said: our father the sun, seeing men live in such a manner which I have just told you about, took pity on them, and sent them from the sky a son and a daughter who would give them principles and laws so that they could live like men in reason and in civilization. He did this also so that they could live in houses and towns, and would know how to plow their fields, cultivate their crops and grains, raise their cattle and enjoy the fruits of the earth and their labor like rational men, and not like beasts.

With this order and mandate our father the sun put these two children in Lake Titicaca, which is eighty leagues from here. He told them to go where they wished, and wherever they went to eat and sleep, they should try to thrust into the earth a golden rod, a half a yard long and two fingers thick. Our father the sun wished that his children would make their capital and court in the spot where this golden rod would sink easily into the earth with one blow.

And at the end of his words he said: after you have reduced these people to your service, you will keep them in reason and justice, with mercy, clemency and gentleness. In all things you shall act towards them as a kind father toward tender and loving children. In doing this you will be imitating me, since I treat the whole world well, and I give my light and clarity so that they can see and do their things, and I heat them when it is cold, and I make their grass and seeds grow; I give fruit to their trees and I multiply their cattle; I make the rains, and I give peace to their time, and I am careful to go around the world once each day to see what the earth needs, to provide for these needs and to help, as the sustainer and benefactor of all peoples. As my children, I want you to imitate this example of mine, and I am sending you to earth solely for the indoctrination and benefit of these humans, who now live like beasts.

4.15: The golden rod

And I therefore name you as kings and lords of all the people who you indoctrinate with your good reason, works, and government. Our father the sun, having expressed his will to his two children, bade them farewell. They left Titicaca, and walked North, and throughout their path, wherever they stopped, they tried to sink the golden rod, but it would not go into the ground. And so they reached a small settlement, which is about seven or eight leagues east of this city, and which is now called Pacarec Tampu, which means "inn of the dawn of the one who sleeps". The Inca gave it this name, because he awoke at dawn at that place. This was one of the towns which this prince later ordered to be settled, and its inhabitants are very proud of the name, because it was given to them by our Inca. From there he and his wife, our queen, came to this valley of Cuzco, which until that time was wilderness.

And there, in Cuzco, the golden rod sank into the ground.

A sample of Quechua and Latin poetry recorded by El Inca Garcilaso de la Vega:

Quechua (Inca)	Latin	English
Cumac ñusta	Pulchra nimpha	Beautiful nymph
Toralláquim	Frater tuus	There is your brother
Puyñuy quita	Urnam tuam	and your urn
Paquir cayan	Nunc infrigit	which he is breaking,
Hina mántara	Cujus ictus	and because of this,
Cunuñunun	Tonat fulget	thunder, lightning;
Illac pántac	Fulminatque	and bolts are hurled.
Camri ñusta	Sed tu Nimpha	You, royal nymph
Unuy quita	Tuam limpham	with beautiful waters
Para munqui	Fundens pluis	will give us rain
May ñimpiri	Interdumque	and sometimes
Chichi munqui	Grandinem, seu	hailstones as well,
Riti munqui	Nivem mittis	and also snow.
Pacha rúrac	Mundi Factor	The Maker of the world,
Pachacámac	Pachacamac	the giver of life,
Viracocha	Viracocha	Viracocha,
Cay hinápac	Ad hoc munus	for that purpose
Churasunqui	Te sufficit	placed you here
Camasunqui	Ac praefecit	and gave you soul.

4.16: Inca tumi (gold scalpel)

5: The Encounter

The Iberians

The Peninsula and its People

"Europe begins at the Pyrenees". The cliché contains some truth, for the Iberian Peninsula has always been different from the rest of Mediterranean (and certainly northern) Europe. The mountains which separate Spain and Portugal from the rest of Europe have tended to isolate the Iberian Peninsula, and the relatively easy access to North Africa across twelve miles of the Strait of Gibraltar has made the southern parts of the Peninsula a transition zone between Europe and Africa. The other important geographic reality is the way in which the Peninsula juts out into the Atlantic, making it the logical launching pad for maritime enterprises to the west or to the south around Africa.

Geography has not been kind to the Iberians, at least as far as the suitability of their soils and climate for agriculture. The land is rough and frequently arid. The central plateau is deeply cut by rivers, which, along with the surrounding mountains, tend to create many small pockets of human population which are cut off from each other. Thus, there is strong regionalism and individualism in the Iberian, characteristics which do not lead to teamwork or easy political control by a central government. The Peninsula's area is about that of the state of Texas. And yet from this relatively small region two countries launched a series of enterprises of exploration and conquest that created in the sixteenth century the largest empires the world had ever seen. To understand this process, we must realize that the Peninsula (and especially Spain) had long been the target of invaders.

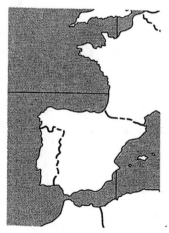

5.1: Iberia

Table 5.1: Encounter and Conquest (Chapters 5, 6, 7, 8)

Cultural- historical framework:	End of the European Middle ages and transition to Renaissance; Humanism The Encounter of two cultures (1492) The conquest (Mexico, Peru, Chile)
Approximate dates:	From the Encounter (1492) through the Conquest to the late 16th Century
Historical Landmarks	Reconquest of Iberia, 711-1492 Search for the eastern route to the Indies by the Portuguese The Spanish and Columbus' enterprise to the west 1492: Fall of Granada; Encounter of two worlds Expulsion of the Arabs and the Jews Treaty of Tordesillas, 1494 Alvares Cabral (Portuguese) reaches Brazil, 1500 Conquest of Mexico, Cortés: 1519-21 Conquest of Peru, Pizarro: 1531-33 Conquest of Chile, Valdivia: 1540-41
Literature	Diaries of the discoverers and the chronicles of the conquerors Inventories of what was seen: emphasis on riches, and the great deeds Christopher Columbus,1451?-1506 Hernán Cortés, 1485-1547 Bernal Díaz del Castillo, 1495?-1584 Alonso de Ercilla y Zúñiga, 1534-1594 Father las Casas, 1474-1566 Guamán Poma de Ayala, 1526?-1614? Anonymous Indigenous authors
The Arts	Architecture: churches, retablos, tiles Military architecture: defensive forts Cultural mestizaje Painting and drawing: the chronicles Copies of classical Iberian paintings Cartography: first simple, then illustrated, with some fantasy

Spain had gone through an extended and difficult struggle to gain its independence from the Muslim world. This latter struggle, known as "La Reconquista"
(the Reconquest) was to shape many of the attitudes the explorers and conquistadores brought from Iberia to the Americas.

The stage for the Reconquest was set by
the Visigoths from northern Europe who
moved into the Peninsula as Roman power
declined in the 5th century. The Visigoths
were a quarrelsome lot, and warfare was frequent among the various local rulers. In the
year 711 one of them invited the Moors to
enter the Peninsula in order to help him defeat a rival. The Arabs, led by Tarik (who
gave his name to Gibraltar) were more than
happy to oblige, but they betrayed their host,
invaded in force and almost conquered the
whole Peninsula by the year 718. Although
the Arab rule was relatively tolerant, the
Christian knights in small mountain strong-
holds in northern Spain launched a struggle

5.2: Moorish Spain

to regain their lost lands and peoples. The Reconquest gradually acquired the
character of a religious crusade, pitting Christian against Arab, especially after
the discovery of what was believed to be the tomb of the apostle St. James (Santiago in Spanish) in northern Spain. The apostle's name became the battle cry of
the Christian knights, and Santiago was cast as the warrior saint, patron of the
Reconquista, and later of the Conquest of America.

There were real heroes as well in the Reconquista. One of them, El Cid
Campeador (Cid the Champion) became the quintessential Spanish hero, a man
who could fight a battle, court a woman, write a poem, and rule a kingdom, with
equal skill, individualism, honor and style. With El Cid as hero, the values of
individual military prowess, religious crusades, conquest, and capture of booty
(including slaves and serfs) became more ingrained in the Iberian character than
the values of hard work or getting one's hands dirty by tilling the soil.

By the middle of the 13th century the Moors had been pushed south to the
kingdom of Granada, where the rugged terrain and isolation favored their defense and gave them another two and a half centuries of presence in Iberia.
When the last Moorish bastion of Granada fell in 1492, the conquering Spanish
kings and knights saw it as perfectly logical and fitting that their God would
reward them with a new world to conquer.

The Renaissance and the Age of Discovery

The fall of Granada, and Columbus' enterprise, coincided with the intellectual awakening of Europe known as the Renaissance. Although Iberia was late

to feel the artistic impact of the Renaissance, in the field of exploration and navigation the Iberians (especially Portugal) were in the forefront.

It is important to note the significance of exploration and discovery in the Renaissance. As humans abandoned the narrow limits of the Church-controlled scholasticism of the Middle Ages, they began to wonder about their natural world and its limits. Thus, the Renaissance was also the Age of Discovery, when humans could defy old superstitions and push the boundaries of geographic knowledge. Most educated people had discarded the old notions of a flat earth, and reasoned that if the earth were a sphere, then it might be possible to navigate around it without running the danger of falling off the edge.

These new notions of geography and cartography became increasingly important when the Turks captured Constantinople in the year 1453 and cut the lucrative European trade route to the far East via the Mediterranean and the Middle East.

The Portuguese and the Eastern Route

By the time of the fall of Constantinople the Portuguese had already made considerable progress in developing a sea route to India and the markets of the Orient. Their sea route went down the coast of Africa and was based on the assumption (valid) that one could reach the southern tip of Africa, go around it, and then sail east to India.

In this enterprise Portugal was favored by early independence from both the Moors and the kings of Castille, who ruled what is today the central part of Spain. By the 14th century Portugal was completing its national consolidation and its rise to become a European power.

An extraordinary Portuguese prince, Henry the Navigator (1394-1460), gathered together the best geographers, cartographers and mariners and organized the exploration of the trade route to the east around Africa. There is some irony in his name, since Henry personally never sailed far from the sight of land.

5.3: The Eastern route

But as a leader he was able to launch Portugal's maritime empire, motivated by his goals of increasing knowledge, exploiting the wealth of the East, developing the slave trade in Africa, and extending the religious crusades of Christianity to new areas. Shortly after Henry's death, in the year 1488 the Portuguese explorer Bartolome Dias rounded the Cape of Good Hope in southernmost Africa and opened up the long-dreamed of trade route to India and the east. And a few years after that, in early 1500, the Portuguese explorer Alvares Cabral was attempting to follow Dias' route but swung far west into the Atlantic, accidentally discov-

Spanish priest who arrived in the New World shortly after Columbus, and it is believed to faithfully reflect the original. Even though the description is straightforward, Columbus reveals some of his motivations (and those of his Spanish sponsors) when he comments that the Indians will make good servants and will soon convert to Christianity.

Diary of Cristopher Columbus

Friday, 12th of October (1492). Because they showed us much friendship, and because I knew that they were people who would join us and convert to our Holy Faith better through love than force, I gave them some trinkets and many other things of little value. They took much pleasure from the red sailor's caps I gave them, and from some glass ornaments which they put around their necks. And they were so quickly ours that it was a miracle.

Afterwards they came swimming out to our ships, where we were, and they brought parrots, and cotton thread, and spears, and many other things. They bartered these things for anything we had, such as bits of glass and rattles. In short, they took anything we gave them, and gave us what they had, with much good will.

5.8: Columbus

But it seemed to me that generally they were very poor people. They went around naked as the day their mothers brought them into this world, even the women, although I only saw one (she was beautiful). All the ones I saw were young, and none were older than thirty, very well built, with nice bodies and very good faces. Their hair was thick as a horse's tail, short and hanging over their brows, except for some who had longer hair which they kept pulled back and never cut...

They did not bring weapons and are not familiar with them, because when I showed them swords they took them by the sharp side and cut themselves out of ignorance. They have no iron. Their spears are rods without iron, and some of them have a fish's tooth at the tip, and others have other tips. All of them are of a good height, with good gestures, and well built. They will be good servants and with good skills, since I can tell that they very quickly repeat what is said to them, and I believe that they will become Christians very soon.

Saturday, 13 October. They are all of a good height, and very beautiful; their hair is not curly, but rather free and thick, and they all have a broad forehead and head, with beautiful eyes, not small, and none black, but rather the color of canaries. ... The island is rather large, and very flat, with many green trees, and much water, and a large lake in the center, with no mountains, and it is all so green that it is a pleasure to see it; and the people, very gentle.

Sunday, 14 October. I later saw two or three settlements, with people who all came to the beach calling out to us and giving thanks to God. Some brought us water, and others things to eat; others, when they saw that we did not land, jumped into the sea and swam out to us. And we understood that they were asking us if we came from the sky. And an old man came out in a canoe. And others, in loud voices, called to the rest, men and women: "Come and see the men who come from the sky; bring them drink and food." And many came, and many women.

The Treaty of Tordesillas, 1494 (excerpts)

And because of this, they, in the interest of peace and concord, and to conserve their relation and love, which said lord king of Portugal has with the said lords king and queen of Castille, and Aragon, etc, as Their Highness wish, and their representatives acting in their name, and by virtue of their powers, they have granted and consented to the following.

That there should be drawn and marked a line straight from pole to pole, that is to say, from the arctic pole to the antarctic pole, which is North to South.

Said line shall be drawn, as it has been established, three hundred and seventy leagues from the islands of Cape Verde, towards the setting sun (West), by degrees or whatever manner can best or more quickly be done, and everything that up to this point has been found and discovered, and which shall be discovered from now on, and found by the said king of Portugal, and by his ships, be the discoveries islands or continents, from this line, as established here going from the line to the rising sun (East), shall belong to the said lord king of Portugal and his successors, for ever and always.

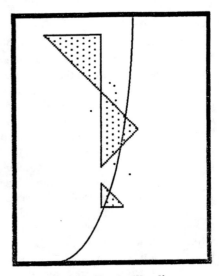

5.9: The Tordesillas line

6: The Conquest of Mexico

The Conquest

The Spanish conquest of their American empires was carried out primarily by individuals who organized and financed their own expeditions after having obtained the permission and authorization of the King by means of a formal contract. The first set of conquerors who agreed to these terms were called *adelantados* (the King's advance men), and it was up to them to persuade the other members of their party to join them, with promises of land, adventure and booty as their reward. This type of enterprise was derived from the patterns which were used in the Reconquest against the Moors, which was generally carried out by small groups of armed men under the authority of one of many

6.1: The Conquest

kings or princes. They fought for the religious purpose of expelling the Moors, but they were also motivated by the desire to take over the lands and serfs held by their enemies. Thus, it was easy for the Spanish, who saw the conquest of America as an extension or a continuation of their Reconquest battles against the Arabs, to use the same methods.

In the Indies (the term the Spanish preferred for their colonies) the motivation could be described as "God, glory and gold", with the religious factor of converting heathens and the personal or royal glory of conquest taking a back seat to the more powerful motive of wealth. The men who carried it out were a mix of nobles (generally the leaders of the expeditions), professional soldiers, young men seeking adventure, and more than a few who were escaping past misdeeds in the Peninsula.

Whatever we may think today of the destruction and changes wrought by the conquistadores, we must acknowledge that the handful of men who crossed the ocean to carry out the conquest performed historically epic deeds as they faced disease, hunger, hardship and hostile terrain to battle large numbers of warriors from two major empires. How were they able to accomplish this in such a short period of time? One explanation lies in the military superiority of the Spanish, both in weapons (steel, armor, gunpowder, the horse, the fighting dog), as well as in tactics (the Spanish had the experience of fierce fighting with the Moors, while to of the Indigenous Americans warfare was something ritualistic and religious, such as the Aztecs' "war of the

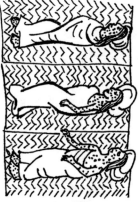

6.2: Smallpox

flowers"). Psychological factors helped as well, since many of the Indigenous empires held the belief of a returning god, such as Quetzalcoatl, coming from the east to reclaim his rightful kingdom on earth. Then there was the factor of biological warfare in the form of diseases brought by the Europeans (measles, smallpox) for which the Indigenous had no immunity. Finally, there was the factor of political divisions and fragmentation between the various groups the Spanish found. A prime example was in the conquest of Mexico, where the Aztec's brutal exploitation of other tribes made it easy for the Spanish to find allies in their fight against the Aztecs.

Art of the Conquest

Art in the early years of the conquest had an important function: to communicate back to the Old World, and especially to the financial backers and the Court, the wonders that were being found in the Americas. Drawings and sketches, accompanied by sometimes exaggerated descriptions in written reports and chronicles, were the only way to show those who stayed behind how valuable the new territories were. Besides illustrating the riches of the New World, art was also used to provide graphic representations of new creatures, foods and flora. This was sometimes done with a reasonable degree of accuracy, but often considerable liberties were taken with reality.

The sometimes very different customs of the Indigenous were also the subject of drawings and sketches, which were frequently done by the conquered ones themselves, with notations and marginal comments provided by the expeditions' leaders, scribes, or priests who accompanied them. This was especially significant in the conquest of the Aztecs, since many of the customs considered sinful by the priests, such as human sacrifice and cannibalism, provided a religious justification for the conquest.

Cartography provided another medium for art. The earlier maps sketched by the first explorers (such as Columbus) were plain and functional. But later ones were profusely illustrated with all manner of new and strange creatures to be found in the Indies. And when these were later copied many times back in Europe, there was a tendency to incorporate fanciful and imaginary details.

Literature of the Conquest

The conquistadores, like the discoverers, were creatures of the Renaissance who had not yet fully shaken off the superstitions of the Medieval period. Further, the Spanish carried with them all sorts of stories, some real and many exaggerated, of their countrymen's exploits during the Reconquest; these undoubtedly influenced the chronicles of the conquest of America. Since the conquistadores were men of action, their writings tended to be direct, descriptive, and matter of fact. The time for reflection, creative esthetics and imagination would come later.

Hernán Cortés and the Conquest of Mexico

Hernán Cortés (1485-1547) was the epitome of the Spanish conquistador in the New World. Of humble origins, he managed to attend the prestigious University of Salamanca in Spain but was a poor student, and was constantly in trouble because of his adventures, including several incidents in which jealous husbands pursued him. After flunking out of Salamanca he decided to find his fame and fortune in the New World. He went first to Hispaniola, and then Cuba, where he married a relative of governor Diego Velásquez. In the year 1517 Velásquez had sent an expedition west from Cuba, and it had explored the coast of Mexico, landing, among other places, on the coast near today's Cancún, where the leader was able to observe the remains of Maya cities; some gold was also found.

His interest piqued, Velásquez in 1519 sent a larger expedition under Cortés, with a total of eleven ships, some five hundred and fifty men, and sixteen horses. On landing in Yucatán and Tabasco, Cortés had the good luck of finding two interpreters who would help him exploit the psychological and political weaknesses of the Aztecs. One was Jerónomo de Aguilar, a shipwrecked Spaniard who had lived among the Mayas for many years.

The second was Malinche, the daughter of a defeated Aztec chief who had been sold as a slave to a Maya family, and thus could speak both the languages of the Maya and the Aztecs. Using the services of these two, Cortés was able to communicate with the principal groups he encountered in Mexico. Furthermore, Malinche (named Doña Marina by the Spanish) became his lover and counselor, providing him with insights, interpretations and military intelligence which Cortés skillfully used in his campaign and in his dealings with the Aztec leadership. Among other things, she gave him details of the legend of Quetzalcoatl and brought him to realize that not only did he look like the god of long beard and white skin, but that he had arrived at a time of many omens, when the return of Quetzalcoatl was expected.

After founding the town of Veracruz on the coast, and making initial contacts with the emissaries of the Aztec emperor Moctezuma, Cortés began his trek inland to the Aztec capital of Tenochtitlán. During his journey he battled (and then forged alliances) with several tribes which had been conquered and exploited by the Aztecs, and which subsequently joined him. He also encountered Moctezuma's ambassadors, who gave him gifts (including gold) and passed on to him Moctezuma's request that he return from whence he came. Unfortunately, the gold only whetted the Spaniards' appetites and guaranteed that they would press on.

Cortés' principal writings were five *Cartas de Relación* (*Letters of Report*) from 1520 to 1526 in which he described the events of the conquest of Mexico to his emperor, Charles I of Spain (Charles V of the Holy Roman Empire). His writings are more elegant and sophisticated than Columbus', perhaps because of his higher level of education, but they have the same credibility stemming from the fact that the author was also the man who performed the historic deeds. The excerpts which follow are from the second of these letters, dated the 30th of October 1520 from Segura de la Frontera, New Spain (Mexico). In this letter Cortés tells the King of his meeting (accompanied by his interpreter and lover Marina/Malinche) with the Aztec Emperor Moctezuma as he enters their capital of Tenochtitlán. In the last section of this excerpt Cortés has Moctezuma de-

scribe the legend of Quetzal-coatl, which was to prove so valuable to the Spaniards in the conquest of Mexico.

Despite the relatively auspicious first encounter with Moctezuma, Cortés' conquest of Mexico was not easy. He gained temporary control of the empire by tak-

6.3: Cortés, Marina and Moctezuma

ing Moctezuma prisoner and claiming that he was indeed Quetzalcoatl who had returned to reclaim his throne. But then came a threat from a different direction: Governor Velásquez of Cuba had never really trusted Cortés, and was beginning to realize that Cortés was acting on his own and was trying to establish a direct link to the King in Spain and set up his own independent domain in Mexico. Velásquez had sent an expedition to bring Cortés back to Cuba as a prisoner, and Cortés learned from messengers that the new expedition had captured his base of operations in Veracruz. Never a passive man, Cortés decided to return to the coast and confront Velásquez' expedition. In doing so he left the city of Tenochtitlán and Moctezuma in the hands of Pedro de Alvarado, who promptly murdered several hundred Aztec leaders. Cortés was able to defeat the expedition Velásquez had sent, and quickly returned to Tenochtitlán, where he found the Aztecs in open rebellion against the excesses of Alvarado. Moctezuma was now discredited and of little use to Cortés, who was forced to retreat from Tenochtitlán in the defeat the Spanish called "La Noche Triste" (the sad or tragic night). Aided by an outbreak of deadly smallpox, Cortés was able to regroup, and complete the conquest by August 1521.

Letter of Report, Hernán Cortés to King Charles V
(The Spaniards enter the city of Tenochtitlán, 1520)

...Having passed this bridge, Lord Moctezuma came out to meet us, with almost two hundred lords, all barefoot and dressed in different livery and manner of clothing, very ornate, much more so than that of the previous ones. They came in two processions, pressed close to the walls of the street, which is very broad, straight and beautiful on both sides; it is about two thirds of a league long, and on both sides there are very large and grand edifices, both houses as well as temples.

Moctezuma walked down the middle of the street with two lords, one on each side. One of the lords was the tall one who had come out to meet me previously, and the other was Moctezuma's brother, the lord of the city of Iztapalapa, which I had departed from the same day. All three were clothed the same way, except that Moctezuma had footwear and the others were barefoot. The two lords were close to his elbows, and when I came near to them I dismounted from my horse and tried to embrace Moctezuma. But his two companions held me back so I could not touch him, and then the three of them ceremoniously kissed the earth...

When I spoke to Moctezuma I first removed a necklace I was wearing made of pearls and glass diamonds, and placed it around his neck. After a short walk one of his servants came with two necklaces, wrapped in a cloth, made from the shells of red snails which they have in abundance. From each necklace hung eight golden shrimp, perfectly made, and very large. After he received these necklaces he turned to me and put them around my neck, and continued down the street until we reached a large and beautiful house, well appointed, which he had set aside for us to rest in.

There he took me by the hand and escorted me to a great hall which faced the patio through which we had entered. There he had me sit in a luxurious drawing room and asked me to wait. In a short while, once all of my company was settled, he returned with many and diverse jewels of gold and silver, and feathers, and perhaps five or six thousand pieces of cotton clothing, very luxurious and woven and crafted in many diverse ways. And after he had given me all these things he sat down and began to speak to me in this manner:

"For a long time we have known from the scriptures that our ancestors wrote that neither I nor all the others who live in these lands are native to it, but rather we are foreigners who have come here from very distant parts. We also know that a Lord brought us to these parts, and that all of us were his vassals, and that he then reverted to his original nature"...

"And we have always believed that his descendants would return someday to dominate these lands and also us, as their vassals. According to the things you tell us about your land of origin, which is where the sun rises, and the things you say about this great lord or king who sent you here, we believe and hold to be true the fact that he is our natural lord. Especially since you tell us that he has known about us for some time. For this reason you may be sure that we will obey you and consider you lord in place of the great lord who sent you. In this there will be nothing held back and no trickery. And in any of my lands you may command at your will, because you will be obeyed, and everything we have is yours to dispose of as you wish."

Bernal Díaz del Castillo

For another perspective of the conquest of Mexico we have the work of one of Cortés' soldiers, Bernal Díaz del Castillo (1495?-1584). He was a lower ranking soldier who had accompanied Cortés in over a hundred battles and skirmishes in Mexico, and he provides us with the viewpoint of the common man instead of the heroic leader. His only work, The True History of the Conquest of New Spain (Mexico), was not published until sixty years after his death, and did not achieve acclaim until many years after that.

In 1518 Bernal Díaz had taken part in one of the early expeditions which explored Mexico's Caribbean coast, and thus was well prepared when he joined Cortés' expedition in 1520. He accompanied Cortés during the key battles in Tenochtitlán, and then later in other parts of Mexico and Central America from 1521 to 1524. As his reward, he was granted an *encomienda* (a large parcel of land along with the Indians living on it) in Guatemala. He lived out his life there in Santiago de los Caballeros (Antigua), Guatemala, where he is buried.

As an old man he read an account of the conquest of Mexico prepared by the priest Francisco López de Gómara, who had served Cortés as secretary in Spain. But Gómara was not present during the conquest of Mexico, and had never served in a conquering expedition. Furthermore, as Cortés' secretary, he naturally gave his employer full credit for all the glorious deeds of the conquest, presenting him in the best light possible. Bernal Díaz reacted with anger at Gómara's account, feeling that it distorted the truth and neglected the common soldier, and began to write his own history of the conquest.

Although Bernal Díaz does not attack Cortés, or try to diminish his glory or fame, clearly he feels that the hero of the conquest is a collective one, namely the conquistadores as a group. Thus, his work is a populist one, exalting the courage and feats of the frequently anonymous common soldier as much as the captains and leaders. In addition, he frequently makes corrections to what he perceives are the errors and exaggerations of Gómara.

Bernal Díaz also gives us a different perspective of the Aztec: he is the enemy, frequently cruel, who must be decisively defeated to permit the success of the Spanish enterprise. But he also expresses admiration for some of the Aztec leaders, especially Moctezuma and Cuahutemoc (the last emperor, who was killed by Cortés). In presenting the common soldier as hero, Bernal Díaz does not accept the criticism of people like Father las Casas, who during this time was bitterly criticizing the excesses of the Spanish conquistadores and early settlers. But Bernal Diaz' account is often frank and direct, and in his stories of the conquest he sometimes does chronicle excesses on the part of his fellow-soldiers.

The first of the two fragments of the True History which follow deals with Marina/Malinche, and stresses the importance of her contribution. The second selection provides details of the Spanish retreat from Tenochtitlán during the "Noche Triste" of 30 June of the year 1520.

True History of the Conquest by **Bernal Díaz del Castillo**
Regarding Doña Marina

6.4: **Bernal Díaz**

Before I get into the matter of the great Moctezuma and his great Mexico and the Mexicans, I want to tell of Doña Marina, and how, from her girlhood, she was a great Lady and leader of the people and vassals, in this manner:

Her father and mother were Lords and chiefs of a town called Painala, and they had other peoples subject to them, about eight leagues from the village of Coatzacoalcos. Her father died when Doña Marina was a little girl, and her mother then married another gentle chief, and they had a son. It seemed that they loved the son very much, and between the father and mother they agreed to give the son their inheritance after their days on earth had passed. In order to avoid any problems with Marina in this inheritance, they gave the girl away one night to some Indians from Xicalango with orders to hide her, and then they put the word out that she had died. At about that time the daughter of a slave of theirs died, and they told everyone that the corpse was that of their daughter Marina. And the Indians of Xicalango gave Marina to those of Tabasco and those of Tabasco gave her to Cortés.

I knew her mother and her half-brother, son of the old lady. He was now a man and governed his people jointly with his mother, because the mother's second husband (his father) had died. After they converted to Christianity the old woman took the name Mary, and the son Lazarus. I know this very well because in the year 1523, after Mexico and other provinces were conquered, and Cristóbal de Olid had rebelled in las Higueras, Cortés went there and passed through Coatzacoalcos. With him and us on that trip were most of the inhabitants of that town, as I will relate in the proper time and place.

Inasmuch as Doña Marina, in all the wars of New Spain, Tlascala and Mexico, was such an excellent woman and good interpreter, as I will explain later on, Cortés always took her with him. On that trip and occasion she married a nobleman named Juan Jaramillo in a town called Orizaba in front of various witnesses. One of them was called Aranda, a neighbor of Tabasco, and he told me of the wedding, and it was not the way recorded by the chronicler Gómara. Doña Marina had a lot of presence, and had absolute say among the Indians of all of New Spain.

Cortés, while in the town of Coatzacoalcos, ordered that all the chiefs of that province be called to have a parley regarding the holy doctrine and its proper treatment. At that moment Doña Marina's mother and her son Lázaro arrived, with the other chiefs. It had been some days since Marina told me that she was from that province, and Lady of the vassals. This was well known to Cortés, and to Aguilar the interpreter, so that when they saw the mother, her daughter, and her brother, they knew right away that she was her mother's daughter because she looked a great deal like her. The mother and son were afraid of Marina because they thought she had ordered them to come so that they would be killed, and they cried.

When Doña Marina saw them crying this way, she consoled them saying that they should not be afraid, because when they had given her away as a young girl to the Indians of Xicalango, they did not know what they were doing, and she forgave them. She gave them much gold jewelry and clothing and told them that they should

6.5: **Marina interpreting**

return to their village, and that God had given her much grace because she no longer worshipped idols, and was a Christian, and was married to a gentleman, who was her husband Juan Jaramillo. She said that even though she might be named chief of all the provinces in New Spain, she would not accept this post, because she placed greater value in serving her husband and Cortés than anything else in the world. All of this which I tell you I heard, and can attest to, and I swear it, amen.

This seems to me similar to what happened to Joseph and his brothers in Egypt, who came to power during that business of the wheat. This is what really happened, and not like Gómara tells it. He also said some other things which I will overlook.

Returning to our subject, Doña Marina knew the language of Guacacualco, which is the tongue of Mexico, and also knew the language of Tabasco, and

Jerónimo de Aguilar knew the language of Yucatán and Tabasco, which is one and the same. They (Marina and Aguilar) understood each other well, and Aguilar would pass the information on in Castillian to Cortés. It was a great beginning to our conquest, and things went our way, glory be to God, in a very prosperous way. I wanted to state all this because without Doña Marina, we would not have been able to understand the tongue of New Spain and Mexico.

The Tragic Night

After we learned of Cortés' decision regarding the way in which we were to leave that night over the bridges, and since it was dark and foggy and drizzly, just before midnight we began to bring the portable bridge and march with the baggage and the horses and the mare and the Tlaxcaltecas loaded with the gold. We put the bridge in place and Cortés and the rest of his group crossed over first, many of them on horse. And at that moment we heard the voices and the trumpets and the shouts and whistles of the Mexicans, who cried out in their language to those of Tatuleco: "Come out with your canoes because the teules (Spaniards) are leaving, and you must grab them so that none will get out alive!" And just when we were not expecting it we saw a great number of squadrons of warriors fall on us, and their lake was filled with uncountable canoes, even though many of our soldiers had gotten through.

And, at that point, so many Mexicans came to remove our bridge and wound and kill our people, that we could not help them. Since fortune is bad in such times, one bad thing happened after another: because it was raining, the horses slipped and fell into the water. When we, and Cortés' group, saw this, we tried to regain control of the bridge, but they had so many warriors that we were unable to, despite our great struggle.

6.6: The Tragic Night

And as a result, there was a water gap where the bridge was supposed to go, and this gap was quickly filled with dead horses and Indians and their women, and the porters and baggage and trunks. Fearing that they would end up killing us all, we pushed ahead along the causeway and ran into many more squadrons who were waiting for us with long spears, and who cried out to us with insulting words, saying: "Oh, you devils, you are still alive!"

Stabbing and thrusting with sword and knife we cut our way through them, although they wounded six of ours. Cortés and his captains and soldiers who had gone first on the causeway on horse, had saved themselves and reached the mainland and made it without losing anyone. They were also able to bring out the horses with the gold and the Tlaxcaltecas, but we, if we waited any longer, would have all been killed, soldiers as well as horses, and none would have gotten out alive. The reason was this: while we were fighting our way along the causeway we were being attacked by the Mexican squadrons, and on one side we had water and the lake full of canoes, and on the other we had houses. We could do nothing, since our firearms and our crossbows had stayed on the bridge, and it being dark and at night, what could we do except what we tried to do, which was to push forward and stab those who tried to stop us, and push through across the causeway. If it had been daylight, it might have been even worse. And those of us who did escape, did so because Our Lord helped us. And for anyone who did not that night see the multitude of warriors who fell upon us, and the canoes which they used to attack our soldiers, it was frightful.

We who pushed on ahead along the causeway reached the town of Tacuba, where we found Cortés and the other captains, Gonzalo de Sandoval and Cristóbal de Olid and the others on horse who had gone on ahead. They were crying out to Cortés: "Sir captain, listen to us, because they say we are fleeing and we are leaving our friends behind to die on the bridges. Let us go back to see if we can protect those who have stayed and have not come out". Cortés' answer was that it was a miracle that any had gotten out. But he decided later to go back to the bridges with the horses and the ones who were not wounded.

They had not gone very far when they came upon Pedro de Alvarado, badly wounded, with a spear in his hand and on foot, because his sorrel mare had been killed, and he brought with him four soldiers as badly wounded as he was, and eight Tlastaltecans, all of whom had bleeding wounds. And while Cortés went along the causeway with the other captains and the Indians of Tacuba, there arrived from Mexico many squadrons yelling out orders to the Tacubans and to those from Atzcapozalco, and they began to hurl lances and stones and arrows and great spears. We made some charges in which we both defended ourselves and attacked.

6.7: Conquistadores

7: The Conquest of Peru and Chile

The Conquest of Peru: Pizarro

The conquest of the Andean Inca Empire is associated with the name of Francisco Pizarro (1470?-1541), a man of more limited education and preparation than Cortés, but who imitated him in a number of ways. Pizarro was the illegitimate son of a minor nobleman in Estremadura, Spain, and spent his youth looking after his father's swine. When the early Spanish explorers began to organize the first expeditions, Pizarro was more than eager to join them. He eventually settled in Panama, where rumors of a rich kingdom to the south in a place called "Biru" were circulating. He launched two small exploratory expeditions which brought back some gold, fine weavings, and a strange animal called a llama. But Pizarro had problems obtaining money and men for a new expedition, and he decided to appeal directly to the Spanish King Charles I.

Pizarro arrived at the Spanish court at a most auspicious time in the year 1528. Cortés had just returned from Mexico with physical proof of the riches of the Aztec Empire, and King Charles was more than willing to believe that a similar fortune awaited an enterprising explorer on the South American mainland. And so he named Pizarro his *adelantado*, a position which included a generous salary (to be collected from whatever riches he found in his adventure). Armed with the King's support, Pizarro returned to Panama and was finally able to mount his definitive expedition in 1531, with some 180 men and 27 horses. He first landed on the coast of what is today's Ecuador, on the northern fringes of the Inca Empire. There he

7.1: **Pizarro and his men**

learned that the Empire was deeply divided and weakened by a long civil war between two claimants to the throne. Although the war had just finished, with the Inca Atahualpa the victor, there were still many Inca subjects who supported his rival. Pizarro sensed that the time was ripe for a quick strike at the heart of the Empire by capturing and holding Atahualpa himself, much as Cortés had done with Moctezuma in Mexico.

And so, reinforced with troops and horsemen led by Hernando de Soto (who was later to discover the Mississippi) he headed to the Inca city of Cajamarca, a difficult march up into the Andes mountains and the heart of the Inca Empire. To their surprise, on arriving in late 1532, Pizarro found Cajamarca deserted, and learned that the Inca Atahualpa had moved his soldiers to a camp near his royal baths. Pizarro sent his brother and de Soto to intimidate the Inca with their horses and invite him to Cajamarca. The events which followed, and which marked the beginning of the end of the Inca empire, are described in the reading later on in this chapter.

7.2: Atahualpa captured

After capturing Atahualpa, Pizarro accepted the Inca's offer of obtaining his freedom in exchange for a room full of gold and one of silver. For two months the Inca's people brought in their precious objects to fill the rooms and then be melted down to make it easier to ship back to Spain. All of Pizarro's men became instantly rich, since even after the King's fifth the lowest ranking soldier's share was some ninety pounds of gold and a hundred and eighty of silver.

The final outcome was not happy. Pizarro was reluctant to release Atahualpa, afraid that he would lead an uprising against the Spanish (several rebellions were in fact mounted). So the Spanish found an excuse to accuse Atahualpa of conspiracy and condemned him to death by fire, a sentence that was changed to garroting (strangulation) when he embraced the Christian faith of his conquerors.

Pizarro moved quickly to seize the Inca capital of Cuzco in 1533, and then founded the coastal city of Lima to facilitate communications with Panama and Spain. Pizarro's men fell to squabbling among themselves over the riches, the land, and the slaves they hoped to control. A series of civil wars between various groups of Spaniards ensued until the King sent a strong Viceroy to impose order. Pizarro himself died in a sword battle against assassins; his remains are on display in the main cathedral of Lima.

Guamán Poma de Ayala's description

Guamán Poma de Ayala (1526?-1614?) was descended from a noble Inca family, but his name symbolizes the process of cultural *mestizaje* (transcultural adaptation or transculturation) that took place shortly after the conquest. "Guamán" means "falcon" in the Quechua language of the Inca, while "poma" is a variant of the puma mountain lion; "Ayala" is a Spanish name. His principal work was titled (with some irony) *The First New Chronicle of Good Government*, and in its 1800 pages and over 300 drawings he presents us a vivid picture of the last days of the Incas, the conquest, and the imposition of Spanish Colonial rule by Pizarro and his men in the decade of the 1530's. His language and style is difficult in the original because of his lack of formal education and his mixed Spanish-Quechua vocabulary. But the book is a unique encyclopedia of the Quechua Inca world of his parents, the history of his race, its origins, kings, customs, feasts, religion, and everyday life. He devotes considerable attention to the arrival of the Spanish (Guamán Poma was about six years old when Pizarro landed in Túmbez in 1532) and to the destruction of the Inca Empire.

The First New Chronicle and Good Government
by Guamán Poma de Ayala

Captain general Rumuiani, ambassador of Atahualpa the Inca, went to the port of Túmbez to meet with Don Francisco de Pizarro, the ambassador of the Emperor (of Spain). Pizarro and Diego de Almagro had many responses and compliments. The Inca's ambassador begged the Christians to return to their lands and he said that he would give them much gold and silver to leave. And they answered that they wished to see and kiss the hands of the Inca king. After that they would go away and tell everything to their king the emperor.

The Inca Atahualpa sent Indian serfs to Don Francisco Pizarro and his men. They gave them beds, rich gifts and women. They also gave gifts to all the horses, because they said that these horses were people who ate corn.

In the year one thousand five hundred and thirty; Pope Clement VII (eleven years of his Pontificate); Emperor Don Carlos the Fifth (of his Empire fifteen years) Don Francisco Pizarro and Don Diego de Almagro march to the city of Cajamarca with one hundred and sixty soldiers against Atahualpa the Inca with one hundred thousand Indians; Hernando de Soto, Sebastián de

7.3: Ambassadors, Pizarro

Balcázar and Hernando Pizarro with twenty knights on horse and Felipe Guancabilca, Indian interpreter, brought for the conquest. They entered Cajamarca and the aforesaid Inca Atahualpa was not there, he was at the baths. Atahualpa sent his ambassador to the city saying that the Spanish Christians should return to their own lands. Don Francisco Pizarro and Don Diego de Almagro responded that they would not return yet. ...

Since the aforesaid Atahualpa was at the Cajamarca baths, Hernando Pizarro and Sebastián de Balcázar went there on their horses, furious and armed, and they carried many bells and plumes and said armed knights dug their legs into their horses' flanks and galloped furiously. They said that this panicked the Inca and the Indians who were at the Cajamarca baths, since they had never before seen this. All the Inca's people were panicked, astonished, and everyone ran away because such huge animals ran towards them, and on top of each animal was a man, something never before seen. Don Francisco Pizarro and Friar Vicente of the order of our Lord San Francisco went to the city of Cajamarca. Atahualpa the Inca went from the baths to the city and court of Cajamarca, with his captains and many more people, one hundred thousand Indians, in the public plaza, in the middle

And then Don Francisco Pizarro and Don Diego de Almagro began to talk to him, using their interpreter Felipe, the Guancabilca Indian. Pizarro said that he was a messenger and ambassador of a great lord, and that he was a friend, and that he had come only for that purpose.

The Inca replied very courteously, and with majesty, saying that it might be true that they came from such a distant land as messengers, and that he believed their king was a great lord, but he the Inca had no need to make friendships, that he too was a great lord in his kingdom.

7.4: The "Requirement"

After this reply, Frair Vicente came in with his approach, carrying a cross in his right hand and the Bible in his left. And he said to the Inca Atahualpa that he too was an ambassador and messenger from another lord, a great friend of God, and who was his friend, and that he should worship the cross and believe in the gospel of God and that anything else was of little importance.

Atahualpa the Inca replied, saying that he had no need to worship anyone except the sun that never dies. And the Inca asked Friar Vicente who had told him what he just said. Friar Vicente answered that the gospel, the book, had told him so.

And Atahualpa said: give it to me, the book, so that it can speak to me. And he took it in his hands, and began to leaf through the pages of the book. And the Inca said that this book is saying nothing to me, and he threw the book down.

Full twenty leagues their boundaries contain,
And sixteen warrior chieftains hold the land.

  Robust and strong, hairless of lip and chin,
Well-grown and tall above the run of men,
Of ample shoulders and capacious breasts,
And brawny limbs thickset with stubborn thews,
Ready and nimble and high-spirited,
Haughty and daring, reckless in assault,
Hardy and tireless, bearing undismayed
Cold, hunger, heat, and all extremities.

  Nor ever has a king by force subdued
This haughty people to his vassalage,
Nor has the foot of an invading foe
Left shameful print upon Arauco's soil,
Nor neighboring tribe so temerarious
To try the battle with their furious hosts.
Untamed and feared by all, they live or die
With haughty neck unbowed to God or man.

  Once in times gone the Inca potentate
Renowned in arms thru all those southern coasts
And eager to subdue new lands and tribes,
Hearing reports of this unconquered race,
Marshaled an army of his chosen braves,
Then, under his best captains, bade them take
The road to Chile; but Arauco's fame
Cooled their hot blood and turned them back again.

Who, with damp mud to the waist,
With two or three fought;
who to show greater boldness,
trying to move, became more enmired;
who, trying his strength and fortune,
to the neighboring enemy held fast
biting him and blinding him with mud
seeking to win in any way he could.

7.9: Incas fight Araucanians

7.10: Santiago, the patron saint of the Reconquest (Santiago Matamoros) and the Conquest of the Americas (Santiago Mataindios)

8: The Indigenous Perspective and "The Defender of the Indians"

The Indigenous Perspective of the Conquest

As we noted previously, in their zeal to impose their will on the conquered peoples of the Americas, the Spanish attempted to suppress all manifestations of the earlier cultures and religions. Since most of the pre-Columbian literature was passed on orally, it was not simply a matter of burning books and destroying libraries. The oral tradition survived in many cases, with poems and stories being re-told time and again out of the hearing of the new Spanish authorities and settlers. And in a few cases these traditions were written down in Spanish by Indigenous and mestizo story-tellers who had learned how to read.

Among the interesting elements of this literature are those pieces dealing with the conquest itself, since they provide the unique perspective of those who lost the battle and paid the price. The authors are anonymous, and we must assume that there may have been important modifications from the original to the versions we know.

The Aztec view of the Conquest
(Anonymous; presumably authored during the conquest of Mexico, around 1521).

And all this happened with us.
We saw it,
we watched it
and with this mournful and sad fate
we were anguished.
In the roads lie broken spears;
our hair is in disarray.
The houses are roofless,
the walls are red with blood.
Worms swarm in the streets and plazas

8.1: Mistreating indigenous

and the walls are spattered with brains.
The waters are red, as if dyed,
and if we drink them, they are salt brine.
In our despair
we beat against the adobe walls
and all that is left of our inheritance
is a net of holes.
Our shields were our defense,
but shields cannot stop desolation.
We have eaten bread of flax seed,
we have chewed salty marsh grass,
and pieces of adobe, lizards, rats,
and dirt dust and even worms.

We ate the meat
when it was barely on the fire.
When it was cooked,
they grabbed it out of the
very coals and ate it.

A price was put on us.
A price for the young man, the priest,
the child, the girl.
It was enough:
for the poor man
the price was two handfuls of corn
or ten cakes of flies;
our price was only
twenty cakes of salty marsh grass.

8.2: Aztec prisoners

Gold, jade, rich cloaks,
quetzal feathers,
all that was precious
was valued as nothing.

The fall of Tenochtitlán:
(Anonymous; first version presumably authored circa 1521)

The cry spreads out,
tears fall there in Tlatelolco.
By water the Mexicans fled;
they are like women
the flight is general.

Where are we going?
Oh my friends! Was it true?
They have abandoned
the city of Mexico:
the smoke rises;
the fog is spreading...
Cry, my friends,
understand that with these events
we have lost the Mexican nation.

The Hundred Years of the People of the Sun
(For comparison with the despair of the last poem,
consider this one, authored before the Conquest)

From where the eagles repose,
from where the tigers rise up,
the Sun is invoked.

Like a shield that comes down
the sun is setting,
In Mexico nightfall is nigh
and war rages all around.
Oh Giver of Life!
War draws near.

Proud of itself
the city of Mexico-Tenochtitlan rises up.
Here no one fears death in combat.
This is our glory.
This is your command.
Oh Giver of Life!
Remember it, oh princes,
do not forget it.
Who can lay siege to Tenochtitlan?
Who can shake
the foundations of heaven?

With our arrows,
with our shields,
the city exists,
Mexico-Tenochtitlan endures!

8.3: Aztec emperor

The "Defender of the Indians": Las Casas

8.4: The Defender of the Indians

Bartolomé de las Casas (1474-1566) came to America in 1502 as a young man in search of his fortune. He was assigned an *encomienda* (grant of land and the Indigenous living on it) in Hispaniola, and he proceeded to exploit the Indigenous in much the same manner as his fellow Spaniards. After a few years, however, he became associated with a group of Dominican priests, entered the priesthood himself, and developed a social conscience on the issue of the exploitation of the Indigenous. He gave up both his lands and his Indians and became a life-long crusader against these wrongs.

One of his approaches was to remind the settlers that the King had given them their *encomiendas* on the condition that they educate the Indians, teach them the Catholic faith, and treat them well, conditions which very few of the settlers complied with. When this approach did not have much effect, Las Casas took his case to the highest authorities in Spain. Here he received a sympathetic hearing, was given the title of "Defender of the Indians", and was instrumental in persuading the King to promulgate the *New Laws of the Indies* in 1542. This new legislation aimed at ameliorating the brutal treatment given to the Indians, and although they did not fundamentally change the situation, they stand as testimony to Las Casas' efforts.

8.5: Las Casas

At one point Las Casas suggested that an alternative to enslaving the Indians would be to bring Black slaves from Africa. He has often been criticized for this idea, but in fairness to him it should be noted that the idea was not originally his, and he quickly repudiated it, arguing that slavery was inherently evil whether it involved the Indian or the Black.

8.6: African slaves on Caribbean sugar plantation

In 1547 he wrote his most powerful tract, the *Brevísima Relación de la Destrucción de las Indias (Brief Account of the Destruction of the Indies)*, in which he presented in gruesome detail the excesses of the Spaniards. Although he exaggerated, his accusations were justified, and they did cause the Spanish Crown to institute reforms. However, his tract also reached the Northern Europeans, who seized upon it as proof of the truth of the so-called "Black Legend", which portrayed Spain in the worst possible light. In a short period of time the work was translated into Latin, English, French, German and Dutch. Here is the subtitle carried in the English translation of 1606: "Popery truly Display'd in its Bloody Colours: Or a Faithful Narrative of the Horrid and Unexampled Massacres, Butcheries, and all manner of Cruelties, that Hell and Malice could invent, committed by the Popish Spanish Party on the Inhabitants of West-India... Composed first in Spanish by Bartholomew de las Casas, a Bishop there, and an Eye-Witness of most of these Barbarous Cruelties; afterwards translated by him into Latin, then by other hands into High-Dutch, Low-Dutch, French, and now Modern English".

Las Casas stands as an example of moral outrage and conscience against the abuses of the early Spanish settlers. Although he unwittingly provided the Northern European enemies of Spain with ammunition for their propaganda, the excesses in their own colonies were also brutal, and there were few voices raised in protest in Northern Europe. His voice of accusation against exploitation was the first to be heard from Spanish America, it and continues to have echoes in the literature of social protest to the present day.

Brief Account of the Destruction of the Indies (1547) by **Bartolomé de las Casas** (extract)

The Island of Hispaniola was where the Christians first entered and began their great ravages and ruination of these people. The Christians first destroyed and depopulated, beginning by taking the women and the children from the Indians in order to have them as servants and to abuse them and take their food which was the fruit of their sweat and their labors. The Christians were not happy

8.7: Abuse of the indigenous

with what the Indians gave up voluntarily on the basis of what each one possessed. The Indians never did possess much, and they barely had enough to survive. What is enough for three Indian households of ten people each for a month is eaten and destroyed by a Christian in just a day. After much violence, force and oppression, the Indians began to understand that these men had not come from the heavens. So some began to hide their food and others their women and children. Others fled to the forests to get away from those hard and terrible people. The Christians would slap and hit them with fists and clubs, and even laid hand on the lords of the people. And this reached such temerity and shameful abuse that a Christian captain forcibly raped the wife of the principal king of the island.

Enriquillo's Rebellion.

8.8: Enriquillo

During this time (late 1518) notable events occurred on this island of Hispaniola, and one of them was the way in which the Indians were dying out, and despite this the Spaniards did not cease to overwork and mistreat them. One of the Spaniards was a young man named Valenzuela who unjustly and tyrannically possessed an inherited *repartimiento* of Indians from his father, and the chief and lord of this *repartimiento* was named Enriquillo.

Enriquillo had been raised as a child in the monastery of San Francisco in the village the Spanish called Vera Paz, in the province, according to the Indian tongue, of Xaragúa. Here ruled Behechio, the principal monarch of the five kings of this island, of whom we have talked much in our first and second book.

The friars had taught Enriquillo to read and write, and had given him the Christian doctrine, and he missed nothing, and knew how to speak our tongue very well, and he always showed in his deeds that he had learned much from the priests (...) This chief and lord of that province of Baoruco, having studied the doctrine of the priests and become a man, married an Indian lady, a noble woman of good lineage, called Doña Lucía, and they were married as Christians in the sight of the Holy Mother Church.

Enriquillo was a tall and gentle man with a well-proportioned body and disposition; his face was neither beautiful nor ugly, but rather was grave and severe. He served the aforementioned young man Valenzuela with his Indians as was required of him, under the law, patiently suffering his unjust servitude and affronts which he received every day. Among the few and pitiful goods which he possessed was a mare, and this mare was taken from him against his will by the tyrannical master he served; and after this, not being content with that armed robbery, he tried to violate the chief's matrimony and rape his wife. And when Enriquillo complained to him, asking why he had done this harm and affront, it is said that Valenzuela beat him with a stick in order to make the proverb come true: "insulted and beaten".

8.9: Priest and indigenous

Enriquillo went to complain of his mistreatment to the governor's lieutenant who lived in that village, by name Pedro de Vadillo. He found in Vadillo that comfort that the Indians always found in matters of justice at the hands of the ministers of the king. Vadillo threatened him, warning him what would happen and what he would do to Enriquillo if he returned with any more complaints against Valenzuela: he told Enriquillo that he would throw him in jail or in the stocks. After he was let go with no satisfaction at the hands of this minister of justice, the saddened Enriquillo decided to come to this city of Santo Domingo to complain to the Audiencia of the injuries and insults which he had received. But he was very poor, tired and hungry, and had no money to remedy his situation.

The head of the Audiencia gave Enriquillo his sympathy, but he sent him back to the aforementioned lieutenant Vadillo with no other recourse; and this too was the consolation which the Audiencias and even the king's Counselor, who resides in Castille, give to the injured and the miserable: to send them back, one should realize, to the very people they had complained about, back to their own enemies.

Once back at the village, which was 30 leagues away, Enriquillo presented his documents, and the justice he received from Vadillo was, it was said, to mistreat him with words and threats worse than the first time. With the approval of his master Valenzuela, he received worse treatment and surprises and beatings and threats of death and other events, based on the ancient disdain in which the Indians were viewed, and the harsh rule which the Spaniards afflicted them with, without any fear of God or justice, so that they would beat them with sticks or blows instead of giving them food as consolation and rest after their voyage.

The chief Enriquillo bore the new injuries and affronts quietly. But then came the period of several months in the year in which the group of Indians working for the Spaniards was to be changed, and it was Enriquillo's role to bring the new Indians and take the first group back. In this process the chief was the one who would endure insults and beatings and even jail if any Indians were missing. And Enriquillo, who by now had little faith in Spanish justice, and more faith in his own land, which was rough, and where horses could not climb, decided to serve his enemy no longer, to send no more Indians, and to defend himself in his own territory. And this the Spanish called, and still call to this day, the "uprising and rebellion of Enriquillo and his followers". In truth, it was nothing more than to flee from his cruel enemies, who had killed and consumed them, in the same way that the cow or the ox flees the butcher. And Valenzuela, when he realized that Enriquillo was not going to send him any more Indians because of his mistreatment, and that he was angry and upset and, as they would say, had risen up, he went with eleven men to bring him down by force and mistreat him some more.

Once he arrived there he found Enriquillo and his people prepared, with weapons, which were spears, clubs with nails and fish bones, and bows and arrows and stones and anything else they could find as weapons. They came out to meet them, with chief Enriquillo at the head, and he told Valenzuela to go back, because neither he nor his Indians would work for him any more. And Valenzuela, who saw him as a slave, and held him in the usual contempt with which the Spaniards saw the Indians, as if they were dung in the plaza, began to call him a dog and many other hurtful words, and then he attacked Enriquillo and the Indians who were with him. But the Indians defended themselves well and quickly, killing one or two of his Spaniards and wounding all of the others, who turned their backs and ran away. Enriquillo did not want to pursue them, but rather let them go, and said to Valenzuela: "Be grateful, Valenzuela, that I do . not kill you. Go, leave this place and never come back. You are warned."

Valenzuela went with his men to San Juan de la Maguana, with his damaged pride, and desire for revenge. And the news ran through the island that

Enriquillo was leading an uprising. The Audiencia determined that men had to put the rebellion down; so some 70 or 80 Spaniards went to find him. These, after many days of hunger and exhaustion, found him in a certain hill; he went out to meet them, killed some and wounded others, and they were all routed and humiliated, and agreed with much sadness and affront to retreat. The fame and victories of Enriquillo were soon known all over the island, and many Indians fled their forced servitude and the oppression of the Spaniards to join the refuge and flag of Enriquillo. He was like an impregnable rocky castle, and they came to him, anguished, oppressed by debts and bitter in their spirits, as if he were David and they were fleeing from the tyranny of Saul, as it appears in the first book of Kings, Chapter 22. And so, because of this resemblance there came to Enriquillo some 300 men who accepted his leadership, although his own people were, I believe, barely 100.

He taught them how they should fight against the Spanish, and how to defend themselves if they should come. And he never allowed them to go out and attack or kill any Spaniard, instead limiting them to defending themselves, and their loved ones, against the Spanish attacks, which many times came to submit him and offend him. This was a just war against the Spanish under his elected leadership; it was like the history of the Maccabeans in the divine Scriptures, or like the Spanish fights which are narrated in the deeds of the prince Don Pelayo, who not only fought a just war of natural defense, but also could proceed to wreak vengeance and punishment for the injuries and harm and death and killing of their peoples and theft of their lands, in the same manner and with the same rights.

As far as natural law is concerned (and leaving aside the teachings of our sacred faith, which is another chapter dealing with the right of Christian self-defense), Enriquillo and his few Indians on this island had just, very just, cause, because they had fallen into the cruel hands and horrible tyranny of the Spaniards, who pursued, destroyed, punished and laid waste to them as if they were their capital enemies, destroyers of their great republics, such as existed on this island, and what they did under natural law was not called war, but natural self-defense.

On the many occasions on this island in which armed groups rose up, they were able to obtain many weapons, and the Indians who rebelled were able to steal weapons from their masters. And all over the island there was an unusual vigilance and diligence and care to protect Enriquillo and all those who were with him, as if all his life he had been a captain in Italy. He had his guards and spies in the ports and other places where he knew that the Spaniards could come to look for him.

When the spies and guards would tell him that there were Spaniards in the area, he would take all the women and children and the old and sick, if there were any, and everyone who could not fight, along with the 50 warriors he always had with him, and he would take them 10 to 12 leagues away, in secret places he had in the hills, where he had cultivated lands and food. He would leave behind a captain, a nephew of his barely a cubit high, but very strong, with all his warriors to wait for the Spaniards. When they arrived, they would fight against the Indians like lions. But then Enriquillo would arrive, fresh, with his 50 men, and he would deal with them as he saw fit, wounding and killing them, so that even though many Spaniards came to fight him, they were always routed, and he always won.

One time it happened that a group of 71 or 72 Spaniards had been routed and they fled to some caves in the mountains in order to hide from the Indians. When the Indians discovered the Spaniards, they wanted to bring firewood and burn them. Enriquillo ordered: "I do not want them burned. Instead, take their weapons and leave them be. Let them go". And so they did, and they obtained many swords and spears and crossbows, even though they did not know how to use these. Of these 70 Spaniards one became a friar in the monastery of Santo Domingo, in the city of Santo Domingo, because of a promise he had made when he believed he would not escape, and I learned of all this from him.

Each day the fame of the victories and diligence, effort and stratagems of Enriquillo and his people spread more and more around the island because, it was said, the Spaniards who went out to find Enriquillo always came back routed. And so the entire island admired him, and there was unrest, and when the Spaniards raised a force to hunt him not all went voluntarily, and they would not have gone at all had the Audiencia not forced them to. All of this lasted thirteen to fourteen years, and the Royal treasury spent more than 80 or 100,000 castellanos on it.

8.10: Abuse of the indigenous (by Guamán Poma de Ayala)

9: The Colonial Baroque

The Colonial Centuries

The accomplishment and the price

For an upper-class Spaniard living in the Colonial Centuries (from the end of the Conquest in the mid 1500's to the early 1800's) there was considerable cause for pride and satisfaction in the accomplishments of his or her nation. In the space of a half a century, a few thousand courageous and adventuresome Spaniards had created the geographically largest empire the world had ever known, stretching from the Golden Gate in San Francisco to the Strait of Magellan, Cape Horn, and unknown territories perhaps as far as the South Pole. Inspired by the success of the Reconquest struggle against the Moors, the Conquest of America was also a religious crusade in which the Roman Catholic religion was brought to millions of converts. And that "instrument of empire", the Castillian language, was the official tongue of this huge extension of territory. In Portuguese America the accomplishments were of lesser magnitude, but almost as impressive. Furthermore, these twin Iberian empires in the New World were to endure for three centuries, giving this region the longest period of stability it had ever known, or was likely to ever experience.

The price, of course, was the profound alteration, and in many cases destruction, of the political, social and cultural structures the Iberians found in America. One immediate effect in the first half-century was the population crash among the Indigenous peoples, followed by the brutality of the Black slave trade. For the rest of the Colonial period the prosperity and pride of the upper class Iberians was paid for by the labor of those who found themselves in the lower portions of the socio-economic pyramid.

9.1: Colonial elites

Table 9.1: The Colonial Baroque (Chapter 9)

Cultural-historical framework:	**The Colonial Baroque: evolution and exaggeration of the Renaissance** **Cultural mestizaje** **The three colonial centuries between the Conquest (16C) and Independence (19C)**
Approximate dates:	**Middle of the 16th Century to Independence, early 19th Century**
Historical landmarks	**Three Centuries of tranquility under the Iberian crowns** **Outbreaks of rebellion; the Precursors**
Literature	**The Baroque: word-plays, artificiality** **Profusion of details** **Twisted phrases, conceits** **Focus on exotic geography, vegetation: cataloguing of types, colors, odors.** **Sor Juana Inés de la Cruz, 1648-1695** **Bernardo de Balbuena (1562-1627)**
The Arts	**Architecture: mainly religious** **Incredible profusion of ornamentation Twisted columns; no straight lines** **Vivid colors, dynamism, movement. Plateresque, Churrigueresque, Mudéjar** **Some Indigenous elements** **use of feathers, symbols and faces** **Painting: religious scenes in Churches** **Sculpture: religious; statues of saints**

The control and domination by the Iberians, although impressive, was not absolute. Behind the new Spanish-style cities, in the small villages and isolated communities of the countryside and mountains, a parallel society developed which preserved, as best it could, the pre-Columbian Indigenous heritage. This heritage was able to find expression in popular culture and even within the carefully controlled expressions of Iberian art and literature in the New World.

9.2: Indigenous

The structure

The key to the structure of Colonial America was the power and authority of the crown and its close ties to the Church. The belief in the divine right of kings was almost unanimous in this society. Power came from God through the Pope (his representative on earth) to the Catholic Kings of Europe. Within Iberia (and America) the Church was closely linked to the crown, and the monarchs had the power to name and control Church authorities. The political-religious system was highly authoritarian and (in theory at least) centralized. The monarchs selected their principal representatives in the Americas, the viceroys, who in turn chose lesser authorities. There was little grass-roots democracy, except in a very limited way at the municipal level in the "cabildos" (local town government bodies).

9.3: Colonial power

In practice, the power of the Iberian monarchs was limited by geographical and political realities. It took a long time to communicate a royal edict from Iberia to America, and by the time it reached those who would actually implement it there were many opportunities for individualism and subjective interpretations to modify the monarchs' intent. A popular Spanish saying captures this spirit: "obedezco pero no cumplo" (I obey, but I do not enforce).

In a sense, this attitude was the continuation of the independent attitudes of the early conquistadores and *adelantados*, who felt that they were the ones who were making the sacrifices, and not the bureaucrats in Madrid or Lisbon. Thus, they deserved the rewards and benefits of their courageous deeds. At first this focused on the looting and pillaging of the precious metals they found in the empires of the Aztecs and the Incas. Once these activities peaked and declined, attention shifted to the profits that would come out of the mines and fields. For this the New World Iberians needed land and labor. Initially the land and labor (in the form of the Indigenous who lived on it) came as a package: the monarch, through the institution of the *encomienda*, awarded the conquistador and his family a grant of land and "commended" the Indians living on it to his care, with the obligation of bringing them the Catholic religion and some limited education. As we have seen, the settler did not hesitate to use the labor and permit the priests to convert. But the amount of "care" he gave his charges was limited, and education for the Indian was almost nonexistent. Power, wealth and social status lay in holding the land and controlling the Indians (and later the Black slaves) who extracted the riches from the land.

9.4: Colonial labor

The paternalistic, authoritarian and centralized nature of Colonial American administration was also closely linked to a caste and racial social system. At the top of the pyramid were the Spaniards or Portuguese who had been born in Iberia, and who were either the initial settlers, or the administrators sent out from Madrid or Lisbon for relatively short tours of duty in the Americas. The loyalty of the former was always somewhat questionable, but the latter were clearly the king's people. Below this top level were the *criollos*, the Spanish and Portuguese born in America. They were ethnically identical to the first group, but their roots were in America, and many of them would live their lives out in the New World without ever visiting Iberia. Toward the end of the Colonial period it was this group who sparked the rebellions that led to independence. Moving down the socio-economic ladder we find the *mestizos* (mix of Iberian and Indigenous), the Indigenous, and the Blacks, as well as various combinations of the last three categories.

Initially there were two Spanish viceroyalties, both based in the regions which had once held the core of the Aztec and Inca empires: New Spain (Mexico) and Peru. Brazil was also eventually a viceroyalty under the Portuguese crown. Toward the end of the Colonial period two additional vice-royalties were created: New Granada (roughly today's Colombia, Venezuela, Ecuador and Panama), and Rio de La Plata (today's Argentina, Uruguay, Paraguay and Bolivia). See map, figure 9-5.

The Colonial Baroque

The State and Church in Colonial Latin America skillfully used the cultural movement known as the Baroque to strengthen their power and reach. The Baroque was characterized by great extravagance of detail and complex intertwined and opposing ideas. Its principal manifestation in Latin America was in architecture, especially church architecture, which emphasized the use of gold, highly curved surfaces, and an incredible amount of lush detail. It is said that the Baroque hated straight and simple lines, be they in literature or in buildings, and that any such straight lines had to be transformed into convoluted spirals and be covered obsessively with complex arguments and details. Unfortunately, this sometimes led to excesses, pedantry, affectation, and artificiality.

Late Renaissance and Plateresque

The Baroque was not typical of the early Colonial period, however, since Iberia was still under the influence of the Renaissance. The architecture of this early period, especially in the first churches and other religious buildings, is characterized by the early settlers' memories of what they had left in Spain: a mixture of remnants of the medieval Gothic, some elements reflecting Moorish influences such as the use of tiles, wood and geometric figures, and mainly the Renaissance. One specific current of the Renaissance in America was the so-called

9.6: Colonial architecture

"plateresque" style, named after the way the delicate working of the stone resembled a silver filigree (*platero* is the Spanish word for "silver-smith").

In designing the early buildings, the first priests and conquistadores also had to take some functional elements into consideration. The threat of a possible attack by rebellious Indians (or raiding pirates from Northern Europe) meant that churches were sometimes built as small fortresses, solid and protective. Much of the military architecture of the Colonial era dates from this early period. In earthquake zones such as Mexico, Central America, and the Andean region (and this covered most of the important areas of Spain's Empire), the Church's architects had to build strong and solid structures with this in mind.

The Baroque

Leaving aside this early period, it is clear that the dominant cultural current in the Colonial period was the Baroque. It began with a mindset that stressed two almost contradictory ideas: on the one hand order and hierarchy (the Church-State linkage), and on the other the exuberance of detail and ornamentation that was exaggerated and sometimes extreme. Tying these two currents together was a sense of cleverness, conceit, indirect allusion and allegory. This was in marked contrast to the cultural current of the conquest period, which was direct, simple, and single-minded.

From the perspective of the Church and the State, the main value of the Baroque was to impress on the population the overwhelming strength and wealth of both institutions. Because the two were closely linked through the theory of the divine right of kings, whatever strengthened one also helped the other. Thus, the awesome and luxurious decorations in the massive churches delivered the powerful message that religion provided the meaning for one's life here on earth, and that the Church supported (and was supported by) God's representatives, namely the authorities of the Church and the Crown. The only path to eternal salvation lay through the Church, and this institutional connection implied obedience to the civil authorities.

It should not be surprising then, that the art that dominated the colonial period was related to the Church and its mission. It began with the architecture of the churches and included the key element of their interior decoration, the heavy use of gold and silver, and the elaborate and extremely realistic representations of Christ and the saints in both carvings and paintings. We know the names and history of the more famous of the Colonial religious statue carvers, such as Aleijandinho in Brazil and Caspicara in Ecuador.

9.7: Church altar

There were an estimated 100,000 churches, cathedrals, chapels and convents built in the colonial period in Spanish America, and the vast majority show the influence of the Baroque in both their basic design, the columns, their altars, and their decoration. Each one of these churches required a full complement of paintings, statues, altars and *retablos* (the often highly complicated decorative elements behind the altar).

Popular versus European currents

Church architecture and art was "official" in that it represented the strictly European viewpoint of the Roman Catholic Church and the Iberian state. The models that were copied and the painters and sculptures that were imitated were those of Spain and Portugal.

But inevitably modifications crept in, despite fairly strict Church control of the artisans and artists involved. We can speak of this process as "cultural mestizaje", since it involves a mixing of the European and the Indigenous. Because the majority of the craftsmen were *mestizos* or Indians, the possibility of deviation from the Iberian models was always real. In some cases, however, understanding priests allowed, and even encouraged, local modifications as a way of making the mestizo and Indigenous feel that the Church was their own. At other times, in a sort of cultural subversion, the local artisan would attempt to sneak in symbols or elements which were American, or even Pre-Columbian. Thus, certain Mexican Colonial churches have versions of the Virgin Mary that have distinctly Indigenous features, and Christ is sometimes represented with symbols that are pre-Columbian. Local fruits, animals and other products often appear among the decorative elements of the Baroque.

As we noted earlier, the Spanish conquistadores frequently built their churches and public buildings using materials from destroyed pre-Columbian buildings, and often in exactly the same sites. Sometimes the destruction of the old was incomplete, and in places like Cuzco one can see Catholic churches built on the visible foundations of Inca temples. Despite the official emphasis on churches and public buildings as the primary place for art to be located, the authorities could not totally suppress popular culture. Much of this popular culture had a strong Indigenous element, especially in the regions where an important pre-Columbian civilization had existed.

Sometimes this popular culture involved materials, such as the use of feathers (an Aztec tradition), even in Church decorations. At other times it involved pre-Columbian handicrafts, such as the use of masks, which were then used in Catholic processions and plays as well as in official celebrations. Sometimes these were even used to mock the colonial authorities and the conquistadores themselves.

Two Colonial writers
Sor Juana Inés de la Cruz:
a Colonial Feminist Poet-Nun

9.8: Sor Juana

Sor (Sister) Juana Inés de la Cruz (1648-1695) was an extraordinary woman, distinguished by her intellectual brilliance as much as by her literary talent. In the male-oriented colonial society of Mexico there were few avenues open to express herself, and she chose to become a nun. This, however, did not stop her from writing emotional and even erotic poetry in which religious ecstasy becomes confused with romantic love.

Her reputation as "America's first feminist" rests on a series of poems and essays in which she defends her sisters and warns them of the double standards employed by men to get what they want from women. The poem cited below is one of the most famous of these. Despite her fame, we know little about the details of her life. We do not know why, for example, she abandoned her poetry and her intellectual pursuits towards the end of her life to tend to the sick (she died while nursing the poor during a plague in Mexico). The portrait we have of her was painted a century after her death with the painter's daughter for a model, and yet it seems to capture the essence and mystery of this remarkable person.

Redondilla by Sor Juana Inés de la Cruz

Stupid men, quick to condemn
Women wrongly for their flaws
Never seeing you're the cause
Of all that you blame in them!

If you flatter them along,
Earn their scorn, their love incite
Why expect them to do right
When you urge them to do wrong?

You combat their opposition
And then gravely when you're done
Say the whole thing was in fun
And you did not seek submission.

You expect from action shady
That some magic will be done
to turn courted courtesan
Quickly into virtuous lady.

Can you think of wit more drear
Than for one with lack of brain
To smear a mirror, then complain
Since it is not crystal clear?

9.9: Colonial authorities (male)

Yet with favor and disdain
You the same results have had,
Angered if we treat you bad,
Mocking if we've loved in vain.

She who's modest cannot hold
Man's esteem. We're all thought naughty.
If we don't accept, we're haughty;
If we welcome you, we're bold. ...

Do not look surprised or rave
When guilt's placed at your own gate!
Love the girls your whims create
Or create the sort you crave.

Tempt us not to acquiesce,
Then with justice can you censure
Any girl who dares to venture
Near you, seeking your caress.

Women need be strong, I find,
To stay safe and keep unharmed
Since the arrogant male comes armed
With Devil, flesh, and world combined.

(In the following poem Sor Juana reveals her inner struggle between the part of her that was obedient nun and the part that was feminist and critic, between heart and mind, between emotion and reason, and between science and religion.)

My soul, confused, is divided in two parts,
One is passion's slave, one is
reason's faithful servant.
Civil war burns
within my bosom. Each of the parts
struggles to win, and in the midst
of such troubled storms, both
parts will perish, and neither
one will prevail.

9.10: Colonial church power

Reply to Sor Filotea by **Sor Juana Inés de la Cruz**

(In this lengthy essay Sor Juana tells of her love of learning and her extraordinary efforts to get an education in the face of the Colonial belief that women did not need to be educated).

... Writing has never been for me a matter of my own will, but rather the result of outside forces; I can truly say that: Vos me coegistis. ("You chose me") What is really true, and I will not deny it (in part because it is obvious, and also because God has been gracious to give me a very great love of truth) is that ever since the first light of reason struck me, I had such a strong and vehement inclination to letters, that not even outside reprimands -of which I have had many- nor my own reflections -and I have made not a few- have been enough to cause me to abandon that natural impulse to write which God has put in me: Your Grace will know why and for what; and will know that I have asked to have the light of my understanding extinguished to the point that all I would have left is what I need to follow His Law, because anything beyond that is, according to some, surplus for a woman; and there even are those who say it is harmful.

Your Grace will also know that this not having been granted, I have attempted to hide my understanding by changing my name, and make sacrifices only to Him who gave it to me; and that no other motive caused me to enter religious orders, despite the fact that the liberty and silence which my studious intentions required were alien to the exercises and company of a religious community. And later, in the community, the Lord knows (as well as the only other person in the world who should know), what I tried to do in order to hide my name, and which was denied me, saying that it was temptation, and so it was.

If I could repay you some small measure of what I owe you, my Lady, I believe I would repay you by telling you this, because it has never come out of my mouth, except to Him who should hear it. But I wish that by opening, one by one, the doors to my heart, making clear its most sacred secrets, you will know that it does not diminish what I owe your venerable person and your many favors.

Continuing the narration of my inclination, of which I want to give you full information, I should tell you that when I was not yet three years old my mother sent my older sister to learn to read in one of those schools called "Amigas", and my sister brought me along out of affection and mischief. And seeing her receive a lesson, the burning desire to learn how to read was so kindled in me that I tricked (or so it seemed to me) the

9.11: Colonial education

teacher, telling her that my mother ordered that I too be given lessons. She did not believe me, because it was not believable, but to comply with my request, she gave me the lesson.

I continued to go to the teacher, and she continued to teach me, but no longer as a joke, because experience had removed that option. And I learned how to read in such a short time that I had to hide it from my mother. The teacher also hid it from my mother because she wanted to surprise her when I was advanced in my studies and could receive the credit for it, along with me. And I kept my knowledge hidden, believing that they would punish me for it since I had done it without permission. My teacher (God bless her) still lives, and can testify to this.

I remember in those days, wanting snacks in a way that is normal at that age, I abstained from eating cheese because I had heard that it would make an idiot out of you, and my desire to learn was stronger than my desire to eat, even though this is very strong among children.

Later, when I was about six or seven years old, and already

9.12: Colonial convent

knowing how to read and write, and with all the other abilities and skills and sewing which women learn, I heard it said that there was a University and Schools in Mexico in which one could study sciences. And as soon as I heard that, I began to pester my mother with constant and insistent pleas that, by dressing up as a boy, I should be sent to Mexico to live with some relatives we had there, in order to study and take courses at the University. She did not want to do it, and it was a good thing, because I satisfied my desire for learning by reading many and varied books which my grandfather had, despite punishment and reprimands and obstacles. And so when I finally came to Mexico, many people admired not so much my knowledge and recollection of information as much as the fact that I knew so much at an age when I barely had time enough to learn how to speak.

I began to study Latin, and I believe I took only about twenty lessons. But I devoted myself so much to my lessons that I made an agreement with myself that I would cut my hair short if I did not learn as much as I should. This was important because it is true that women, and especially those in the flower of their youth, place great emphasis on the natural adornment of their hair, and I would cut off four to six finger's lengths of hair, and made a deal with myself that if by the time it grew back I had not learned as much as I had planned, I would cut it back even further as punishment for being so stupid. And what happened was that my hair grew rapidly, but my learning did not grow as fast, so I kept cutting it back as punishment because it did not seem right to me to have a head that was well dressed with hair and so naked of knowledge, which was a far more important adornment.

I went into the convent even though I knew that convent life had some things (I refer to secondary things and not the basic formal ones) which were very repugnant to my personality. But in all, and especially considering my total negation of matrimony, the convent was the most suitable and most decent thing I could choose, in matters of the security that my salvation desired. And so in this regard (because it was the most important goal) I surrendered and bowed my neck, and gave up all the little impertinences of my nature, among those the desire to live alone, and not to have any obligatory occupation which might inhibit my freedom to study, nor any noise from the community which might interrupt the deep silence of my books.

This caused me to vacillate somewhat in my determination, until some learned persons enlightened me, and I overcame my hesitation with divine grace, and I took the state of sisterhood which I now so unworthily hold. I thought that I was fleeing from myself. But, woe is me! I brought myself with me and I brought my own worst enemy with me, and I don't know how to determine if it was a gift or punishment from Heaven, because as the exercises of religion tried to snuff out or block my studious inclination, it exploded like gunpowder, and in me was confirmed the saying: "privation is the cause of appetite."

I returned (better said, I never left), and I persisted in my studious tasks (which for me were a rest and break in every moment left after my obligations). I read and read some more, I studied and studied some more, with no teacher other than my books themselves. And I realize how difficult it is to study those soulless letters, lacking the live voice and explanation of the teacher; but in all this work I suffered with pleasure, because of my love for letters. Oh, if it had been for the love of God, which was the one sure thing, how much I would have deserved it!

It was a good thing that I attempted to raise my learning up and direct it to His service, because the goal which I was seeking was to study Theology. It seemed to me a stupid inability, being Catholic, not to know everything one could in this life, through natural means, about the divine mysteries. And being a nun and not a secular person, I should therefore due to my ecclesiastical state, profess letters, and being a daughter of Saint Jerome, and Saint Paula, it would not be right for such learned parents to have an idiot for a daughter. This is what I proposed to myself, and it made sense; if it was not (and this was most likely) to satisfy and applaud my own inclination, then to propose it as an obligation in and of itself.

First Dream (excerpt) by Sor Juan Inés de la Cruz

(This very dense and impenetrable poem is typical of the mystical and religious nature of much Baroque writing).

Pyramid-like, mournful, from the earth
born as shadow, heading to the sky
the high peak of vain obelisk attempting to reach the stars;
and their beautiful lights -always exempt, always brilliant-
but the gloomy war with black vapors threatened
the fearful fugitive shadow and mocked the distant lights.

Bernardo de Balbuena (1562-1627)

Born in Spain, Balbuena came to the New World at any early age, studied theology, and rose within the Church to become one of the early Bishops of Puerto Rico. Despite his priestly duties, he found time to write long and elegant verses which are excellent examples of the Baroque tendency to heavily load (and sometimes overload) poetry with highly detailed descriptions.

Perhaps his best work is *La Grandeza Mexicana (Mexico's Grandeur)*, in which he replies in elegant and lyrical verse to a nun who asked him for a description of the young Spanish city of Mexico. Balbuena takes advantage of this opportunity to

9.13: Balbuena

present a detailed inventory of the complicated, luxurious and beautiful city as he knew it almost 100 years after the arrival of Cortés. The details he provides include physical geography, the climate, the surroundings, the architecture, the vegetation, the different human types, the animals, all in great detail. The poem is high-sounding, but at the same time simple; it is direct, but also contains complicated metaphors, word plays, majestic adjectives, and a rich catalog of the lexicon. Balbuena's works represent some of the best of the Baroque's love of color, detail, ornamentation and intellectual playfulness. It also stands as a monument to the pride in the New World that many transplanted Spaniards shared with the *criollos* (the Americans descended from Spanish or Portuguese families).

Mexico's Grandeur (1604) by **Bernardo de Balbuena**
Of the famous Mexico the seat,
origin and grandeur of edifices
horses, streets, treatment, complement,
letters, virtues, variety of professions.

  gifts, occasions of contentment,
immortal spring and its indications,
illustrious government, religion, state,
all in this speech is written. ...

  It is ordered that I write you some indication
that I have arrived in this famous city,
center of perfection, hinge of the world;

  its seat, its populous greatness,
its rare things, its riches and its treatment,
its illustrious people, its pompous labor.

  in all, a most perfect portrait
you ask of Mexican Greatness,
be it expensive, be it modest.

  Be aware, it is a grave and heavy task
which you impose on such weak ability
but I desire and wish to serve you.

  And so, in response to your pleasure
and mine to comply with your law,
here are of Mexico the signs:

Bathed in a temperate and cool breeze
where no one believed there was a thing
it enjoys its lush and gifted seat.

Almost under the fertile tropics,
which bestow the flowers of Amaltea
and impregnates the deep sea with pearls,

within the zone where the sun passes,
and the tender April goes, wrapped in roses,
sowing perfumes made of livery;

on a delicate and soft crust,
which lies atop two clear lagoons,
fenced in by waves from all sides,

forged in great proportion and worth
of towers, spires, and vantage-points,
its superb machine is presented.

9.14: Colonial city

With most beautiful distant views,
outings, recreations and country-feasts,
orchards, farms, mills, and groves.

malls, gardens, thickets
of various plants and fruits
in flower, in blossom, immature and ripe.

There are not as many stars
in the sky, as flowers in her garland
nor as many virtues in it than her.

This great city built on water has
strong causeways, on which its many people
as capable as they are, come close together;

and not even the Greek horse made a bridge
so full of arms as the Trojan wall,
nor did prudent Ulysses guide so many;

not even when Arctus' frigid wind blows
and denudes the trees, and with stripped
leaves covers the hard soil,

as in these roads and causeways
in every time and every occasion.
one can see the mass of people crossing.

Draught animals, coaches, carts, wagons,
of gold, silver, riches, provisions
laden go out, and enter in multitudes.

Of various paths and various movements
various figures, faces and visages,
of various men, of various thoughts;

muleteers, officials, contractors,
Spaniards, soldiers, merchants,
Courtiers, gentlemen, litigants;

9.15: Colonial church

clergy, friars, men and women,
of various colors and professions,
of various states and various appearances;

different in tongues and nations,
in purposes, goals and desires,
and even sometimes in laws and opinions;

and all by short-cuts or roundabouts
in this great city they disappear
from giants they become pygmies.

Oh, immense sea, where grow
so many waves and avenues of things,
which disappear and are not similar!

This is the sun that gives life to the world;
that conserves, governs and grows it,
protects, defends and fortifies it. ...

hyacinths and daffodils, which as hostages
of your coming to the orchards were given
as hope and promise of flowery goods;

joyful flowers, which in another time
were monarchs of the world, nymphs and shepherds
and in bloom they stayed; in bloom they left;

birds of most beautiful hues
of various songs and various plumages,
skylarks, popinjays, nightingales. ...

Thus this hidden force, live source
of political life, and breath
that can revive the most still and frigid chest.

among others of its goods gives the seat
to this distinguished city on hills of water,
and in her edifice opened the first foundation.

And so whatever the human genius forges
and art reaches, and desire practices
in it and its lake is poured
and is returned agreeable, illustrious and rich.

9.16: Mexico City cathedral

10: Independence and Neoclassicism

Independence and the tradition of protest

Despite the surface appearance of tranquillity in the three centuries of Colonial rule, there were always undercurrents of protest which eventually culminated in the move for Latin American Independence in the early 1800's. In this lesson we will take a look first at two examples of the protest tradition during the Colonial period, and then the Independence movements themselves.

A Baroque protester: Juan del Valle y Caviedes

Caviedes (1652?-1697?) belongs chronologically to the Baroque Colonial period, but he shares little with the Baroque writers we considered previously (Sor Juana and Balbuena). He is instead a sharp social and political critic, pointing out to the traditional and smug Spanish American colonial administrators their shortcomings and hypocrisies.

10.1: Caviedes

As a writer he does share some characteristics with several of the writers of Spain's Golden Age, such as Quevedo and Góngora, because of his satirical, biting, vulgar, popular, and picaresque wit. But behind this criticism is a sharp social and moral attack on the abuses, injustices, and double standards of the Colonial period.

He was born in Spain but came to Peru at an early age and settled in the mining area, where life was hard even for a Spaniard at the top of the social pyramid. It appears he quickly dissipated his fortune on gambling, drink, and the women of dubious morals who were drawn to the money and debauchery of the mining fields. Apparently he contracted a venereal disease, and was badly treated by the primitive doctors in the town, many of whom had minimal training and were basically charlatans. This illness gave rise to one of Caviedes' major themes: the damage done by physicians and their indifferent and rapacious attitude toward their patients.

Independence and Neoclassicism (Chapters 10-11)

Cultural-
historical
framework:
	The Independence period and its precursors.
	The need to break away from the intellectual
	  and cultural influences of Iberia (especially Spain),
	  and the colonial Baroque.
	French influences: Enlightenment, Revolution
	Patriotic themes

Approximate dates:	Late 18th Century until Independence is completed (1826)
Historical landmarks	Penetration of the ideas of the Enlightenment Independence of the United States (1776) The French Revolution (1789) Independence of Haiti (1804) Napoleon's invasion of Iberia (1807-08) The "Cabildos" (1810) Battles for Independence, 1814 to 1824 Peaceful independence of Brazil (1822)

Literature	Neoclassicism: reaction to the Baroque
	Classical Greek and Roman models
	
	Compared to the Baroque, Neoclassicism is rigid,
	  objective, colder, rational.
	Little sentiment; the mind controls the heart.
	
	Unity of time, place, action (rules)
	  Precursors:
	Baroque protester: Juan del Valle Caviedes 1652-97?
	Rebel: Tupac Amaru (1742-1781)
	
	Independence writers:
	  Simón Bolívar (1783-1830)
	  José Joaquín Olmedo (1780-1847)
	  Andrés Bello (1781-1865)

The Arts	Architecture: classical simplicity Greco-Roman inspiration. Straight lines, more rigid, colder Themes of nativism and regionalism Painting: patriotic themes in the classical style Influence of the Academies, especially French

He later moved to Lima where the targets of his biting satire included not only doctors, but also the Lima aristocrats and even the Vice-regal court. He attacked the clergy, lawyers, tailors, and street women, with an emphasis on the grotesque, the scatological, the ugly, the pornographic and the immoral. The scandalous aspects of his work made publication difficult during his lifetime, and it was not until years after his death that they were collected in a book titled *Diente del Parnasso (Tooth of Parnassus)*, a reference to the biting and harsh nature of his satirical criticism and protests against the injustices of his era.

Juan del Valle y Caviedes: *Colloquium that a seriously ill doctor had with Death* (From: *Diente del Parnaso*)

The whole world is witness
my dear Death,
that you have no reason
to mistreat me this way.
Reflect: I am your friend
and your one-eyed shots
with my help hit the target;
excuse the note,
but for every month of my life
I'll give you thirty-one dead.

Death, if the farmers
always leave seed for the future
who do you wish to wipe out
the seed of doctors?
We give you major fruits,
because with purges and ointments
we give your scythe enough business
to keep your stretcher-trolleys full,
and for each doctor you collect
ten bushels of deceased.

Don't ignore me
nor use your wiles with me,
because Death without doctors
is not death, it's half-life.
Poor, lazy and destroyed
you'll end up that way,
with nothing in your quiver
and it will be your great flaw
to have a poor little death,
or a death of bad death.
Death with doctors is uncivil,

10.2: Colonial types

it would be like, I infer
a musket without a musketeer,
sword or spear without a hand.
They will fear you in vain,
even though you be Death,
it will be just as they see it,
you'll be pushed aside
because no one is really dead
unless the doctor shakes him first.

   Unjust Death, you'll drag
me too by the nipple,
but I know it's no marvel
to poorly pay he who serves well.
I swear by Galenus, whom
I venerate, that if your rigor
is not converted into love,
and changes in a hurry,
and I die in this accident
I will no longer be a doctor.

   Take care that in your eagerness
if you treat doctors this way
you'll force the priests and sacristans
to go on all fours.

10.3: Colonial town

Because neither sunstroke nor excess
or the worst parents-in-law
fruit or snow without liquor,
bullet, stockade or song
kill in one year as many
as the best doctor.

Privileges of the poor by **Juan del Valle y Caviedes**

The poor man is stupid, if he is quiet,
and if he speaks he is foolish;
if he knows, he is just a talker,
if affable, he is tricky.

   If courteous, he is an intruder,
when he suffers not, he is arrogant;
a coward, when he is humble,
and crazy when he is resolved.

If he is brave, he is rash,
presumptuous, if discrete;
a flatterer, if he obeys;
and if he excuses himself, he is gross.

If he attempts, he is insolent,
·if he is deserving, he is worthless
his nobility is nothing seen,
and his court dress is shoddy.

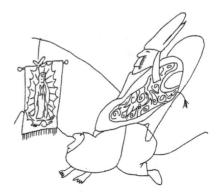

If he works, he is greedy,
And, in the contrary extreme
lost, if he rests.
Behold these great privileges!

10.4: Priest leading peasant

How to find your fortune in the palaces by Juan del Valle y Caviedes

To find esteem in the palace
you have to be a little bit tricky,
one and a half parts flatterer
and two parts complete buffoon,

three parts and a bit gossiper
and four parts procurer who collects
five parts and a bit charlatan,
censuring works and actions.

It will be a continuous amen to anyone who speaks
to the lord, the viceroy, or whoever you serve;
and even more if the words are rubbish.

you will need to applaud with greater strength;
and if you go on with this soft job,
in the palace you'll have anything you want.

Early armed rebellion: the Tupac Amaru uprising

Towards the end of the eighteenth century a series of rebellions and upris-ings challenged Spanish rule in the New World. These were seen as serious threats by the Spanish authorities, who acted swiftly and relentlessly to put them down and make dramatic examples of the leaders. The most important of these rebellions was that of José Gabriel Condorcanqui (1742-1781), who took the name of the last Inca ruler Tupac Amaru, executed by the Spanish in 1572.

Tupac Amaru II was in fact descended from his namesake, and was a man of some status and education. By taking the Inca name he appealed to the large Indian population of the Andean region. But he was also careful to appeal to the *criollos* by stressing the grievances they bore against the Spanish administration, especially the *Corregidores* (local authorities). His uprising had some initial success, and in the process several Spanish authorities were killed. But he was finally captured, tried, and cruelly executed in the main square of Cuzco. In death he became a symbol of native rebellion against authority, and the name "Tupamaro" was used by many who would lay claim to this precedent. These included groups who fought against the Spanish from Northern Argentina to Colombia, as well as twentieth century leftist guerrillas, such as the Tupamaros of Uruguay.

10.5: Tupac Amaru II

The documents that follow show two sides of the Tupac Amaru rebellion. The first is one of his proclamations in which he lays out the grievances he and his followers had against the Spanish colonial authorities. The second document is the death sentence pronounced by the Spanish *Visitador* (special emissary), which was carried out in the main square of Cuzco in 1781.

Proclamation of Tupac Amaru Published in Silos.

Don José I, by the grace of God, Inca, King of Peru, of Santafé (Bogotá), Quito, Chile, Buenos Aires and the Continent of the Southern Oceans, Duke of

10.6: Execution of Tupac Amaru I

la Superlativa, Lord of the Caesars and Amazons, with dominion in the great Paititi, commissioner and distributor of divine grace, from the source without peer. Inasmuch as it has been agreed by my Council, in full session, on repeated occasions, some secret and some public, that the Kings of Castille have usurped the crown and the dominions of my peoples for close to three centuries, burdening my vassals with unbearable taxes and tributes, pilferages, customs houses, alcabalas (taxes), monopolies, contracts, tithes, royal fifths, viceroys, audiencias, corregidores and other ministers, all equal in their tyranny, selling justice at auction, with the collaboration of the notaries, some more and some less, in such a way that the ecclesiastical and secular agents of the Crown have entered into this, taking the lives of those they could not or knew not how to rob, all of this worthy of the most severe punishment.

Because of all this, and because of the just complaints, which have reached the Heavens, in the name of God Almighty, I command that none of these tributes be paid and that the intrusive European ministers not be obeyed. Only the priests shall be given respect, paying them the tithe and other tributes immediately as if they were being given to God. The tributes to the King shall be given to the natural Lord, and this with due moderation. For the prompt remedy and protection of all the aforesaid, I order that the oath to my royal crown be repeated and published in all the cities, towns and places of my dominions, and that we be informed at the earliest of those vassals who are prompt and faithful so that they may be rewarded. And equally we shall be informed of those who rebel against us, so that they may receive the punishment they deserve.

SENTENCE pronounced in the City of Cuzco by the Visitador don José Antonio de Areche, against José Gabriel Tupac Amaru, his wife Micaela Bastidas, sons, and other culprits of the uprising.

In the criminal case which is pending before me, and which has followed the procedures of Royal Justice against José Gabriel Tupac Amaru, cacique of the town of Tungasuca, province of Tinta, for the horrendous crime of rebellion

or general uprising among the indians, mestizos and other castes, for five years now, and carried out in almost all the territories of this viceroyalty and that of Buenos Aires, with the idea (of which he is convinced) that he wishes to be crowned their Lord, and liberator of the so-called misery of those classes of inhabitants which he was able to seduce, and which began with the hanging of his corregidor Don Antonio de Arriaga. ...

... in order to assure the earliest possible tranquility of the provinces subverted by him, the notice of the

10.7: Execution of Tupac Amaru II

execution of this sentence and his death shall be published in order to end the various ideas which have circulated among almost all the nation of the indians, full of superstitions, that inclines them to not believe that he will receive capital punishment because of his high character, believing him to represent the main trunk of the Inca tree, as he has titled himself, and by this absolute and natural owner of these dominions and their vassals. I also consider the nature, condition, low customs and poor education of these same indians, and of the other castes of the people, which have contributed to the ease by which the aforesaid culprit José Gabriel Tupac Amaru has carried out his depraved intentions....

Considering, then, all of this, and the ways in which this vile insurgent urged the indians and other castes to join him, even offering the slaves their freedom, and reflecting also on the unhappy and miserable state of the provinces which he stirred up, and which will require much effort to correct, and that many years will be required to repair the harm done by the aforementioned José Gabriel Tupac Amaru, with the detestable statements that have been made, and adopted by his nation and their partners to their horrible ends; and observing also the remedies which the tranquility of these territories requires, the punishment of the guilty, justice, subordination to God, the King and his ministers, therefore:

I must and do condemn José Gabriel Tupac Amaru to this: that he be taken out to the principal public plaza of this city, dragged to the site of the execution, where he will presence the execution of his wife, Micaela Bastidas, of his two sons, Hipólito and Fernando Tupac Amaru, his uncle Francisco Tupac Amaru, and his brother in law Antonio Bastidas, and the other principal captains and helpers of his perverse project, who shall die that same day. Once these sentences are finished, the executioner shall cut out his tongue ... and his body shall be quartered by four horses, each heading to a different corner of the plaza.

The Independence of Latin America
The Independence movements

The Independence of Spanish and Portuguese America was deeply influenced by the strong currents of new ideas of the Enlightenment which surged through Europe (mainly France, but also Spain) and North America in the mid and late 1700's. Just as the Renaissance had challenged the archaic ideas of the Middle Ages, so did the Enlightenment look with a deeply critical eye at the conservatism epitomized by colonial rule, the divine right of kings, and the closely interrelated institutions of Church and State.

10.8: Independence!

The Enlightenment stressed reason, study and analysis. It emphasized the need to know and understand the natural physical, economic and political world here on earth more than metaphysical and religious abstractions of what might lie beyond life on earth.

The emphasis on science and nature coincided with a growing appreciation of the resource wealth and natural wonders of the New World, and how they had for centuries been exploited and pillaged to serve the empires of the Old World. This feeling of pride in one's American land and roots grew into regional pride and a nativism that reinforced the notion that Americans (and especially the *criollos*) were just as good, if not better, than the Europeans. Art and literature contributed to this nativism and regionalism by focusing on the beauty and wealth of the continent.

Beyond the new ideas of the Enlightenment, there were many other causes which came together in the movements for Independence in Latin America in the late 1700's and early 1800's. The Independence of the United States and the French Revolution were examples of the power of the new ideas against the old monarchical system. There was growing resentment against the restrictions on trade and commerce imposed by the mercantilistic economic systems favored by Spain and Portugal. And among the *criollos* there was the resentment of centuries of being made to feel that they were inferior to their masters in Madrid and Lisbon.

10.9: Napoleon

The spark for most of the Independence movements was Napoleon's invasion of the Iberian Peninsula in 1807. His armies headed first for Lisbon, but the Portuguese Court was able to escape to Brazil with the assistance of their old ally (and Napoleon's nemesis), England. The Spanish king was not so lucky. Charles IV was taken prisoner and briefly replaced by his son Ferdinand VII, who was removed by Napoleon and replaced by his brother Joseph Bonaparte. French control of the Peninsula was not complete, however, and a rump Spanish government was established in a series of *Juntas* (independent local governments) in southern Spain.

The news of the Napoleonic invasions traveled slowly to America, but by early 1810 the various Viceroyalties and lesser administrative units were faced with the choice of accepting Napoleon's authority or aligning themselves with the fragmented and marginally functioning Juntas in southern Spain. In several cities in Spanish America (Mexico, Caracas, Santiago, Buenos Aires) the creoles seized control of the Cabildos (municipal governments) and declared their independence from Napoleon in Madrid. Initially they were cautious not to declare a complete break from Spain, and most of them continued to recognize the deposed King Ferdinand VII as sovereign. But as confusion reigned in Spain these local Cabildos became more and more independent, finally declaring, in one form or another, their complete independence and full break from Spain. By 1814, when Napoleon was defeated and Ferdinand VII restored to the throne in Spain, he launched an all-out campaign to regain control of the rebellious colonies, and a devastating war of Independence raged for ten years in Spanish America.

The major centers of the Independence movement in South America were at the two extremes: Caracas (Venezuela) and Buenos Aires (Argentina). Each had a major military hero (Simón Bolívar and José de San Martín, respectively), and from these two cities the military campaign to liberate the rest of Spanish South America was launched. The center of Spanish power (and loyalty to the king) was Peru. The military aspects of the campaign for Independence can be summarized as a double thrust from Buenos Aires and Caracas through various other newly forming nations to meet in Peru, where the Spanish finally surrendered after the battle of Ayacucho in 1824.

The battles were between Spanish troops on one side and mixed armies of criollos and mestizos on the other. But the criollos were in the leadership positions, and when Independence was won they quickly moved into power, replacing the Spanish colonial power structure with a creole elite power structure, a shift which fostered little economic, social or political effect on the life of the mestizo, Indigenous or Black majority.

The norm: Creole elite rebellions

The struggle for Independence in the early part of the 19th Century had different meanings for individuals at different levels of the socio-economic pyramid. The Indigenous peoples and the Blacks had the most deeply-rooted reasons for rebelling, but despite their large numbers they had few means and opportunities to organize and focus their grievances. The Colonial administrators lived in fear of such uprisings, and they took careful steps to make sure communications were difficult among the different groups that might rebel, and that access to weapons and subversive ideas was strictly controlled.

For the mestizos and other racially mixed groups there were greater opportunities to channel dissatisfaction and the feeling of being rejected by both their European and Indigenous ancestors. But they too were disorganized and kept away from the means to make good their protests. They did, however, become a powerful force for social, economic and political change later in the national period, in revolutions such as the Mexican.

And so the remaining group, the criollos, were the best prepared for protest and finally rebellion. But the criollos never wanted a profound revolution that would change the basic social-economic order in which they had grown up. Rather, they wanted to remove the "peninsulars" and take their positions of power and authority for themselves. For most of Latin America, the Independence movements of the early 19th Century were really only a change in the elites from the Peninsular-born Spanish and Portuguese to their criollo descendants. The change in elites had relatively little impact on the vast numbers of Indigenous, Blacks, and *mestizos*.

Four exceptions

There were four exceptions to this pattern of victory by the new creole elites. In Haiti a slave revolt against the French in 1804 led to the creation of the first Black republic in the Americas. Despite an attempt by Napoleon to put the revolt down, the Haitians under military leaders such as the former slave Toussaint l'Ouverture, using their knowledge of their island and the tropics against the French expeditionary force, were able to defeat Napoleon.

In the landlocked nation of Paraguay a strong autarchic movement stressed local self-sufficiency based on the idea that the outside world meant only trouble and interference. Paraguayan Independence thus was achieved not simply against the Spanish crown but also against Buenos Aires, which wanted to incorporate Paraguay into what would later become the Argentine Republic. Paraguay successfully resisted both, and for many years shut itself off from almost all outside influences and turned inwards.

10.10: L'Ouverture

In Mexico the 1810 Independence movement began as a true popular uprising which brought together large numbers of mestizos and Indians in what could have been a profound social, political and economic revolution aimed at getting rid of not only the Spanish power structure, but also the criollos'. As such the Independence movement served to briefly unite the Spanish "peninsulars" and the *criollos*. The Revolution was led by two parish priests, Father Miguel Hidalgo and Father José María Morelos, who owed their loyalties not to the Spanish-oriented official church based in Mexico City but to their flocks of mestizos and Indigenous. Unfortunately for Hidalgo and Morelos, their military skills were not up to the challenge posed by the coalition of Spaniards and criollos, and they were defeated on the battlefield and executed. Mexico's Independence movement was then co-opted by the criollo elites, who turned against the Spanish and achieved Independence in a fashion similar to that of the rest of Spanish America.

10.11: Hidalgo

The fourth exception was Brazil. The Portuguese Court had escaped Napoleon's control and established itself in Rio de Janeiro, Brazil, under British protection. The Portuguese king in Rio raised the status of Brazil to a kingdom, (at the same level as Portugal), and the court was well received by the Brazilians, who felt that equality had been achieved. After Napoleon's defeat and the return of the Court to Lisbon in 1821, the Royal family left behind Prince Pedro as regent. When Lisbon attempted to reassert its prior control over Brazil, the Brazilians staged a bloodless rebellion and named Pedro I emperor of independent Brazil in 1822.

There was, however, no fighting, and little animosity between the two reigning branches of the same dynasty in Rio and Lisbon. This peaceful transition from colony to Independent Empire saved Brazil the years of destructive fighting suffered by Spanish America and gave Brazil the great advantage of stability and well-being for many years. The principal benefits of this well-being, however, accrued to the creole elite in Brazil, who retained a position in power similar to the creole elites in Spanish America after Independence.

Art of the Independence period

There was little time or energy left for cultural pursuits during the struggles for Independence. Much of the writing that went on was political, aimed at supporting the thrust for Independence (we will take a look at an example later on). The prevailing literary form was the essay, with a major focus on propaganda and the economic, political and social grievances against the mother country and Napoleon.

The art that was produced tended to stress the themes of nativism and pride in the beauty and wealth of the Americas. The intellectual thrust of the Enlightenment meant that the heavy Colonial Baroque emphasis on Church art and architecture was finished, and that new models would have to be found and used; these would take the form of the Neoclassical movement which reached its peak shortly after Independence as the new nations sought to find their identities. The relatively few paintings and other works produced during the period of Independence itself (1810-1824) tended to focus on the themes of struggle, battle, and the major heroes of the process of breaking from the mother countries.

A Liberator/writer: Simón Bolívar

Although Simón Bolívar (1783-1830) is justly remembered as a military man and national leader, he was also an important geopolitical analyst and writer of political essays in which he supported the Independence cause, analyzed the options available to the new republics, and made some startlingly accurate predictions of the fate of America and its different nations. In the selection which follows, Bolívar makes use of his profound knowledge of each of the Spanish American nations and of the influence of geography on politics to predict the rise of Argentine militarism, Peru-

10.12: Bolívar

vian instability, and the probable success of democracy in Chile.

These are fragments from the *Jamaica Letter* of 6 September 1815, written by Bolívar while he was on the island of Jamaica attempting to obtain arms, men and other support for the revolutionary cause. The letter was probably addressed to the British Governor of Jamaica, the Duke of Manchester. Displaying remarkable geopolitical vision, in this letter Bolívar makes a frank assessment of the problems and possibilities which the geography and politico-military situation of Spanish America were presenting to the newly-emerging republics. He shows a realistic mix of optimism, idealism, and despair. In 1826 Bolívar eventually did convene the American Congress he speaks of (it was called the Amphyctionic Congress, and was held in Panama), but its results were fleeting and disappointing. Four years later Bolívar died, a broken and disappointed man, lamenting that "he who serves the revolution plows the sea".

The Jamaica letter by Simón Bolívar

I fear that until our compatriots acquire the political talents and virtues which distinguish our brothers to the North, then entirely popular political systems are likely to take us to ruin rather than be favorable to us. Unfortunately, these political qualities appear to be distant from us, at least to the required degree. On the contrary, we are dominated by the vices which one inherits under the direction of a nation such as Spain, which has been outstanding only in its ferocity, ambition, vengeance, and greed. ...

10.13: Independence battle

I wish, more than anything else, to see in America the greatest nation in the world, not so much because of its size and riches as its liberty and glory. Although I hope for the perfection of the government of my nation, I am not persuaded that the New World should, for the moment, be governed by a great republic. At the same time, I do not wish a universal monarchy for America, because that project is not only useless but impossible. The abuses which exist at present will not be corrected and our regeneration would be fruitless. The American states presently need paternal governments which will heal the wounds and ills of despotism and of war. The metropolis or capital of such a single America, for example, might be Mexico, which is the only one which could fulfill this function because of its intrinsic power, without which there is no metropolis. Let us suppose that the capital would be on the Isthmus of Panama, which is the central point for all the far-flung corners of this continent. But if this were so, would they not continue to languish in their present state of decay and disorder? In order for a single Government to give life, to animate, to put into motion all the levers of public prosperity, correct, illuminate and improve the New World, it would be necessary for it to have all the attributes of a god, or at least the brilliance and virtues of all men.

10.14: Map, nations in 1826

The partisan spirit, which at present is agitating our states, would then burn with greater ferocity in the absence of the source of power, which is the only thing that could repress it. Furthermore, the magnates in the capitals would not suffer the preponderance of those from the metropolis whom they would consider as just other tyrants; their jealousy would reach the point where they would compare them with the hated Spanish. And so, a monarchy like this would be a deformed colossus, whose very weight would cause it to collapse at the smallest convulsion.

M. de Pradt has wisely divided America in fifteen to seventeen independent states, governed by as many monarchs. I am in agreement on the first point, because America lends itself to the creation of these seventeen nations. But the second point, although it might be easy to achieve, is less useful, and thus I am against the proposal to have American monarchies. ...

... By the nature of the location, riches, population and character of the Mexicans, I would imagine that they would attempt at first to establish a representative republic, in which the Executive Power will have great attributes. These would be concentrated in one individual, who if capable of carrying out his functions with sureness and justice, would almost naturally come to have a lifetime authority. If his lack of skill or violent administration would excite a triumphant popular commotion, that same Executive Power might perhaps diffuse itself in an assembly. If the dominant party is military or aristocratic it will. require, probably, a monarchy which at the beginning would be limited and constitutional and later, inevitably, would decline into absolutism. This is because there is nothing more difficult in the political order than to conserve a mixed monarchy, and it is also necessary to recognize that only a people as patriotic as the English is capable of containing the authority of a king, and to sustain the spirit of liberty under a scepter and a crown.

The states of the Isthmus of Panama, as far as Guatemala, will perhaps form an association. Their splendid position between the two oceans could make them, with time, the emporium of the universe. Their canals would shorten global distances and would strengthen the commercial bonds between Europe, America and Asia, thus bringing to that happy region the tributes of the four corners of the earth. Perhaps only there in the Isthmus could there someday be established the capital city of the Earth, as Constantine hoped Bizantium would be for the ancient world.

Nueva Granada (Colombia) will join with Venezuela, if they agree on forming a central republic, whose capital might be Maracaibo or a new city with the name of Las Casas, in honor of that hero of philanthropy, which might be founded on the border between the two countries, in the superb port of Bahia-honda. That place, although little known, is very advantageous in all respects. Its access is easy and its situation so strong, that it could be made impregnable. It has a pure and healthy climate, a land as propitious for agriculture as for the raising of cattle, and a great abundance of wood for construction. The savages which inhabit it would be civilized, and our possessions would increase with the acquisition of the Goagira area. This nation would be called Colombia, as a trib-ute of justice and gratitude to the creator of our hemisphere. Its government could imitate the English, with the difference that in place of the king there would be an elected executive power, perhaps life-long, and never hereditary if they want a republic, with a legislative house or senate which could be heredi-tary which in the political storms could interpose itself between the popular waves and the rays of government. There would also be a popularly elected leg-islative body, freely elected, without any restrictions other than those of the English house of commons. This constitution would have all the good aspects and I would wish it to have none of the vices of government.

Since this is my own homeland, I have the incontestable right to wish for it what in my view is best. It is very possible that Nueva Granada will not agree in the recognition of a central Government, because it is extremely addicted to fed-eration, and it would then form a state by itself, which, if it endures could be very rich because of its great resources of every type.

We know little of the opinions which prevail in Buenos Aires, Chile, or Peru. Judging by what filters through, and by appearances, in Buenos Aires there will be a central government, in which the military will have primacy, as a result of their internal divisions and external wars. This constitution will degen-erate, necessarily, into an oligarchy or a monarchy, with fewer or greater re-strictions, and whose denomination no one can guess. It would be painful if this were to occur, since those inhabitants deserve the most splendid glory.

The land of Chile is called, by the nature of its situation, by the innocent customs and virtues of its residents, by the example of its neighbors, the fierce republicans of Arauco, to enjoy the blessing showered upon it by the just and sweet laws of a republic. If there is any one nation that will remain a long time in America, I am inclined to think that it will be the Chilean. The spirit of liberty has never been extinguished there; the vices of Europe and Asia will arrive late or never to corrupt the customs of that extreme of the universe. Its territory is limited; it will be always out of unfortunate contact with the rest of humanity, and it will not alter its laws, uses and practices, but rather will preserve its uniformity of political and religious opinions. In a word, Chile can be free.

Peru, in contrast, encloses two elements which are the enemy of any just and liberal regime: gold and slaves. The first corrupts all; the second is corrupt in and of itself. The soul of a serf rarely reaches an appreciation of healthy liberty: either it becomes furious in the tumult or it is humiliated in its chains. Although these rules would be applicable to all America, I believe that with greater justice they are deserved by Lima, because of the ideas I have expressed and because of the cooperation that it has offered to its lords against its own brothers, the illustrious sons of Quito, Chile and Buenos Aires. It is a constant that he who aspires to obtain liberty, should at least attempt it. I suppose that in Lima the rich will not tolerate democracy, nor will the slaves and mestizos tolerate the aristocracy. The former will prefer the tyranny of a single person in order to avoid the tumultuous persecutions and to establish a tranquil order. Much will be achieved if it could recover its independence.

From everything we have said here, we can deduce these consequences: the American provinces find themselves struggling for their emancipation, and will eventually obtain it. Some will become federal and centralized republics in a sregular fashion. Monarchies will be almost inevitably established in some of the larger areas, and some of these will be so unfortunate and unhappy that they will devour their elements in revolutions, be they the present or future ones. A great monarchy will not be easy to consolidate, and a great republic impossible.

It is a grandiose idea to attempt to form throughout the New World a single nation with a single bond which will tie together all its parts into a single whole. It would seem that their common origin, their single language, customs and religion would lead to a single government which would confederate the various states that might make it up. But this is not possible because of the remote locations, different climates, diverse situations, opposing interests and dissimilar natures which divide America. How beautiful it would be if the Isthmus of Panama would be for us what Corinth was for the Greeks! Would that someday we could have the good fortune of installing there an august Congress made up of the representatives of the republics, kingdoms and empires, to deal with and discuss the high issues of peace and war, with the nations of the other three parts of the world!

11: Neoclassicism - Forging the New Nations

Creating the new nations

The first problem faced by the newly-independent Latin Americans was the dilemma of what kind of nation they wanted and what political system they would adopt. Or put another way, what would replace the Spanish colonial system and what would fill the power vacuum. (We noted previously that the Brazilian solution was, at least for most of 19th century, to continue a monarchy, but independent from Portugal).

Unfortunately for the Latin Americans, there had been little experience with democracy before Independence. Unlike English North America, there was little grass-roots self-rule in the Colonial period, except for a very limited amount in the *Cabildos*. There were, however, a great many political theorists and lawyers who had read much about the French and United States Revolutions and who attempted to create constitutions in Latin America based on those foreign models. The individuals who had to make these foreign constitutional models work, however, knew little about these imported systems or their theoretical foundations. The end result was a period of considerable chaos and instability for the first fifty years after Independence.

11.1: In case of democracy break glass

Inevitably, the military heroes of the fighting period filled the power vacuum. While in some cases handing power over to men with proven track records as leaders worked out well, military skills were often quite different from skills required by the constitutions and their abstract political theories. In the end, the generals tended to rule with a heavy authoritarian hand, and were prepared to sacrifice theoretical democratic ideals to the daily needs of pragmatic politics. And so began Latin America's long and frequently unhappy experience with the "caudillo", the strongman, frequently a military officer, who governed all too often as a dictator.

Much of the political debate in this period polarized around two positions loosely defined as "liberal" or "conservative". A 19th Century Latin American "liberal" would most likely favor a republican system, limits on the power of the Church, free trade with the outside world, and a decentralized federal arrangement of states or provinces. In contrast, the "conservative" might argue for a native monarchy (or at least a strong executive), a large role for the Church in education and issues involving public morality, restricted trade, and a centralized system in which the national executive would control the provinces. Conservatives stressed how well the Colonial system had functioned, and attempted to preserve as much of it as possible. Liberals pointed to the Colonial system's failures, exalted the examples of the new republics in France and the U.S., and demanded as much change as possible.

11.2: Landowner, officer, priest

The end result was a long struggle between these two camps, which had local variants in each nation. The energies that could have gone into building the new nations were wasted in political bickering, and all too often the reins of power were held by caudillos. These tended to ally themselves with the landowning elite and with the Church, and thus were drawn into the conservative camp. The alliance of military, landowner and priest was a powerful one that was to dominate Latin American politics for many years, and in some cases continues into our own times.

The new Latin American nations were also severely challenged by centrifugal forces. Based at times on regional pride, and at times on the ambitions of local caudillos or politicians, this centrifugal tendency was reinforced by geography, distance, and difficult communications from the national capital to the farthest provinces. And so we note that in the early years of the Independence period the Central American Confederation broke away from Mexico and then divided into five separate nations: the nation of Gran Colombia broke up into Colombia, Venezuela, and Ecuador (and later Panama); Bolivia, Paraguay and Uruguay were carved out of the successor states of the two Viceroyalties of southern South America. (See map, Figure 10.13). Only Brazil, blessed with more favorable geography and the stability of a monarchical system, was able to successfully resist this tendency toward fragmentation.

From outside came the threat of the Holy Alliance (made up of conservative absolutist monarchies in Europe) to restore the Spanish colonial system by force. This threat was one of the reasons for the U.S. declaration of the Monroe Doctrine in 1823, although the United States had little power to enforce it for many years. The Monroe Doctrine was a unilateral US declaration of policy, taken without consultation with the rest of the Hemisphere. Latin American critics of the Doctrine also argue that its first violation occurred when Great Britain took the Falklands/ Malvinas Islands by force in 1833, and that the US did nothing to stop it.

Neoclassicism

The predominant cultural movement in this early national period was Neoclassicism, which had arrived in Latin America in the late 18th Century as the esthetic expression of the Enlightenment. The Neoclassical traditions stressed the Greco-Roman foundations of European culture and required a fairly rigid treatment of certain standard themes. Although local writers and artists could introduce their own variants of these themes, they were expected to fit them into the rules of Neoclassical literature and art.

11.3: Neoclassicism

Because of its link to the Enlightenment and to the French Revolution, Neoclassicism quickly took root in Latin America around the time of Independence. It was also seen as the best way of rejecting the old Spanish Colonial baroque esthetic tradition, which was no longer acceptable because of the way it had been used to buttress the power of the king and the conservative Church. Neoclassicism's Greek and Roman roots were also used to emphasize, somewhat idealistically, the democracy of those Mediterranean cultures. Thus, when it came time to design the public buildings for the new nations, it seemed highly appropriate that a new congress or government building should be modeled after classical Greek or Roman ones.

In contrast to the Baroque, Neoclassicism stressed simplicity and clarity of design, restraint in detail, rationality, and organization. There was little room for the exuberance of colors and lushness of details that characterized the Baroque. In literature and painting the rules of Neoclassicism inhibited excesses of emotion or subjectivism; the mind clearly dominated the heart.

The principal mechanism for transmitting Neoclassicism and its rules and standards was the institution known as the Academy. The first Academy of Fine Arts had been established in Mexico in 1785 (it was the only one founded in the Colonial period). Others were created soon after Independence. They were based on French models, and they established what was and what was not acceptable in the world of art, writing, and architecture.

A number of prominent European intellectuals, especially naturalists such as Charles Darwin and Baron Alexander von Humboldt, visited the New World in the early and middle part of the nineteenth century, and these figures left their impact in their scientific fields as well as the literary ones. This, coupled with local pride, helps explain the neoclassicists' priority of countryside and agriculture over cities and urban life. This was also a reflection of the Enlightenment's emphasis on the "noble savage" and the purity of life in the state of nature.

Popular art and literature was not favored by the Neoclassic standard-setters and the elites who held political and economic power. They viewed it as uncultured and distant from both the French models as well as the Greco-Roman roots of Neoclassicism. Although undoubtedly local artisans and painters continued to produce their craft, it was considered inferior by the elites and given no official sanction or protection; little of it has survived.

Neoclassical literature in Latin America borrowed heavily from Latin models and made frequent allusions to classical images from Greek and Roman mythology. Good writers who carefully followed the standards produced high-sounding and inspiring works. Unfortunately, there were many Neoclassical writers who could not achieve these goals and their product tends to sound artificial and even bombastic, especially when translated into a non-Latin language. Because of the historical period of Independence, Neoclassical literature focused on the great heroes of Independence and their exploits. Themes exalting the natural wonders of America also prevailed. These currents were seen as helping to forge the new nations by emphasizing the break with the Colonial past and exalting the beauty and wealth of the New World.

José Joaquín de Olmedo (1780-1847).

This Ecuadorian poet epitomizes the Neoclassical emphasis on glorious deeds, Independence, classical references, high-sounding oratory, and carefully structured verse. Olmedo knew Bolívar personally, and after the important battle of Junín the Liberator asked him to write a heroic poem in the Latin tradition. While Bolívar did not ask for a poem that would glorify him personally, it was obvious that he would figure prominently in the poem since he had been present at the battle. The poem is indeed a hymn to Bolívar, elevating him to the level of a conquering Roman Caesar as well as extolling his republican virtues.

By the time Olmedo was finishing the poem another important battle, that of Ayacucho, had

11.4: Olmedo

taken place, and he felt it should be included in the work. This created a problem for the poet, since Bolívar had not been present at Ayacucho. Olmedo solved it (and complied with the Neoclassical rule of unity and logic) by writing the poem in two parts and introducing the figure of the last Inca, Huayna Capac, as a sort of commentator who would tie the two parts, corresponding to the two battles, together. Huayna Capac does this by glorifying Bolívar, castigating the Spanish for their cruel conquest and Colonial rule, and then presenting the second half of the poem, which deals with the battle of Ayacucho. Bolívar was not pleased with the end result, apparently because he felt Huayna Capac was too prominent a figure and that the inclusion of the second battle detracted from his role in the first.

Bolívar might also have been concerned over the symbolism of the Inca. At the moment the poem was written (1825) the debate over republicanism versus monarchy was raging in Spanish America, and some felt that the creation of a local monarchy based on a descendant of the Inca Emperor might be a logical solution. Bolívar himself was known to have been considering the advisability of a British-style parliamentary monarchy (with himself as a possible monarch or president for life) as a way of fighting the centrifugal tendencies he had perceived. Thus, the prominence of Huayna Capac had a heavy political meaning when the poem appeared.

The first lines of the poem are also an excellent example of onomatopoeia, and were meant to suggest the thundering of distant cannon in battle. They are frequently used to torture English-speaking learners of Spanish who have an inherent difficulty in rolling the Spanish "r".
The original Spanish lines are:
> "El trueno horrendo que en fragor revienta
> y sordo retumbando se dilata...

The Junín Victory: Bolívar's Anthem
by José Joaquín Olmedo

The horrendous thunder throbs and rumbles
and rolls in swelling waves
across the globe in flames,
announcing to God that He rules in Heaven.
The bolt that at Junín crashes and scatters
the Spanish multitude
who fiercer than ever were threatening
eternal slavery through blood and fire.

11.5: Independence battle

And the hymn of victory
which with a thousand deafening echoes reverberated
through deep valleys and to the craggy peaks
proclaims that Bolívar is on earth
the final judge in peace and war.

The arrogant pyramids which skyward
human art had dared to raise
to speak to centuries and nations;
temples, where hands of slaves
deified in pomp their tyrants,
are mocked by time, who with weak wings
touches them, and brings them down,
after which the fleeting wind easily
erases their lying inscriptions;
and below the confused ashes
between the shadows of eternal oblivion,
oh what an example of ambition and misery!
lies the priest, the god, and the temple.

But the sublime mountains, whose face
to the ethereal region is raised,
who see the storms at their feet,
flash, growl, break, dissipate;
the Andes: the enormous, stupendous
mounds seated on bases of gold,
the earth with its weight balancing,
shall never be moved. They mock
alien envy and stubborn time.
fury and power, they shall be eternal
heralds of Liberty and Victory,
who with deep echo

11.6: Soldier

shall say to later ages:
"We saw the field at Junín;
we saw that with the deployment
of Peruvian and Colombian flags
the arrogant legions grew restless,
and the fierce Spanish panicked and fled,
or surrendering, sued for peace.
Bolívar triumphed; Peru was free;
and in triumphal pomp sacred Liberty
was placed in the Temple of the Sun" ...
Who is that who with slow pace moves
over the mount that dominates Junín?
Who from there measures the field, the site
of combat and victory designated?
Who observes the enemy host, counts
and in his mind breaks and routs,

and the bravest condemns to death,
like an eagle who commands
the high skies to sight its prey
who in the flock uneasily grazes?
Who is it who now descends
prepared and ready for the fight?
Tremendous clouds pregnant with storm
surround him; the flash of his sword
is a living reflection of glory;
his voice thunder; his look a lightning bolt.
Who, when the battle is joined
proud as a messenger of victory
carries his impetuous load tirelessly
running to and fro here and there?
Who, but the son of Colombia and Mars!

His voice rang out: "Peruvians.
behold there the harsh oppressors
of your homeland. Brave Colombians,
victors in a hundred cruel battles,
behold there your fierce enemies
whom you have sought since Orinoco:
theirs is the power, the courage is yours:
yours shall be the glory;
because to fight bravely for the homeland
is the best presage and omen of victory.
Attack: because he who dares most
always is victorious:
and he who does not expect to win has already lost."

Andrés Bello (1781-1865)

Latin America's most notable Neoclassical
figure was the writer, linguist, philologist, educator and law-maker Andrés Bello. He worked
closely with Simón Bolívar in his youth and spent
many years in Europe (especially France and
England), steeping himself in the Neoclassical
tradition and eighteenth century European ration-
alism. In 1810 he accompanied Bolívar as his
interpreter and advisor on a diplomatic mission to
London. Although it was supposed to be only a
short visit, Bello remained in England for almost
twenty years, marrying twice. He spent many

11.7: Bello

hours in the British Museum studying the Greek and Roman classics and debating politics with his British hosts and exiled Spanish liberals.

His knowledge was truly encyclopedic and broad-ranging. Among other things he wrote the best Spanish grammar text of his time and drafted many of the documents which created the Chilean legal system and the foundations of Latin American international law. He spent the last part of his life in Chile, where he was the first rector (president) of the University of Chile. In Santiago he engaged in hot debates with a number of writers, especially Argentines such as Sarmiento, who were prominent figures in the Romantic movement. The Romantics, as we shall see in following lessons, viewed the Neoclassicals as too deeply rooted in rigid foreign rules and standards to capture Latin American reality. As a result of these debates Bello is sometimes seen as an inflexible defender of Neoclassicism, but in truth he was open to new ideas, as we shall see in the essay on the Spanish (Castilian) language which follows.

One of his best poems is a Neoclassical ode to American agriculture. His naturalist's eye (and nose) provided him with keen tools with which to describe the exotic elements to be found in the New World's countryside. The poem is thus a combination of art and science. His pen is placed here at the service of the new nations of the Americas, in their search for their own identity and natural history. Bello clearly prefers the countryside and the bucolic life to the city, which, in the tradition of the Enlightenment, he sees as potentially corrupting. In this poem Bello includes lines which invite the post-Independence military to lay down their weapons, return to the fertile countryside as productive farmers, and participate in the political life of the new nations as civilians. These lines are often interpreted as a warning against the caudillo and the dictatorial role that the military all too frequently played in Latin American politics.

The Castilian language in America by **Andrés Bello**

I do not claim to write for the Castilians. My lessons are directed to my brothers the inhabitants of Spanish America. I judge it important to conserve the language of our fathers as pure as possible, as a providential means of communication and a fraternal link between the various nations of Spanish origins scattered over two continents.

But it is not a superstitious purism which I dare to recommend to you. The prodigious advances in all the arts and sciences, the spreading of intellectual culture, and the political revolutions, cry out each day for new words to express new ideas. And the introduction of brand new words, taken from ancient and foreign languages, has ceased to offend us, so long as it is not manifestly unnecessary, or as long as it does not reveal the affectation and poor taste of those who think

11.8: Castilian

they are adorning the language by writing this way.

There is a worse vice, which is to borrow new meanings for familiar words and phrases, multiplying in this way the number of words with several meanings which to a greater or lesser degree afflict all languages today (and especially those languages which are most in use), because of the almost infinite number of ideas which one must accommodate with a necessarily limited number of words.

But the worst evil of all, and the one which if not stopped will deprive us of the great advantages of a common language, is the road of constructed neologisms, which floods and muddies a great part of what is written in America. By altering the structure of the language they tend to convert it into a multitude of irregular dialects, which are unfettered and barbarous embryonic stages of future languages. These, in a lengthy elaboration would reproduce in America what was the dark period in Europe while Latin was being corrupted. Chile, Peru, Buenos Aires would each speak their own language, or better said, various languages, as happens in Spain, Italy and France, where certain provincial languages dominate, but next to them are other languages, and this places obstacles to the spread of ideas, to the execution of laws, to the administration of the State, and to national unity. A language is like a living body: its vitality does not consist of the constant identity of elements, but rather in the regular uniformity of the functions that these carry out, and whose procedure forms the characteristics which distinguish it from others...

Do not feel, when I recommend the conservation of Castilian, that I am criticizing as false and vice-ridden all that is peculiar to the Americans. There are authentically pure words that in the Peninsula are now considered antiquated, but which traditionally continue to be used in America: why proscribe them? If according to the general practice of the Americans the particular conjugation of a given verb is more suitable, for what reason should we capriciously prefer the usage that prevails in Castile?

If from Castilian roots we have formed new words using the normal procedures for word derivation which Castilian recognizes, and which it has continuously relied on (and continues to rely on) to increase its stock of words, why should we be ashamed of using such words? Chile and Venezuela have as much right as Aragon and Andalucía to tolerate their accidental divergences, when they are provided by the uniform and authentic customs of educated people. In this procedure we sin much less against the purity and correctness of the language, than in the use of frenchified words, which one can see spattered across even the most highly esteemed works of Peninsular writers.

The Agriculture of the Torrid Zone by Andrés Bello (fragment)

Hail, fertile region
where the beloved sun in his daily rounds
envelops you as you conceive every living thing

that stirs in every kind of climate
caressed by its life-giving light!

You weave the summer's garland
from the heavy-leaden heads of grain.
You give the grape to the bubbling cask.
No shade or hue is missing in your fruit
or in your gorgeous forests:
neither purple, nor red, or yellow.
And the wind drinks in your flowers
a thousand varied scents.
Flocks without number
graze thy green majesty,
from the never-ending plain
to the surging uplifted mountains
with their ever-white snowcapped peaks.

You give the beautiful cane
from where honey is refined,
which the world prefers to honeycombs;
you in coral urns thicken the almond
that runs over the foaming jug;
in the prickly pears boils living carmine
that would rival Tyre's purple
and the generous ink of your indigo
copies the sapphire's light.

Yours is the wine, which the wounded maguey
pours for the sons

11.9: Countryside

of happy Anáhuac, and the leaf is yours
which, when from gentle
smoke in errant spires it flees,
the fastidious will solace inert idleness.
You dress in jasmine
the coffee plant,
and give it the perfume that in feasts
will temper the insane fever of Lieo,
for your sons the high palm
its varied feudal growth,
and the pineapple seasons its ambrosia;
the yucca its white bread,
the potato educates its blond fruit;
and cotton opens up to the faint dawn
golden roses and snowy fleece.

Stretched out for you the fresh passionflower
in bowers of abundant green
hangs from its climbing shoots
nectarous globes and fringed flowers;
and for you the maize, arrogant chief
of the tasseled tribe, swells its grain;
and for you the banana tree
faints under the weight of its sweet load
the banana, first
of all the beautiful gifts conceded
by Providence to the people
of happy Ecuador, with a generous hand.
No more obliged by human arts
the fruitful prize it gives;
not to the pruning knife, or the plow
it owes to the fruit;
little industry is enough, since it can
steal from its work a slave's hand;
it grows quickly, and when it ends exhausted
adult progeny replace it all around.

Oh, if to the treacherous sound
that calls him from his home
the simple laborer
far from being stupid and vain
is the pomp and false glitter
of the pestilent laziness of the city!
By what dark illusion
do those whom fortune made lords
of such lucky, varied and abundant earth
which the citizen abandons
and to the mercenary faith
the inherited motherlands
and in blind tumult are imprisoned
in miserable cities
where obstinate ambition
fans the flame of civil bands. ...

The luxuriant heart
which scorns a happy darkness
which in the bloody luck of combat
beats with happiness,
and covets power or glory,

11.10: American plants

and loves noble dangers;
let it esteem insult and affront
the honor that the motherland does not receive
the liberty sweeter than an empire,
and more beautiful than the olive's laurel.

Citizen soldier
put aside your livery of war:
the branch of victory
should be hung from the motherland's altar
and alone adorn the merit of glory.
Of its triumph, my motherland,
shall see Peace the longed-for day
Peace, at whose sight the world fills
its soul with serenity and joy:
man returns inspired to his tasks,
the ships hauls anchor, and to her friends
commends soft breezes,
the workshop hums, the countryside boils,
and sickle cannot cut all the grain there is.

O young nations, who lift your brows
girded with early laurels
over the gaze of the marveling West.
Honor the fields and the simple life
of the farmer and his frugal openness.
Thus liberty will forever live in you,
ambition will be restrained,

11.11: Caudillo

and the law will have a temple.
The people will be not stray from the path
to immortality, arduous and hard;
they will take heart from your example.
Your posterity and your new names
adding to your fame and glory
as the cry rings out:
"These are sons, sons
(the voice will preach to all mankind)
of those who as victors overpowered
the highest peaks of the Andes;
sons of those who in the battle of Boyacá
and in the arena of Maipú,
and in the glorious campaign of Apurima,
knew how to humble the Spanish lion".

12: Civilization and Barbarism

The Theme: Civilization and Barbarism.

One of the predominant themes in nineteenth century Latin American literature (as well as politics and sociology) was the struggle between the European-oriented "civilized" city and the native "barbaric" countryside. This theme was especially noteworthy in Argentina, where it also took the form of the political struggles between the one large city (Buenos Aires) and the vast expanses of fertile countryside, and is captured in the writings of the two authors considered in this chapter, Domingo F. Sarmiento and Esteban Echeverría.

To appreciate the significance of the works of authors such as Sarmiento and Echeverría it is necessary to understand the historical development of Argentina in this period. After Independence, which started in 1810 and was consolidated in 1816, Argentina was the scene of a bitter struggle between the city-port of Buenos Aires and the caudillos of the interior. Buenos Aires was the symbol of the cosmopolitan and refined "civilized" side of the nation, with a strong orientation outwards to France and England. In

12.1: Gauchos

sharp contrast, the pampas (plains) of the interior represented the tough and sometimes cruel "barbaric" side of life in Argentina.

The political tendency called the "Unitarians" argued for a strong centralized and unified government under the leadership of Buenos Aires. Their political adversaries were the Federales, who wanted a decentralized system with considerable autonomy for the provinces. Between the years 1830 and 1850 the Federals had the upper hand, and one of them, the caudillo of the Province (not the city) of Buenos Aires, Juan Manuel de Rosas, took the city and launched a harsh dictatorship, persecuting the Unitarians without mercy.

Romanticism (Chapters 12, 13)

Cultural-historical framework:	Struggles between liberals and conservatives, between federalists and centralists Forging of the new nations and cultural identity Conflicts between the "civilization" of the European-oriented cities and the countryside "barbarism" Romanticism displaces Neoclassicism: triumph of the heart over the mind
Approximate dates:	Approximately 1830 to late 19th Century
Historical landmarks	Independence of Spanish America affirmed with the last battle (Ayacucho, 1824) Rise of the caudillos and the struggles against them Juan Manuel de Rosas in Buenos Aires, 1829-52 British occupy the Falkland/Malvinas Islands, 1833 European and American travelers: Cook, Humboldt, Catherwood, Darwin
Literature	Romanticism as a reaction to Neoclassicism. Sentimentalism, freedom, subjectivism, individualism Democratic and liberal political ideas Struggle against the caudillos Stress on the exotic. Use of the imagination Storms of nature reflect storms of human emotions Idealization of the Indigenous, the countryside. Idealization of "types": bandits, gauchos, the noble savage Domingo F. Sarmiento, 1811-1888 Esteban Echeverría, 1805-1851 José María Heredia, 1803-1839 Jorge Isaacs, 1832-1894 Gertrudis Gómez de Avellaneda, 1814-1873
The Arts	Painting (some sculpture): emotional, subjective Painting at the service of science: the travelers/observers Idealization of the Indian, the countryside. Storms of nature reflect emotions Use of exotic, emotional, imaginative themes Romantic travel painting and landscapes Architecture continues to rely on Neoclassicism The Academies continue to stress Neoclassicism, but begin to shift to Romantic themes and approaches

Sarmiento (1811-1888)

Domingo F. Sarmiento was an Argentine writer, politician, diplomat and educator who fought against the tyranny of the dictator Juan Manuel de Rosas and became president of his country. One of his principal works, *Facundo, or Civilization and Barbarism*, is a sociological study of his divided nation as well as a biography of the gaucho caudillo Facundo Quiroga. It had a further political purpose as a weapon in his struggle against the caudillo Rosas.

12.2: Sarmiento

Sarmiento was personally able to bridge some of the gaps in his divided nation: he was an educated and cultured man, yet he was from the interior and supposedly less civilized area of his country. He presents the figure of Facundo with brutal realism, and yet also with some sympathy as a tragic individual who is the simple product of his environment. Sarmiento's prescription for Argentina, however, is very clear: the age of the animal-like caudillos must give way to progress, civilization, and massive immigration from Europe. In this process education should play a major part.

In an attitude that was not shared by all his countrymen, Sarmiento greatly admired the United States. He served as Argentina's ambassador in Washington, and became friendly with a wide circle of American political and intellectual figures. Sarmiento was much impressed by the American educator Horace Mann, and after he became president he brought New England schoolteachers to Argentina to strengthen the public education system.

Facundo: Civilization and Barbarism
by Domingo F. Sarmiento (fragment)

Chapter I: Physical Features of Argentina, and the Characters, Habits, and Ideas which it Engenders.

The immense spaces of the far reaches of the nation are totally unpopulated, and the country's navigable rivers have not yet been penetrated by even small craft. Argentina's basic problem is size and empty space. The emptiness surrounds us and permeates our innermost self. The border between one province and another tends to be the empty space between them, without any human habitation. There we have immensity: immense plains, immense forests, immense rivers, with an always uncertain horizon obscured by fog and distance so that from a far perspective it is not possible to tell the point at which the earth ends and the sky begins. To the South and North we are threatened by savages, who wait for moonlit nights in order to fall, like a pack of hyenas, on the cattle that graze near the undefended hamlets. When the teamsters of the solitary caravans of wagons that slowly traverse the pampas must stop to rest and build their small fires they are always alert to danger. The slightest whisper of wind in the dry grass turns their gaze south, where their scanning tries to penetrate the dark shadows of the night to seek the sinister shapes of the savage horde which could surprise and assault them from one moment to the next.

If they hear nothing, if their gaze cannot penetrate the dark veil that covers the quiet solitude, then the men seek reassurance by observing the ears of the horses near the fire to see if they are relaxed and casually tilted to the rear. Only then do they continue their interrupted conversation, or tear off chunks from the slab of half-raw beef which is their food.

If it is not the closeness of the savage which disturbs the men of the pampas, it is the fear of the stalking tiger, or of the snake that might be stepped on. The insecurity of life, which is habitual and permanent in the countryside, imprints, in my view, a certain stoic resignation in the Argentine character towards violent death. Death is but one of the inevitable turns of fate and life; one form of death is like any other, and this may perhaps explain the certain indifference with which they receive or cause death, even though there are profound and long-lasting impressions left among those who survive. ...

Chapter V: Life of Facundo Quiroga.

(Sarmiento tells a series of anecdotes regarding Facundo, including one when he was trapped in a tree by a tiger for many hours.)

Facundo was also called "The Tiger of the Plains", and indeed this name suited him well. Phrenology, or comparative anatomy, has well demonstrated the relationship between external appearances and moral tendencies, between the physiognomy of mankind and of certain animals which might resemble their character. ... Quiroga's black eyes, full of fire and shaded by heavy brows, caused an involuntary feeling of terror among those who might receive his glare, because Facundo rarely looked directly at anyone. Because of his habit, his skill, or his desire to always seem fearsome, he usually inclined his head forwards and peered out through his

12.3: Facundo

eyebrows, like Montvoisin's Alí Bajá. Cain, as represented by Ravel's famous company, arouses in me the image of Quiroga, leaving aside any artistic merit, which does not seem appropriate. The rest of his physiognomy was normal, and the pale darkness of his skin nicely matched the thick shadows which framed him. ...

When driven by rage, he could kick a man to death, or smash someone's brains in over a gambling dispute; he once pulled both ears off a lover because she asked him for thirty pesos to celebrate a wedding he had agreed to; he opened his son Juan's head with a hatchet because there was no other way to make him shut up; he beat a beautiful young woman in Tucumán because he could neither seduce or force her to fulfill his desire. In all these acts he showed himself to be a man-beast, although not stupid, and not without some purpose. Since he was incapable of being admired or esteemed, he relished being feared, and this relish was exclusive, dominant, to the point where he arranged all the actions of his life so as to produce terror around him, among the people as well as his soldiers, among the victims about to be executed as much as among his wife and children. In his inability to manage the levers of civil government, he used terror as the expedient to replace patriotism and sacrifice. Ignorant, surrounded by mysteries, and impenetrable, making use of a native cunningness, an uncommon capacity for observation and an appreciation for the credulity of the masses, he pretended and assumed great accomplishments, which gave him prestige and reputation among the vulgar people.

The repertoire of popular anecdotes about him is unending. His sayings, his orders, have the stamp of originality that is common to certain Oriental viziers, with a certain air of solomonic wisdom, in the mind of the people. What difference, in effect, is there between the famous device of Solomon to divide the disputed child in half in order to discover the true mother, and the trick that Facundo used to discover a thief among his men? This is what happened: an object had been robbed in one of his companies, and all the attempts to find the thief were fruitless. Quiroga then assembled the troops, and had one short reed cut for each soldier. These he distributed, and with a sure voice, said: "Tomorrow morning the reed held by the thief will have grown an inch, and I will know who the thief is". The next day Quiroga reassembled the troops and proceeded to inspect and compare the size of the reeds. There was one soldier whose reed was one inch shorter than the others. "You are the thief!" Facundo yelled at him with a fearsome voice. And indeed, he had caught the thief, who quickly broke down. The explanation is simple: the credulous gaucho, believing that his reed would grow an inch, had cut an inch off to compensate. This incident showed Quiroga's certain superiority and sure knowledge of human nature in using these methods.

Esteban Echeverría, 1805-1851

Along with Sarmiento, Esteban Echeverría epitomizes the romantic liberal's struggle against despotism and the caudillos, offering us another glimpse at the tensions between "civilization and barbarism".

Echeverría lived a scandalous youth and never finished his studies in Argentina. However, after the death of his parents he settled down and took life more seriously. He traveled to Europe, where he absorbed the writings of the French and English romantics, and he determined to fight to the end against the Rosas dictatorship his country was enduring. Even though he wrote poetry, essays and novels, he is best remembered for one short story, *El Matadero (The Slaughterhouse)*, which is a bitter attack against Rosas.

Echeverría and many other intellectuals were the objects of special attention and oppression by Rosas and his followers, the most brutal of whom formed gangs called *mazorcas*. Echeverría wrote a series of essays protesting the excesses of Rosas, and he was forced to flee the city, hiding first in the countryside and then exiling himself to Uruguay. In that period he wrote his powerful critique of the Rosas dictatorship, *The Slaughterhouse*. It is a relatively short account, but it became important because of the explicit metaphor in which the Rosas dictatorship is equated with a brutal and savage slaughterhouse.

12.4: Echeverría

One might well ask what this story has to do with Romanticism. The answer is that Romanticism was tied to the liberal struggle against political dictatorships, and many Romantic writers were also political essayists, such as Echeverría and Sarmiento. Beyond that, the story's central event is the capture and torture of a young Unitarian who is, in essence, a tragic romantic hero who dies with dignity in the face of overwhelming odds. Some critics have also seen in *The Slaughterhouse* some elements which were to appear in later literary movements. These include "Costumbrismo" because of the attention paid to the typical customs of the gauchos, and Naturalism because of the use of realistic details which are brutal and even obscene in an attempt to bring attention to intolerable socio-political circumstances and thus provoke change.

The themes employed by Echeverría (as well as Sarmiento) were used much later in a parallel struggle against the dictatorship of Juan D. Perón, who governed Argentina from 1945 to 1955. Both Rosas and Perón came from interior Argentina, and governed with a heavy hand, raising the banner of Argentine nationalism against foreigners. Both were married to intelligent, strong and beautiful women who died at an early age and who were actively involved in the political process.

The Slaughterhouse by Esteban Echeverría

The slaughterhouse of the Convalecencia, or of El Alto, located among the farms to the south of the city, is a great open area in the form of a rectangle, located at the far end of two streets, one of which ends there; the other continues to the east. This open area, with a slope to the south, is intersected by a ditch cut by the flow of rainwater. On the edges of the ditch are innumerable rat holes; and the ditch caries in time of rain all the dry or recent gore from the Slaughterhouse. In one corner, to the east, is found what they call the "casilla" or little house, a low building, with three rooms and a flat roof and a porch which faces the street, and a hitching post for tying up horses. Behind the casilla are several corrals made of ñandubay wood, with strong gates to lock up the cattle.

In the winter these corrals are veritable mud-holes, in which the animals are so bogged down they can hardly move. In the casilla the taxes for the use of the corrals are collected and fines are levied for violating regulations. Here we find the Judge of the Slaughterhouse, an important person, chief of the butchers, who exercises his power in that little republic, by authority of The Restorer. It is easy to figure out what kind of person is required to fill that post. The casilla, for its part, is such a dilapidated and tiny building that one would hardly notice it next to the corrals were it not associated with the terrible judge, and were it not for the bright red slogans on its white walls: "Long live the Federation", "Long live the Restorer and the heroic doña Encarnación Ezcurra", "Death to the savage Unitarians". These are very meaningful slogans, symbols of the political and religious faith of the people of the Slaughterhouse. But perhaps some readers might not know that the afore-mentioned heroine is the deceased wife of the Restorer, a very dear patron to the butchers, who, now that she is dead, is venerated for her Christian virtues and her federal heroism in the revolution against Balcarce. It happened that on an anniversary of that memorable achievement of the mazorca the butchers were celebrating with a splendid banquet at the casilla. The Heroine and her daughter attended, along with other federal ladies, and there, in the presence of many, she offered the butchers in a solemn toast her federal patronage. For this reason the butchers enthusiastically proclaimed her their patron, and placed her name on the walls of the casilla, where it will remain until erased by the hand of time.

12.5: Rosas

The appearance of the Slaughterhouse from a distance was grotesque, full of movement. Forty-nine steer carcasses were laid out on their hides, and close to two hundred people wandered around the dirt soaked with the blood of their arteries. Around each steer there was a group of human figures of different skin and race. The most prominent figure in each group was the butcher, with his knife in hand, bare-chested, with long and disheveled hair, with shirt and trousers and face spattered with blood. Behind him there milled around, following his every movement, a gang of young men, and Black and Mulatto offal collectors whose ugliness rivaled that of the legendary harpies. Mixed in with them were enormous stray dogs, who sniffed, growled and snapped at each other as they fought for scraps. Forty-odd carts, covered with blackened hides, were scattered at random around the open area, and a few riders, with their ponchos thrown over their shoulders and their lassos hanging on their saddles, cast their indifferent eye over the various groups surrounding the butchered animals.

Overhead a flock of white and blue gulls, who had returned from their migration when they smelled the blood and flesh, whirled around, spreading their discordant cawing over the sounds and voices of the slaughterhouse, and projecting a clear shadow over that field of horrible butchery. This was all to be seen at the beginning of the slaughter. ...

Suddenly, the hoarse shout of a butcher cried out:

"Here comes a Unitarian".

And upon hearing such a memorable word, that whole mob stood still as if struck by lightning.

"Don't you see his U-shaped sideburns? And he is not wearing the insignia on his coat, or the sign of mourning on his hat"

"Unitarian dog"

"That little dandy"

"He rides a gringo saddle"

"Give him the mazorca"

"The shears!"

"Let's beat him up"

"He even has pistol holsters to show off"

"All those Unitarian dandies are show-offs"

"We dare you to grab him, Matasiete"

"You dare me?"

"Yeah"

Matasiete was a man of few words and a lot of action. When the matter at hand had to do with violence, with agility, with skill with the axe, the knife or the horse, he used actions and not words. They had challenged him: he spurred his horse and galloped with loose reins to meet the Unitarian.

The Unitarian was a young man of about twenty-five years, of elegant and

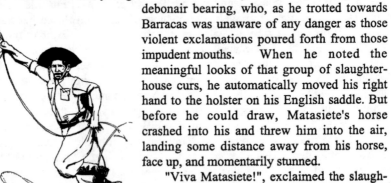

debonair bearing, who, as he trotted towards Barracas was unaware of any danger as those violent exclamations poured forth from those impudent mouths.   When he noted the meaningful looks of that group of slaughterhouse curs, he automatically moved his right hand to the holster on his English saddle. But before he could draw, Matasiete's horse crashed into his and threw him into the air, landing some distance away from his horse, face up, and momentarily stunned.

"Viva Matasiete!", exclaimed the slaughterhouse gang, running toward the victim like scavenger birds falling on the bones of an ox . devoured by the tiger.

12.6: Gaucho, lariat

Still confused, the young man, casting a fiery glance on those fierce men, moved toward his horse, who was standing still a short distance away, going for his pistols that would give him vindication and revenge. But Matasiete jumped off his horse, cut him off, and with his burly arm grabbed him by the necktie, threw him to the ground and at the same time drew his knife and brought it to the Unitarian's throat.

A tremendous guffaw and new stentorian "Vivas" saluted Matasiete.

What nobility of soul! What Federal bravery! They always moved together in gangs when they fell like buzzards on a hapless victim.

"Cut his throat, Matasiete; he wanted to draw his pistols. Cut his throat like you did the bull's"

"Unitarian scoundrel. Let's shave him"

"He has a good throat for the violin"

"Let's play the violin on him. Better yet, give the Slippery-one"

"Let's try it", said Matasiete, and with a smile he ran the edge of his knife over the victim's neck, while he pressed his chest with his knee and held him by the hair with his left hand.

"No, no, don't cut his throat" came from afar the imposing voice of the Slaughterhouse Judge who drew near on horse.

"Take him to the casilla. Yes, the casilla. Prepare the noose and the shears. Death to the savage Unitarians! Long live the Restorer of the laws!"

"Long live Matasiete"

"Long live!" "Death to him!" the spectators cried out in chorus, and tying the unfortunate young man's elbows together, rained blows on him, dragging him to the torture table, like the executioners of Christ.

The main room of the casilla had in the center a large and solid table where glasses and cards were constantly present except for when the table was needed for the torture and executions carried out by the Slaughterhouse's Federal executioners. Over in the corner was a smaller table, with a writing desk and a notebook, and a bunch of chairs among which one stood out: it was the Judge's armchair. One man, apparently a soldier, sat in one of the chairs, singing with his guitar "La Resbalosa", a tune which was immensely popular among the Federals. Then the mob burst in, hitting and shoving the young Unitarian to the center of the room.

"You're going to get the Slippery One"
"Commend your soul to the devil"
"He's furious, like a wild bull"
"The stick will tame him"
"We'll take care of him"
"For now the stick and the scissors"

12.7: Gaucho, whip

"If not, the candle"

"Better yet, the noose".

"Shut up and sit down" yelled the judge, dropping into his armchair.
They all obeyed, while the young man,   standing and facing the judge,   cried out
in a voice full of indignation:

"You bastard executioners! What are you going to do to me?"

"Take it easy", said the Judge, smiling. "No need to get upset. You'll see".

The young man, in effect, was beside himself with fury. His whole body
seemed to be convulsed. His pale and mottled face, his voice, his trembling lip,
all showed the convulsive beating of his heart and the agitation of his nerves.
His fiery eyes seemed to bulge out of their sockets, and his long black hair bris-
tled. His bare neck and open shirt front showed the violent beating of his arteries
and his anxious breathing.

"Are you trembling?" asked the Judge.

"Out of rage, because I can't choke you"

"Would you have the strength and courage to do that?"

"I have more than enough will and courage to do that, you bastard"

"Get my horse shears and shave him Federal-style"

Two men grabbed him, one by the rope tying his arms together, and the
other by his hair, and in a minute they had cut the sideburns and beard which
framed his face, to the raucous laughter of the spectators.

"Give him a glass of water to cool him off" ordered the judge.

"I'd give you a glass of gall, you bastard".

A short Black man stood in front of him
with a glass of water in his hand. The young
Unitarian kicked his arm and the glass flew up
and hit the ceiling, spattering its contents on the
astonished faces of the spectators.

"This fellow is incorrigible!"

"We'll calm him down"

"Silence" said the Judge. "Now you are
shaved Federal-style, and we just have to take
care of the mustache. Don't forget it. Let's get
down to business. Why aren't you wearing the
insignia?"

"Because I don't want to"

"Don't you know that the Restorer has ordered it?"

"That insignia becomes you, slaves, but it is
not for free men"

12.8: Gaucho, mate

"Then we'll force free men to wear it"

"Yes, force and bestial violence. Those are
your weapons, you bastards. The wolf, the tiger, the panther, also are strong like
you. You should walk like them, on all fours."

"Aren't you afraid the tiger will chew you up?"

"I'd rather have that happen, than be tied up and have you tear out my guts, little by little".

"Why aren't you wearing the sign of mourning for the Heroine?"

"Because I carry the sign of mourning in my heart for the Motherland, the Motherland that you have destroyed, you bastards."

"Don't you know the Restorer has ordered it?"

"You decided that, you slaves, to flatter the pride of your lord and give him your bastard vassal tribute"

"Insolent! You are getting very brave. I'll have your tongue cut out if you say another word. Pull this wise guy's pants down, tie him to the table, and beat his bare ass."

No sooner had the Judge ordered this, when four blood-spattered executioners grabbed the young man and laid him out on the table, holding down his limbs.

"Rather cut my throat than strip me, you bastards".

They muzzled him with a handkerchief and started to strip off his clothes. The young man struggled, kicked, ground his teeth. His limbs for an instant were as flexible as reeds, then as stiff as iron, and his spinal column was the axis of movement that seemed like a snake's. Beads of sweat beaded his face, as large as pearls; his eyes burned, his mouth foamed, and the veins in his neck and chest were dark in contrast with his pale skin as if they were bursting with blood.

"Tie him first" exclaimed the Judge.

"He's roaring with rage" said one of the executioners.

In an instant they had his feet tied to the table, and his body turned face down. It was necessary to do the same thing with his hands, and for this they loosened the bonds that held his arms together and compressed his shoulders. Feeling his arms free, for a short instant in which he seemed to spend all his energy and vitality, the young man jerked upright, leaning first on his arms, and then up on his knees. But then he collapsed, murmuring:

"Rather cut my throat than strip me, you bastards"

His strength had been drained. Immediately they tied him to the table as if on a cross and began the task of stripping him. Then a torrent of blood bubbled out of the young man's mouth and nose, and streamed out over both sides of the table. The executioners stood still, and the spectators were stunned.

"The savage Unitarian burst from rage" said one.

"He had a river of blood in his veins" said another.

"Poor devil. We only wanted to have a little fun with him and he took it too seriously" exclaimed the Judge, scowling his tiger's brows. "We have to file a report. Untie him and let's go"

They carried out his order: then they locked the door and in a moment the gang scurried behind the horse bearing the Judge, downcast and taciturn. The Federals had wound up one more of their innumerable deeds of courage.

In those days the cut-throat executioners of the Slaughterhouse were the apostles of the Rosas Federation, who propagated the word with club and knife. It is not hard to imagine what kind of a federation would emerge from their heads and their knives. They would call a "savage Unitarian" (according to the jargon ordered by the Restorer, patron of the gang) anyone who was not a cut-throat, butcher, savage, or thief. They would use this term for any decent man with a good heart, any patriot, enlightened friend of knowledge and of freedom. And from the events here described we can clearly see that the roots of the Federation were in the Slaughterhouse.

12.9: Gaucho, boleadora

13: Romanticism

The Romantic Movement

This important literary and cultural movement quickly emerged in Latin America in the early part of the 19th Century as a strong reaction against the rigidity and perceived coldness of Neoclassicism. Thus, it was a sort of cultural emancipation from the excessive order imposed by Neoclassical rules. However, it was not antagonistic to the political ideals of the Enlightenment (which was one of the foundations of Neoclassicism) because political liberalism was an important part of Romanticism as well as the Enlightenment.

Romanticism appealed to the exuberant, passionate, individualistic and rebellious side of the Latin. It also included an important amount of nativism or regionalism which glorified the wonders of the Americas, albeit in a somewhat idealized way.

13.1: Romantic love

In literature (and to a lesser extent in painting), what mattered were the emotions of the individual, "*el yo*" (the "I"). Romantic heroes tended to be eccentric and sometimes incapable of functioning effectively within the normal rules of society. Because of this inability, the Romantic hero was frequently tragic, often exiled, or suffering from a disastrous or unrequited love affair. The death of the lover, especially if at an early age, and suicide, were frequent themes in Romantic literature.

Romanticism tended to idealize scenery and character "types" (the bandit, the pirate, the savage, the Indigenous). In Europe the Romantics idealized their past, such as the Middle Ages in the writings of Sir Walter Scott. Not having a similar past, the Latin American Romantics idealized the exotic things they had at hand: the countryside, the jungle, and nature in its most exaggerated and dramatic aspects (storms, waterfalls, high mountains, volcanoes).

Victor Hugo once stated that Romanticism was to literature what liberalism was to politics. The political facet of Romanticism took the liberal side against the conservatives, and found expression in the struggle against dictators, tyranny, and religious obscurantism. This aspect was especially prominent in Argentina (Echeverría, Sarmiento) and Cuba (Heredia, Martí), where the Spanish were able to maintain a colony until the War with the United States in 1898.

The historical moment

The historical period of Romanticism comprises the first few decades after Independence, although in some countries it extended until late in the 19th Century. It was the period in which the new nations were consolidating their political and socio-economic systems, and searching for an identity that would be distinctly theirs. Although Latin American Romanticism was obviously linked to the same European movement, it had uniquely regional and native characteristics that served this purpose of reaffirming the special nature of these new countries. For example, Romanticism allowed local vocabulary and forms of speech which deviated from the Neoclassical norms of the Royal Academy of the Spanish Language; it also emphasized regional types such as the gaucho, country folk, and the Indigenous population. By so doing it also allowed each nation or region to pay homage to its own unique characteristics, thus strengthening national identity. This was also the age of the caudillos, who all too often imposed their iron-fisted rule in local areas or in whole countries; thus, Romanticism (via political liberalism) played an important part in the history of these years.

Art in the Romantic Period

Academic Art: from Neoclassicism to Romanticism

13.2: Garden

The academies continued to dominate and control much of the art that was produced in this period. But Romanticism itself began to penetrate the academies and slowly shifted their conservative Neoclassical emphasis to art that was more consistent with Romanticism. Sometimes this took the form of illustration of the favorite themes of Romantic writers: unrequited love, tragic early death, exotic human types. At other times it focused on the uniqueness of the American landscape in all its extreme forms. Frequently Romantic painting used nature to mirror human passions. Thus, a violent tropical storm or a thundering waterfall would be presented in painting as metaphors for the deep passions of love or the pro-

found sorrows of unbearable tragedy. In the process the cold rules of Neoclassicism gave way to the emotional swings of Romanticism. The heart had regained
its control over the brain and emotion subdued reason.

The shift to Romantic art can be seen in the way many of the Indigenous
peoples were portrayed. A Neoclassical painter would have presented them in
ways that suggested ancient Romans or Greeks, while a Romantic would have
idealized the Indigenous, softening the body forms and stressing sensuality and
harmony with an equally idealized and sensuous natural world.

Romantic travel painting and landscapes

One very popular genre of painting in the Romantic period was that gener-
ated by travelers or explorers. Although consistent with many of the Romantic
currents we find in literature, it had other purposes of its own, such as the communication of scientific knowledge and the relationship of humans to the land
they lived on in ways that today we would include under the term "ecology".

The aspects of the travelers' and explorers' painting which came closest to
Romanticism focused on the extremes of nature, especially at its most raw and
unbridled. However, landscape painting also included scenes that were tranquil
and subdued. Themes that were more sociological in nature, such as realistic
presentations of the ways in which a variety of people lived in the period, were
also prevalent. They were not "Romantic" because they portrayed reality, and
not the idealized version of reality that would be favored by Romantics.

The scientific aspect of painting in this period derived from the fact that
without the technology of the photographic camera, art was still the only way to
convey a visual image of the flora and fauna of the New World, as well as its
archaeological past. The linking of science to art in this period was grounded in
the European Enlightenment in the sense that it rekindled human interest in the
natural world, after many centuries in which art's major function (especially in
the Baroque years) was to serve God.

The earliest scientific painters were Europeans who felt awe at the natural
wonders of the New World and sought to capture and preserve what they saw as
best they could with their pencils and brushes. One of the first in this period who
touched the New World was Captain James Cook, who in the year 1776 landed
on the Island of South Georgia in the South Atlantic and claimed it for King
George III. Cook had several scientists and artists on board, and they faithfully
recorded the flora and fauna of this exotic island, with its vast quantities of seals
and penguins. As we shall see later on, the Island of South Georgia acquired
later significance as the "gateway to Antarctica", and the place where an incident
set off the 1982 war between Argentina and Great Britain.

Other scientific traveler-painters included Baron Alexander von Humboldt
(who concentrated on the Andean region), Frederick Catherwood (who recorded
the marvelous ruins of the Mayas in Central America), and Charles Darwin on
board HMS Beagle, who spent considerable time in the Galápagos Islands, the
Beagle Channel in Southern South America, and the Falkland/Malvinas Islands.

The scientific writings of these Europeans was richly supplemented by fine drawings, water-colors and oil paintings of the unique sights and life-forms they saw in their travels. Besides recording these wonders, the European explorer-painters of the Romantic period also inspired local scientific study and painting by a number of Latin Americans who thus employed art to educate their countrymen in the richness of their own emerging nations.

Popular art in the Romantic period

Popular art fared better in the Romantic period than in the previous ones. The focus on the countryside and local types eventually led to the current (in both art and literature) known as "costumbrismo", i.e., the focus on local customs and types. During the Romantic period there was a renewed respect for the Indigenous peoples and their ways. The Romantics tended to exaggerate and idealize and were not above distorting history and current conditions .to suit their vision of the way the world should be. Nevertheless, they did not have the negative view of the Indigenous that was generally held by the Spanish colonial Baroque artists or the European-inspired Neoclassics. The Romantics also valued the artistic contribution made by folk art from all sources, and all levels of the socio-economic structure.

Two Romantic Poets

José María Heredia (1803-1839)

13.3: Heredia

Like many of his fellow early Romantics, Heredia was forged in the Neoclassical mold, but he quickly abandoned this current while still young to embrace Romanticism. He personally had many characteristics of the Romantic hero: he fought political battles against the Spanish in his native Cuba, was exiled, had tragic love affairs (his principal lover married another man), and was awe-struck by the wonders of wild American nature. As a typical Enlightenment revolutionary, he joined a secret Masonic lodge, and because of his anti-Spanish political activities became an exile at the age of nineteen. He spent most of his exile in the United States, earning his living as a Spanish teacher in a New York academy.

Heredia traveled extensively, and on one of his trips to Canada (in 1824, at age twenty) visited Buffalo and saw Niagara Falls. His reaction to the Falls was pure Romanticism, and it produced one of his best poems: he found in the awesome power of the Falls the reflection of his strong emotions, especially the pain of exile far from his beloved Cuba.

On another occasion a tropical storm served to remind him of his passions and his pain over Spanish oppression of his country. Heredia was also capable of writing expressive poems of love that are among the best of those written in the Romantic period. Heredia eventually settled in Mexico, where a sympathetic government gave him several diplomatic posts. He was able finally to return to his Cuban homeland, but he became disillusioned at the apparent inability of his countrymen to rebel against the Spanish, and he once more went into exile. He died young and embittered.

Niagara by José María Heredia

Tune my lyre, let me have it, for I feel
my soul shaken and agitated
and burning with inspiration.
    Oh! How much time
it spent in the shadow without my face
glowing in its light! Sinewy Niagara,
only your sublime terror could
bring back the divine gift that
the sorrow of an impious hand took away.

13.4: Waterfall

    Prodigious torrent, be calm, still
your terrifying roar; draw back a little
the shadows that wrap around you;
let me contemplate your serene visage,
and fill my soul with burning enthusiasm.
I am worthy enough to see you; always
I have scorned the common and the poor,
I wished for the terrific and sublime.
When the furious hurricane poured forth,
and lightning crashed in front of me,
I enjoyed, trembling. I saw the Ocean
whipped up by the southern storm,
and beat against my craft, and 'neath my feet
the boiling vortex opened, and I loved the danger.
But the fierceness of the sea
in my soul did not produce
the deep impression of your grandeur.

    You flow serene and majestic; and then
breaking on sharp rocks,
you violently balance, then burst forth
like blind and irresistible destiny.
What human voice could describe
the roaring danger
of your terrifying face? My soul

in vague thought is confused
when it sees that burning current,
which in vain wants to follow,
turbulent scene in its flight to the dark edge
of the high precipice. A thousand waves
like rapid thoughts pass,
crash, are maddened,
and another thousand and another reach them
and in foam and thunder disappear. ...
    Powerful Niagara!
Farewell! In a few years
the cold grave will have devoured
your weak bard. May my verses last
as long as your immortal glory! May piously
seeing you some traveler,
give a sigh in my memory!
and when Febus drops into the western sky
happy I fly to where the Lord calls me
and listen to the echoes of my fame,
rise up in the clouds of your radiant face.

To my wife by José María Heredia

    When in my fervid veins there burned
fiery youth, my song
poured out painful tears
and the stormy wishes of my passions.

    Today I dedicate them to you, my wife,
when love, now freer of illusions,
inflames our pure hearts,
and the day seems serene and peaceful to me.

    And so lost in turbulent seas
the miserable navigator implores to heaven,
when the furious storm afflicts him;

13.5: Heredia's wife

    and free of the shipwreck, on the altar
consecrates faithful to the adored deity
the damp relics of his ship.

In a storm by José María Heredia

Hurricane, hurricane, I feel you coming,
And with your burning breath

I enthusiastically inhale
The breath of the lord of the skies.

  Suspended on the wings of wind
I see it roll through the immense space,
Silent, tremendous, irresistible,
In its rapid course. The earth in its calm
Sinister, mysterious,
Contemplates with fear its terrible face.
Do you not look upon the bull? Pawing the ground
With the unbearable ardor of wounded feet:
The powerful face lifted up,
And fire pouring from the swollen nose
Calls out the storm with its roars.
What clouds! What fury! The sun trembles
Watching with sad fear your glorious face,
And its clouded disk pours out only
A shadowy and funereal light,
That is neither night nor day...
Fearful color, veil of death!
The little birds tremble and hide
When the roaring hurricane approaches,
And the distant mountains resonate
And the woods hear, and they too respond.

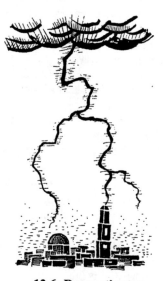

  It comes now... Don't you see it? Look how
its fearful and majestic cloak unfolds!...
Giant of the air I salute you...
In fierce confusion the wind agitates
The ornaments of its dark vestments...
Look...! On the horizon
The arms rapidly unfold into arcs
And with them embrace
Everything I can see from hill to hill!

13.6: Romantic storm

  Universal darkness...! Your blowing
Lifts up in whirlwinds
The dust of the agitated fields...
In the resonating clouds is hurled down
The chariot of God, and from its wheels
Bursts forth the speedy lighting,   precipitated
Wounds and terrifies the ground,
And its livid light floods the sky.

What is that rumor? Is it rain...? Unleashed

It falls in torrents, it darkens the world,
And all is confusion, profound horror.
Sky, clouds, hills, dear woods,
Where are you...? I seek you in vain:
You have disappeared... The dark storm
In the sky scrambles an ocean
That buries everything...
In the end, fatal world, we separate:
The hurricane and I are alone.

Sublime tempest! As in your bosom,
From your solemn inspiration swollen,
To the vile world and miserable oblivion
And I raise my face full of pleasure!
Where is the cowardly soul
who fears your roar...? I rise up in you
To the Lord's throne: I hear in the clouds
The echo of his voice; I feel the earth
Listen to him and tremble. Feverish tears
Descend my pale cheeks,
And your high majesty I tremblingly adore.

To Cuba's Star by **José María Heredia**

Liberty! Now never over Cuba
Will your divine lights shine.
We lack even the poor crumbs
Of the honor of the sublime enterprise.
Oh dark and senseless pity!
Woe to he who is human and conspires!
Long fruit of blood and ire
He will reap from his miserable error.

When our eloquent voice sounded
All the people in fury embraced,
And Cuba's star rose up
More fiery and serene than the sun.
We shall respect with clemency the lives
Of traitors and vile tyrants
When with a little blood shed
Liberty toasted us and honor.

Today the people wounded with vertigo
Give us the insolent tyrant
And with cowardice and stupidity

13.7: Cubans, flag

Has not wanted to draw the sword.
  Everything lies dissolved, lost!
Because I despair of Cuba and myself,
Against the terrible, severe destiny
My asylum shall be a noble tomb.

  We struggle with a fierce tyranny
Combined with perfidious treason,
And Cuba's star is eclipsed
For the century of horror that remains.
  Because if a people their harsh chains
Do not dare break with their hands,
It is easy to exchange tyrants
But they will never be free.

  The cowards hide their faces,
The vile masses bow to the tyrant
And he arrogantly threatens, fulminates,
And enjoys his fatal victory.
If the gallows await me, in its heights
I will show my bloodied head
Monument to Spanish ferocity,
Drying in the rays of the sun.
  Execution does not defame the patriot
And from it my last cry
Will hurl against the tyrant's ear
A fierce wish of eternal hatred.

Gertrudis Gómez de Avellaneda (Cuba, 1814-1873)

"La Avellaneda" was one of the most prolific and lyrical of the Romantic poets. She shares with Heredia her love of Cuba, and bitterness over Spanish oppression and the seeming inability of Cubans to liberate themselves. She had unbridled and passionate love affairs, which always seemed to turn out badly, leading to Romantic tragedy and the frequent scandalizing of her contemporary society.

13.8: La Avellaneda

At the age of twenty-two she was forced to accompany her parents to Spain, and she expresses her pain at leaving Cuba in the lyric and eloquent poem "Departure". She had literary success in Spain, but her ardent emotional life led to rejection by Madrid society and made it impossible for her to be accepted by the Royal Academy. She fell in love with Ignacio de Cepeda, but it seems that he, either because of fear or envy of her artistic and intellectual ability, abandoned her to marry another, a circumstance which led to the sad and bitter poem. "To him".

In addition to her poems, Gómez de Avellaneda is noted for an anti-slavery novel and her feminist essays. Late in life she was able to return for a few years to Cuba, where she was proclaimed the National Poet of the country.

Departure by Gertrudis Gómez de Avellaneda

Pearl of the sea! Star of the West!
Beautiful Cuba. Your brilliant sky
covers the night with its opaque veil
just as pain covers my sad face.

I am leaving. The diligent crew
to rip me from my native soil,
raises the sails, and soon they will fill
with breezes from your ardent zone.

Farewell, happy motherland, beloved Eden!
Wherever fate in its fury impels me,
your sweet name will please my ear!

13.9: Ship at dock

Farewell! The swollen sail is groaning...
the anchor is raised... the boat, shuddering,
cuts through the waves and silently flies!

Romance (Fragment) by Gertrudis Gómez de Avellaneda

(Answering one from a young lady).

I am neither magician nor siren,
nor cherub nor enchantress
as in your gallant verses
you called me today, beautiful girl.

Gertrudis is my name,
given to me at the baptismal font;
my mother calls me Tula,
and my friends imitate her.

Leave aside then, I beg you,
all the Safos and Corinas,
and simply call me
Gertrudis, Tula or friend.

No, I have no noble ambition,
as you mistakenly imagine,
that in the pages of glory
my humble name might be written.

I sing as the bird sings,
as the branches are moved,
as the fountains murmur
as the golden skies sigh.

I sing because heaven was pleased
to give me the inspiration that moves me
as it gave brilliance to the stars
as it gave harmony to the world.

I sing because in my breast
there are secret chords that vibrate
to each affection of the soul,
to each chance of life.

13.10: Romantic thoughts

I sing because there is light and shadows,
because there is sadness and joy,
because there is fear and hope,
because there is love and there is treachery.

I sing because I exist and feel,
because that which is great I admire,
because that which is beautiful enchants me,
because that which is bad irritates me.

I sing because my mind sees
infinite concordances,
and mysterious pleasures,
and hidden truths.

I sing because every being
has its precise conditions:
the water flows, the bird flies,
the wind whistles, and the sun shines.

I sing without knowing myself
what the song means,
and whether for the listening world,
it inspires astonishment or pity.

13.11: Romantic poetry

The nightingale has no ambition
to be applauded when it trills...
Its nocturnal melodies
are heartbeats from its bosom.

Moderate, therefore, your praise,
and from my forehead withdraw
the imperishable crown
which your love places there.

The prize should go to noble efforts
of more heroic temples
because when I sing I only fulfill
the condition of my life.

To him by Gertrudis Gómez de Avellaneda

The link no longer exists: all is broken.
Heaven wanted it that way: Blessed be it!
Bitter chalice exhausted with pleasure;
My soul is finally at rest, it desires nothing.

I loved you, I love you no more: think about it at least.
Never, if it were error, did I look at truth!
Let the many years full of bitterness
Be swallowed up by oblivion; the heart breathes.

You have destroyed it without pity: my pride,
Time and time again, you stepped on it insanely...
But never did my lips exhale a murmur
To accuse your tyrannical proceeding.

Of grave faults you are the terrible avenger,
You calmly fulfilled your mission. Do you realize?
It was not your power which irresistibly
Prostrated before you my victorious forces.

13.12: Couple

God wished it and it was so: Glory to his name!
All is finished: my spirit is recovering.
Angel of vengeance!, now you are man..
I feel neither love nor fear when I contemplate you.

Your scepter fell, your sword was blunted...
But, oh! What a sad liberty I breathe!

I made a world of you, today it is annihilated,
And in a deep and vast solitude I look at myself.

May you live happily! If someday
You see this goodbye which I eternally send you
You will know that you still have in my soul
Generous forgiveness, tender affection.

A Romantic novelist: Jorge Isaacs (1832-1894)

Isaacs is the author of the novel *María*, the most widely-read book of the 19th Century in Latin America, and a classic example of its genre. He was the son of an English Jew who prospered as a landowner and farmer in the Cauca Valley of Colombia near Cali. There, in a farm called *El Paraíso*, which still exists as a monument to the author, he grew up in a calm and bucolic atmosphere. The novel is autobiographical and simple: young Efraín falls in love with his cousin María when he returns to his homestead near Cali after years of study in Bogotá.

13.13: Isaacs

Efraín and María spend a few months in the chaste delirium of first love, but their parents are opposed to the match, and María is suffering from a fatal disease. In the hopes of helping her, Efraín goes to Europe to study medicine, but by the time he eventually returns, María has just died. Tragic young death shows up frequently in Romanticism.

The popularity of *María* in its time lay in its simplicity, its profound emotions, the few brief moments of joy, and then finally its tragic and inevitable outcome. The auguries, the symbols and the foreshadowing leave the reader no room for doubt about the premature death of María. The countryside is a protagonist in the novel, which combines realism along with a heavy dose of idealization. The "costumbrista" current which evolved from Romanticism is also present in the presentation of local country types from the Cauca Valley and the city dwellers of Cali.

María by Jorge Isaacs

(Fragments from Chapters LXIV and LXV, which are the final ones of the novel: Maria has died. Efrain has returned from Europe to the home of his parents, and Emma, Maria's cousin, tells him of Maria's final hours. Efrain goes to his room, crushed by the tragedy).

...Holding in my hands Maria's braided hair, and lying on the sofa on which Emma had heard Maria's last words, I heard the clock strike two: the very same clock had measured the hours of that anguished night before I left on my trip, and it was now to measure the last hours that I would spend in the home of my elders.

I dreamt that Maria was now my wife: this most chaste delirium had been and would continue to be the only pleasure left in my life. She was wearing a vaporous white dress and a blue apron, blue as if it had been formed by a splinter from the sky. It was the same apron which so many times I had helped her fill with flowers, and which she knew how to tie so prettily and casually around her restless waist. I had found her braids wrapped in this apron. She opened the door to my room carefully, being sure not to make the slightest sound with her clothes, and then she kneeled on the rug at the foot of the sofa. After looking at me with a little half smile, as if she was afraid that I was only pretending to sleep, she touched my forehead with her lips as soft as the velvet of Paez. Less fearful now of my little deceit, she let me feel for a moment her warm and fragrant breath. But I waited in vain for her to press her lips against mine. She sat on the rug, and as she read some of the pages spread out on the floor, she rested her cheek on one of my hands which was resting on the cushions. Feeling that hand move, she turned towards me and gazed with a look full of love, smiling as only she could smile. I drew her head against my chest, and reclining thus she searched for my eyes as I adorned her forehead with her silken braids or breathed her basil perfume with pleasure.

A cry, my own cry, interrupted this dream. Jealous reality disturbed my dream as if that instant had been a century of pleasure. The lamp had burned out; through the window I felt the cold wind of dawn. My hands were stiff and pressed those braids, the only thing I had left of her beauty, and the only reality of my dream.

During the afternoon of that day, during which I visited all the sites which were dear to me, and which I would never see again, I prepared to begin my trip to the city, passing through the Parish cemetery where Maria's tomb was located. Juan Angel and Braulio had gone on ahead to wait for me, and José, his wife and daughters

13.14: Efraín and María

now surrounded me to receive my farewell. At my invitation, they followed me into the chapel, and all kneeling, all crying, we prayed for the soul of she who. we had loved so much. José interrupted the silence which followed that solemn prayer with a plea to the protector of pilgrims and travelers.

Now in the corridor, Transito and Lucia, after receiving my good-bye, sat on the pavement and sobbed, covering their faces. José, turning his face away to hide his tears from me, was waiting for me, holding my horse by the halter at the foot of the steps. Mayo, the old family dog, wagged his tail and lay in the grass, watching all my movements as he did in his days of vigor when we hunted partridges.

I could not find my voice to speak a final kind word to José and his daughters; nor could they have found words to respond.

A few blocks from the house I paused before starting down into the draw and looked one more time at that dear mansion and its surroundings. From the hours of happiness that I had spent in the house I only carried with me memories; of Maria, and the gifts she had left me at the edge of her grave.

Mayo arrived then, and fatigued, he paused at the edge of the torrent which separated us: twice he tried to ford the stream and both times he had to retreat. He then sat on the grass and howled so painfully that it almost seemed as if his cries were human, as if he was trying to tell me how much he had loved me, and to reproach me for abandoning him in his old age.

13.15: Unrequited love

An hour and a half later I dismounted at the gate to a sort of orchard, isolated on the plain, and fenced in with boards: it was the local cemetery. Braulio, receiving my horse and sharing the emotion which he saw in my face, pushed open the gate and stopped. I passed through amidst the brush and the crosses of wood and bamboo that were raised up above the growth. The setting sun pushed through the intertwined branches and the overgrowth with a few rays, which threw their yellow light on the brambles and the foliage of the trees that shaded the graves. Coming around the edge of a group of thick tamarinds I stood in front of a white and rain-stained pedestal, on which there was raised a cross of iron; I drew near. On the black plate which the poppies were already half-covering, I began to read: "Maria..."

In that terrible monologue between the soul and death, of the soul that asks, that curses ... that begs .. that calls out for her ... and the answer from the cold and deaf tomb was all too eloquent, as I embraced it and washed it with my tears.

The sound of steps on the dry leaves made me raise up my face from the pedestal: Braulio came closer and handed me a wreath of roses and lilies, a gift from Jose's daughters. He stayed there as if to tell me that it was time to leave. I stood up to place the wreath on the cross, and I embraced the tombstone again to give Maria and her sepulcher one final good-bye...

I mounted my horse, and while I shook hands with Braulio a bird flew over us, beating its wings and giving out a sinister caw well known to me. The bird interrupted our farewell: I saw it fly to the cross of iron, and resting on one of its arms, beat its wings again and repeated its frightful song.

Shaking, I fled at a gallop in the middle of the solitary plain, whose vast horizon was blackened by the falling of night.

13.16: The Cauca Valley of Colombia

14: Costumbrismo

Costumbrismo

Latin American literature and culture has always been rich in the local or regional aspect. Some of the first writings to come out of the New World were descriptions of things that were new and different in the discoverers' experience. In later centuries, writers continued to record and chronicle the special and sometimes quaint ways and customs of the inhabitants of the continent's different regions. This current has had many variants; for example, the cattle culture produced its own strong regional literature in Argentina and elsewhere. The genre known as "Costumbrismo" is sometimes used to describe these various currents, which reached their peak in a movement bridging the gap between the unbridled Romantic movement in

14.1: Regionalism

Latin America (mid-19th Century) and the less emotional currents of the latter part of the century (Realism, Naturalism, and Modernism).

Costumbrismo has its roots in the art and descriptions of the European travelers and explorers of the early Independence period, but it differs from much of their work in that it focuses on the custom or the local type, without a great deal of regard for the scenery or the exotic nature of the surroundings. Generally costumbrismo found subjects in the countryside or the innumerable small towns of Latin America. Wherever there was an important cattle culture, there was likely to be costumbrista art and writing focusing on the Latin American equivalent of the North American cowboy. But the cities also provided fertile · ground, and here we can find costumbrista descriptions of street persons (beggars, lottery sellers, night watchmen, etc), shopkeepers, and even priests, such as Fray (Brother) Gómez in the short story which follows.

Costumbrismo (Chapter 14)

Cultural-historical framework:	Continuing consolidation of national identities, which are sought through customs and ways of being of the different regions of each nation, especially the countryside and small towns
Approximate dates:	Middle and late 19th Century, but always present to some degree
Historical landmarks	Many post-Independence caudillos. Recovery from destruction of the Independence Wars "Closing" of the Argentine pampas by barbed wire and the railroads as the country enters the international export economy (sending wheat and meat to Europe) French intervention in Mexico (Maximilian)
Literature	Costumbrismo: focus on quaint, picturesque customs Regionalism: habits and customs of each region. Both evolved from Romanticism The custom is more important than the individual, or the scene. Is a bridge between sentimentalism of Romanticism and the more objective tendencies which follow (Realism, Naturalism, Modernism) Ricardo Palma (1833-1919) José Hernández (1834-1886) Luis Carlos López (1883-1950)
The Arts	Painting: primitivism, provincialism Renewed respect for folk art: clay figures, pottery, woodcarving, primitive painting, "ex-votos" The elites continue to prefer Academic art

Folk art found renewed acceptance in Costumbrismo. Wax and clay figures, pottery, woodcarvings and even primitive paintings were popular among the lower and middle classes of this time. The elites, however, continued to prefer European art, or the academic art still heavily influenced by European models. One important form of folk art was the *ex-voto*, or votive offering. Sometimes it represented a single scene (along with a short narration) of a miracle.

The miracle would have been performed by the Virgin Mary or a particular saint. Sometimes the same format was used to present a prayer or special plea for mercy or a miraculous cure. The ex-voto also took the form of small metal or clay figures which had some relationship to the prayer or miracle involved. Thus, if someone had a broken leg the figure would be a realistic representation of a leg. A prayer for a successful amorous outcome might take the form of a small metal heart.

The historical period (middle of the 19th century) was one of continuing national consolidation and recovery from the devastating fighting of Independence. The search for a strong cultural basis of national identity also continued, and Costumbrismo supported this search by generating pride in one's own region or nation through portrayals of typical ways of being and customs.

Ricardo Palma, 1833-1919: Costumbrista

Among the Costumbristas, Ricardo Palma of Peru distinguished himself by creating his own sub-genre, the *tradición* ("tradition"). At the risk of great simplification, the "Peruvian Tradition" created by Palma can be described as a short historical anecdote, frequently with a surprise ending or a moral which captures a small vignette of life in colonial Peru. Palma himself described his recipe for the *tradición* as follows: "The *tradición* is a romance and is not a romance; it is history and it is not history. The

14.2: Palma

form has to be light and airy; the narration, quick and humorous. What I had in mind was to sugar-coat pills and give them to the people to swallow, without letting any silly nun's scruples slow me down. Some lying, and even a little more than some, with an equal dose of truth, as infinitesimal as it might be: a lot of care and polishing of the language; and there you have the recipe for writing the *tradiciones*."

Although his topics ranged from the Peru of El Inca Garcilaso through to his days of the War of the Pacific with Chile in the late 19th Century, his favorite era was the eighteenth century of the Vice-regal capital of Lima. He was especially fascinated with the scandalous era when the viceroy's concubine, Micaela Luján, exercised great influence. She was the subject of various "tradiciones", and her nickname (given by the disapproving upper crust of Lima society) was "La Perrichola", derived from "perra" (female dog) and "chola" (Indian half-breed). Palma himself was of mestizo blood, and his "tradiciones" may also have been a response to his own experiences with the snobbishness of upper-class Lima.

Friar Gomez' Scorpion by **Ricardo Palma**

When I was a boy I frequently heard old women exclaim, as they talked about the value and price of a piece of jewelry, that "it was worth as much as Friar Gomez' scorpion". I have a little girl, good and full of grace, with mischievous eyes, and I have nicknamed her, in my fatherly exaggeration, "Friar Gomez' little scorpion". And now I propose to explain both the old wives' saying as well as my daughter's nickname.

Here is the inscription under his portrait in the monastery: "Venerable Friar Gomez. Born in Extremadura, Spain, 1560. Took his vows in Chuquisaca in 1580. Came to Lima in 1587. He was a nurse for forty years, exercising all of the virtues, blessed with heavenly favors and gifts. His life was a continuous miracle. He died the 2nd of May, 1631, with the fame of sainthood. The next year his remains were placed in the chapel of Aranzazú, and on the 13th of October 1810 they were moved to the main altar, to the crypt where the fathers of the convent are buried."

14.3: Fray Gómez

One morning Friar Gomez was in his cell in the monastery, deep in meditation, when there was a discreet knock at his door, and a humble voice said, "Deo gratias ... Praise be to God!" "For ever, amen. Come in, little brother", replied Friar Gomez. The door of this most modest cell opened and a ragged old man entered. His clothes were in tatters, but his face showed the proverbial honesty of the people from Old Castille. The furniture in Friar Gomez' cell consisted of four rawhide chairs, a dirty table, a cot without a mattress, sheet or blanket, and with a stone as a pillow.

"Have a seat, brother, and tell me straight out what brings you here" said Friar Gomez.

"Father, I am an honest man..."

"I can see that, and I hope you continue that way so that you will deserve the peace of your conscience on this earth, and your blissful reward in heaven".

"I am a peddler, with a large family, and my business is not doing well because I have no capital, and not because of any laziness or lack of effort on my part."

"I am glad to hear that brother, because God rewards he who works honestly."

'But it seems, father, that up to now God has been a little deaf, and has not been in a hurry to help me..."

"Do not despair, brother, do not despair."

"Well, but I have knocked on many doors seeking a loan of five hundred pesos, and all the doors have been closed to me. And last night, as I was worrying about it, I thought I would come to ask Friar Gomez for the money, because even though he has no money he will find me a way out of my troubles."

"And how could you imagine, my son, that in this sad little cell you would find that kind of money?

"To tell you the truth, father, I don't know how to answer that question. But I have faith that you will not let me go without consolation."

14.4: The scorpion

"Your faith will save you, brother. Wait just a minute."

Friar Gomez let his eyes wander over the bare white-washed walls of his cell, and his glance fell on a scorpion who was calmly crawling on the window sill. Friar Gomez tore a page out of an old book, went over to the window, carefully wrapped the insect in the paper, and turning to the old Castillian said:

"Here, my good man, take this jewel and pawn it. But do not forget to return it to me in six months." The peddler spilled over with expressions of gratitude, said good-bye to Friar Gomez, and rushed over to the store of the usurer.

The piece of jewelry was magnificent, befitting a Moorish princess, to say the least. It was a pin in the shape of a scorpion. The body was a splendid emerald in a gold setting, and the head was a large diamond with two rubies for eyes. The usurer, who was a cunning man, eyed the pin with greed, and offered the peddler a loan of two thousand pesos for it. But our Spaniard refused to accept any loan greater than the five hundred pesos for six months, even though the interest was high. The necessary papers were drawn up and signed, and the pawnbroker consoled himself with the thought that the peddler would soon be back for more money, and that in the long run the larger loan and the high compound interest would mean that he would never be able to redeem his pin. And then the pawnbroker would be the owner of a piece of jewelry which would be valuable for its uniqueness as well as for its beauty.

The peddler took his little capital and prospered in his business so much that at the end of the six months he was able to redeem his pin. He wrapped it in the same old paper in which he received it, and returned it to Friar Gomez. The Friar took the scorpion, placed it on the window frame, blessed it, and said: "Go, little animal of God, continue on your way." And the scorpion crawled happily and freely on the walls of the cell.

José Hernández, 1834-1886: Gaucho Poet

This writer is typical of those Costumbristas who concentrated on the cattle culture, although the quality of his verse and the originality of his work make him stand out. He had lived for many years among the gauchos of interior Argentina, and he had come to respect and love the lifestyle of those free souls of the open pampas. He also was a witness to the abuse of the gauchos (as well as the few remaining Indigenous peoples) by the centralized government in Buenos Aires as the pampas were being exploited for their beef and grains in the international market. This commercialization brought in the railroad, barbed wire, and the commercial rancher, who saw the gaucho all too often as an obstacle to progress. Hernández

14.5: Hernández

fought against the Rosas dictatorship, but he also opposed Sarmiento because he believed that Sarmiento's European and US orientation was a threat to the gaucho's freedom.

Hernández' major work, "Martín Fierro" can be seen as an epic poem, with some characteristics of Romanticism, since the hero is at times a tragic Romantic figure. But the special feature of "Martín Fierro" lies in the way it preserves and transmits the sayings, folk wisdom, language, and lifestyle of those men of the pampas.

Hernández had little formal education, and one of his purposes in writing the poem was to give the gaucho something that he would want to read and thus educate himself. There were many inexpensive popular versions of Martín Fierro, and every little store in small-town Argentina made them available to those who wanted to read. It was popular literature for the masses, not the elites or outward-looking inhabitants of the port city of Buenos Aires. This translation is by Walter Owen, an Englishman who lived in Argentina and translated several epic poems (including "La Araucana") so that his countrymen would learn more about the unique cultural contribution of that part of the world.

Martín Fierro by José Hernández
(Translation adapted from Walter Owen's)

I sit me here to sing my song
To the beat of my old guitar;
For the man whose life is a bitter cup,

With a song may yet his heart lift up,
As the lonely bird on the leafless tree,
That sings 'neath the gloaming star.

May the shining Saints of the heavenly band,
That sing in the heavenly choir,
Come down and help me now to tell
The good and ill that me befell,
And to sing it true to the thrumming strings;
For such is my desire.

Come down ye Saints that have helped me
In many a perilous pass;
For my tongue is tied and my eyes grow dim,
And the man that calls, God answers him,
And brings him home to his own roof-tree,
Out of many a deep morass.

14.6: Around the fire

O many singers have I seen,
That have won a singer's wreath
That have talked a lot as they passed the pot,
Of the songs they sang and the songs they wrought
Till their voices rusted in their throats,
As a knife rusts in its sheath.

Now all that a son of the plains may do,
To none shall I give best;
And none may dunt with a windy vaunt,
Or bristle my scalp with a phantom gaunt,
And as song is free to all that will,-
I will sing among the rest.

Tis little I have of bookman's craft,
Yet once let me warm to the swing
And the lilt and beat of the plainsman's song,-
I will sing you strong, I will sing you long,
And the words will out like the tumbling rout
Of waters from a spring.

With my mellow guitar across my knee,
The flies even give me room,
And the talk is stilled, and the laugh and jest,
As I draw the notes from its sounding breast;
The high string, and the middles weep,

And the low strings mourn and boom.

I am the best of my own at home,
And better than best afar;
I have won in song my right of place,
If any gainsay me -face to face,
Let him come and better me, song for song,
Guitar against guitar.

I step not aside from the furrowed track,
Though they loosen their hilts as they come;
Let them speak me soft, I will answer soft,
But the hard may find me a harder oft;
In a fight they have found me as quick as they,
And quicker far than some.

When trouble's afoot-now Christ me save,
And Christ me save from sin,-
I feel my heart grow big and strong,
And my blood rise up like a rolling song,
For life is a battle, it seems to me,
That a man must fight to win.

A son am I of the rolling plain,
A gaucho born and bred;
For me the whole great world is small,
Believe me, my heart can hold it all;
The snake strikes not at my passing foot,
The sun burns not my head.

I was born on the mighty Pampas' breast,
As the fish is born in the sea;
Here was I born and here I live,
And what seemed good to God to give,
When I came to the world; it will please him too.
That I take away with me.

14.7: Gaucho weapon

And this is my pride: to live as free
As the bird that cleaves the sky;
I build no nest on this careworn earth,
Where sorrow is long, and short is mirth,
And when I am gone none will grieve for me,
And none care where I lie.

I have kept my feet from trap or trick
In the risky trails of love;
I have roamed as free as the winging bird,
And many a heart my song has stirred,
But my couch is the clover of the plain,
With the shining stars above.

And every one that hears my song,
With this he will agree:
I sought no quarrel, nor drew a knife,
Save in open fight and to guard my life,
And that all the harm I have done to men
Was the harm men wished to me.

Then gather around and hearken well
To a gaucho's doleful story,
In whose veins the blood of the Pampas runs,
Who married a wife and begat him sons,
Yet who nevertheless is held by some
as a bandit grim and gory.

Martín Fierro, VII by José Hernández

So many old friends at the dance
I met again that night,
That we all let go, and I'm sorry to say
That soon your friend was tight.

I never before, for picking a fight
Was feeling so inclined
When a guy arrived in a swell rig-out
With his gal riding up behind.

14.8: Gaucho recreation

When she got off, I sidled up,
And I looked at her most polite,
And as she went past I said to her:
"It's a little bit ... chilly tonight."

She took me up, and to choose her words
She didn't stop to bother
For like a flash she answered me:
"The bigger bitch your mother!"

With a tail like a vixen she bounced inside

And rolling her saucer eyes,
And showing a bunch of gleaming teeth
Like a mouthful of fresh-cooked maize. ...

The guy was gathering up his rage,
And was almost ready to bark
I could see his eyes beginning to glow
Like lanterns in the dark.

I saw him beginning to paw the ground,
I knew how to make him bellow;
I said to him: "Keep your temper in;
You look like an ass...tute fellow."

The fellow he gave a jump;
I could see he was seeing red;
"You're the only ass that's loose tonight
You drunken beast," he said.

And on the word he came in blind.
And sure would have done me in,
If I hadn't brought him to a stand
With a whack from the crock of gin.

Luis C. López: Costumbrista Poet

Although this Colombian Costumbrista poet comes quite late in the period, we include him because of the way he provides us with a sample of small-town Costumbrista themes. He gives us a series of authentic vignettes and caricatures of local types, such as the mayor, the barber, the shopkeepers, and the lonely spinsters.

The Barber

The village barber, who wears straw hats,
dance slippers, jackets of piqué,
and is a passionate card player,
who hears mass on his knees
and speaks well of Voltaire.

A tireless reader of El Liberal. He works
happily like a glass of muscatel wine,
stitching together, as he wipes the sharp razor

14.9: The barber

gossip, all the gossip of the mystical flock.

With the mayor, with the veterinarian,
good people who pray the rosary
and speak of the miracles of San Pedro Claver,

he talks in the canteen, argues in the cock-ring,
his scissors cutting from life's newspaper clippings
happy as a glass of muscatel wine.

The Mayor by Luis Carlos López

The mayor, with his dirty straw hat
wrapped with a three-color silk ribbon,
big stomach like a Capeto, loose clothes,
he walks through the town with his bull-dog profile.

A man with hair on his chest, blonde as flax,
he signs with the point of machete. And at
night as takes his local soup
of thin spaghetti and garlic, he loosens his belt...

His wife, a nervously pretty girl,
who has him wrapped up like a clamp,
likes the dog-eared works of Paul de Kock,

she loves beads and paints her eyebrows,
while her consort shows off in the streets
with his belly, his "I saids" and his fierce face.

14.10: Small town

Spinster girls by Luis Carlos López

Spinster provincial girls,
who stitch through the years
reading booklets
and watching closely from balconies and windows...

Provincial girls,
the ones with needle and thimble, who do nothing
but drink at night
their coffee-and-milk and papaya juice...

Provincial girls,
who go out -if they leave home at all-
very early to church
with the walk of domesticated geese...

Provincial girls,
soft, etcetera, who sing
melancholically
from sun to sun: "Susana, come ... Susana"

Poor girls, poor
girls so useless and chaste,
who make the Devil say,
with his arms crossed- "Poor girls!"

14.11: Gaucho

15: Positivism, Realism, Naturalism

Positivism: Order and Progress

By the last quarter of the 19th Century, once national identities were consolidated and the age of the early post-Independence caudillos had begun to wane, Latin America came under the influence of another set of European ideas which were to have profound social, economic and cultural implications. The philosophical current was Positivism, which had originated in France under Auguste Comte.

15.1: Comte

The Positivists argued that humans and nature are subject to certain natural laws which determine not only the functioning of the physical world, but also humanity's destiny. If humanity goes against these laws the result will be disorder, anarchy and disaster. The function of science, literature, art and philosophy is to discover these natural laws and transmit them to everyone so that fundamental problems can be rationally analyzed, and logical solutions worked out.

15.2: U.S. technology

To a great many people Positivism had an attractive scientific foundation, was linked to best intellects of the Enlightenment, and seemed consistent with the most advanced thinking of the day by people such as Charles Darwin and Herbert Spencer. However, some European Positivists (and their elitist Latin American followers) carried these ideas to extremes such as Social Darwinism and Spencerianism. These argued that geography and ethnic origin played a key role in determining humanity's destiny.

Positivism, Realism, Naturalism (Chapter 15)

Cultural-
historical
framework:
	The ideology of Positivism arrives from France:
	(Auguste Comte)
	Stress on "order and progress"
	
	Economic expansion in many Latin American
	  nations using the Positivist model.
	
	Use of Naturalism to focus on social problems
	  and then attempt to correct them
	
	Rational and "scientific" progress based
	on Positivism

Approximate dates:	Late 19th Century

Historical
 	
landmarks
	Porfirio Díaz in power in Mexico, 1877-1911
	
	Brazil removes Pedro II and becomes a Republic,
	  1889, with the words "order and progress"
	  in the new flag)
	
	Invention of the photographic camera

Literature	Realism: objective, "photographic" representation
	  of reality, with no distortions.
	Focus equally on bad and good.
	No emotional, philosophical or political distortions
	
	Naturalism: focus on the ugly, sordid detail with
	  political and social purposes of bringing change.
	Influences:
	Emile Zola, France; Alexis Gorki, Russia
	
	Baldomero Lillo (1867-1923)

The Arts	Mainly in painting: "photographic" Realism and
	  Naturalism focusing on the ills of society
	
	Popular art is neglected and rejected by the elites
	
	Academic painting continues, portraits, landscapes
	  with use of Positivist symbols (railways, progress)

To them, mid-latitudeCaucasian cultures such as the European were inherently superior to the non-Caucasian cultures of much of the rest of the world. These ideas appealed to the European-oriented white elites in Latin America, who saw the material progress of Europe and the United States towards the end of the 19th Century and credited Positivist thinking and laws for their successes.

Positivism was also very consistent with capitalist entrepreneurism, which regarded the ownership of property and private wealth as sacred and relegated the state's role to imposing the order and stability that would allow technical and material progress. The shining example of that progress was seen in the European and US industrial revolutions, which were increasingly demanding both raw materials and international markets in which to place the output of their industrial machinery. Latin America was to supply both, and in this process underwent a profound transformation.

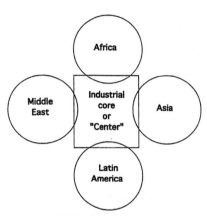

15.3: Center-periphery

The transformation involved inserting many of the Latin American nations in the world economy in a center-periphery dependency relationship in which the "center" (industrialized Europe and the United States) provided the industrial base and exported machinery and manufactured goods. The "periphery" of Latin America, and what would later come to be called the underdeveloped third world, would provide raw materials for the center, as well as markets for much of the center's manufactured goods.

To extract and move the raw materials out of the periphery it was necessary to develop Latin America's infrastructure, especially transportation, agriculture, mines, and other extractive pursuits. The years 1880-1910 saw a great boom of European investment in Latin America aimed at this extraction of raw materials and foodstuffs. British (and to a lesser extent US and other European) investors poured large sums into the construction of railways in Latin America for the purpose of moving raw materials to the ports where they could be trans-shipped to Europe. The railway became the symbol of this late 19th Century progress, and of Positivism itself.

Positivism was especially strong in the larger and richer countries of Latin America. In Mexico it formed the intellectual and ideological base of the 34 year long dictatorship of Porfirio Díaz, who neglected his own lower classes and provided all kinds of facilities to the foreign investors, thus setting the stage for the 1910 Mexican Revolution. In Brazil Positivism was a key element in bringing down the Empire and in creating a Republic led by technocrats and military officers; when their leaders designed the Brazilian flag they placed in its center the Positivist slogan of "order and progress". In Chile Positivism was the driving force behind the development of the mining industry, especially copper and ni-trates. In Argentina British-financed railways fanned out from Buenos Aires into the fertile pampas, extracting the bountiful grain and beef.

15.4: Positivist symbol

From the perspective of the landowners, the capitalists and the technologically inclined elites in Latin America, Positivism was good and was equated to material and social progress. But the larger masses saw little benefit from this progress and frequently felt the negative effects of authoritarian governments determined to impose the order and stability required by the foreign investor.

Realism and Naturalism

In the world of culture, still dominated by the elites, Positivism was associ-ated with Realism and Naturalism. These replaced the emotional and dramatic excesses of Romanticism, and the quaint country ways of "Costumbrismo", which to the elites seemed to be hopelessly old-fashioned and detrimental to the scientific and technological progress offered by Positivism. Popular and folk art, as one might imagine, were looked on with disdain by the Positivists, who saw them as the product of inferior, or at least backward, ethnical groups.

Realism can most simply be described as a straight photographic represen-tation of the world, with no particular axe to grind and no special emphasis on any one theme, or service to a particular ideology or purpose. It is just the world as it is, without the emotion or drama of romanticism. It sought to present a hon-est and direct portrayal of life and nature as it really was.

Naturalism, on the other hand, had a social and political purpose, and came to Latin America linked to the Positivist philosophy which stressed that there were natural laws which had to be discovered and respected. These natural laws governed passions and emotions and presented humans with limits within which progress must be sought through order and discipline. One of the functions of Naturalist literature in Latin America was to focus on the sordid, the bad, and the violations of natural laws so that appropriate steps could be taken to correct these situations. Just as Latin American Positivism was shaped by a French philosopher (Auguste Comte), so too was Naturalism, which took many of its ideas from the French Naturalist Emile Zola, and Russian authors such as Alexis Gorki.

Latin American Naturalist writers found fertile ground and many themes in the exploitation of workers and their families in cities, the countryside, and the mines. Although this literature is grounded in Positivism, it also belongs to the current of social protest literature in Latin America, which goes back to the Conquest writings of Father Las Casas, and continued through the literature of Echeverría's *Slaughterhouse*. This protest current of literature (and art) was later to take revolutionary overtones in the 20th Century.

Art in this period included an academic current which continued to follow the European models, stressing carefully rendered portraits (mainly of high society women), as well as technically perfect landscape painting. The latter frequently included symbols of Positivist progress, such as railroads, bridges, and transportation facilities. Popular art was officially neglected, especially by the elites, but continued its traditional focus.

A Naturalist author: Baldomero Lillo

Social protest was the main theme of the best of the Naturalist writers, the Chilean Baldomero Lillo 1867-1923). Lillo's father had gone to California to participate in the Gold Rush, but he returned with no fortune. He did learn much about mining, and he moved to northern Chile to work the nitrate mines. Baldomero Lillo grew up in these mining communities and worked the mines himself. He was exposed to the writings of the French author Emile Zola, who used the philosophy of Positivism and the literary current of Naturalism to try to change the terrible conditions of French

15.5: Hand mining

coal miners. Lillo was able to observe similar conditions in the Chilean mines and set out to improve the conditions of the workers by dramatizing their plight. Lillo wrote many short stories (collected in two major books, Sub Sole and Sub Terra) which sparked the interest of social activists who were appalled by the conditions in the mines. The story that follows is typical of his efforts.

In *The Devil's Tunnel* the miners are seemingly trapped by their destiny to live out their squalid and exploited lives, which are dominated by the need for raw materials and the machinery of the Europeans. At the story's end there is a strong contrast between the clean, pure and benevolent sky, and the underground monster that devours the humans who dare to penetrate its dark lair.

The Devil's Tunnel by **Baldomero Lillo**

In a low and narrow room the foreman on duty sat at a work table facing the registry book, checking off the workers as they descended into the mine shaft that cold winter morning. Through the open door could be seen the elevator with its human cargo, which, once full, would disappear, silent and quick, through the damp entrance of the pit. The miners arrived in small groups and as they took their lanterns off the hooks on the wall the foreman checked their names off in his registry. Suddenly, he spoke to two workers who were moving quickly toward the elevator: "You two, stay here."

The pair turned, surprised, and a vague feeling of unease ran across their pale faces. The youngest, barely twenty years old, freckled, with abundant red locks that earned him the nickname "Copperhead", was short, strong and chunky. The other, taller, a little thin and bony, was already old and had a weak and sickly appearance. Each held a lamp in their right hand, and in their left a handful of short pieces of cord with buttons and bits of glass of distinctive colors: these were the markers which the miners placed in the wagons of coal to indicate their origin and receive credit for their work.

The clock on the wall slowly rang out the six bells of the hour. From time to time a sweaty miner would burst through the door, grab his lamp and head toward the elevator, glancing timidly at the foreman who, without moving his lips would mark the latecomer's name in the book with a large "X".

After a few minutes of silent waiting the foreman gestured to the two miners and said:

"You two are miners from La Alta, right?" "Yes, sir", they replied.

"I'm sorry to have to tell you that there is no work for you. I have orders to cut back the work force in this shaft."

The workers did not answer and there was a profound silence for a while. Finally the older one said: "But will there be work for us somewhere else?"

The boss closed the book firmly, and leaning back in his chair, replied in a grave voice: "It doesn't look good, we have too many people in all of the mines".

15.6: Mining

The worker kept at it: "We would take anything you give us; we'd work as maintenance, shorers, whatever".

The foreman shook his head: "I've just told you, there are too many workers and if the demand for coal doesn't increase, we will have to slow down production in some other mines as well".

A bitter and ironic smile pulled back the miner's lips as he cried out: "Come on, Don Pedro, level with us, and tell us straight out that you want to force us to work in the Devil's Tunnel".

"No one forces anyone here. Just as you are free to turn down any work you don't like, the Company has the right to take whatever measures are good for it".

During his explanation, the two miners listened quietly with downcast eyes. Seeing their humble demeanor the foreman softened his tone: "Look, even though I have strict orders I'll try to help you two out. In the New Tunnel, or the Devil's Tunnel as you call it, there are two openings for miners, but you had better take them now. Tomorrow will be too late." ...

15.7: The entrance

The deal was made. The workers accepted their new assignments without objection and a moment later were in the cage, hurtling down the depths of the mine like lead weights.

The shaft of the Devil's Tunnel had a sinister reputation. It had been opened to give access to a new seam of coal, and in the beginning the shoring had been done correctly. But as the shaft penetrated, the rock grew more porous and unpredictable. The percolating water, which had been minimal at the beginning, increased to the point that the stability of the ceiling was precarious and could be made safe only with much wooden shoring. As the digging progressed the immense amount of wooden beams required for the shoring increased the cost of the mined coal considerably, and management began to take shortcuts. The shoring continued, but it was inadequate and sloppy as they tried to economize as much as possible.

The results were predictable: there were frequent accidents. Injured and even dead miners were a common occurrence as the ceiling would break away due to the lack of support and the treacherous action of the unseen waters. This constant threat to the lives of

15.8: The price

the workers took its toll, and more and more of them refused to work in the fatal corridor. But the Company very soon overcame their resistance with the bait of a few centavos more in salaries, and the work continued. Later, however, the pay raises were cancelled and the Company resorted to the kind of tactic the foreman had just used on the two miners.

Copperhead returned home much later than usual that night. He was silent and taciturn, answering with monosyllables the gentle questions his mother asked him about the day's work. In that humble home there was a certain decency and cleanliness, rare qualities in those hovels where men, women and children, in repugnant promiscuity, were all thrown together along with the company of so many animals that they suggested a vision of Noah's Arc.

The miner's mother was a tall, thin woman, with white hair. Her pale face had a resigned and sweet expression which sof-

15.9: Bagging ore

tened the brightness of her eyes, where tears seemed always ready to spring out. Her name was María de los Angeles. Daughter and mother of miners, she had aged prematurely under the strain of terrible disasters. Her husband and two sons had been killed one after the other by mine collapses and gas explosions. These were the tributes that her loved ones had paid to the insatiable voracity of the mine. All she had left was that young man for whom her heart always ached. Always fearful of an accident, her imagination never for an instant left the misty coal seam that was possessing the only thing she had left, the only thing she lived for....

Copperhead went to work the next day without telling his mother of his new assignment in the Devil's Tunnel. There would be plenty of time to give her the bad news. With the indifference so typical of those his age he gave little thought to the dangers or the fears of the old woman. A fatalist, like all his comrades, he believed that it was useless to try to change the fate which each human had been assigned as his destiny. ...

15.10: Mining

As the noon hour approached the women in their hovels prepared their men's lunches. Suddenly the shrill sound of the alarm bell made them drop their tasks and desperately leave their rooms and run to the pit entrance. ....

A strong wooden barrier surrounded the mouth of the shaft, and the multitude of running women crashed against it in their desperate efforts to reach their men. On the other side of the fence a few grim miners, silent and taciturn, held back the women who screamed and shouted, pleading for news of their loved ones, of the number of dead and the site of the disaster.

One of the engineers peered out of the doorway of the machinery room. He was a fat Englishman, with a pipe in his teeth, red sideburns, and an air of indifference as he surveyed the scene. Upon seeing him, a hundred voices wailed: "Murderers, murderers!"

The women raised their arms and shook their fists, insane with rage. The engineer who had provoked that explosion of fury blew a few puffs of smoke, turned his back, and left.

The news coming from the miners slowly calmed the throng. The event was not as bad as past catastrophes: there were only three dead, names yet unknown. It was almost not necessary to mention that the roof collapse had taken place in the Devil's Tunnel, where for two hours rescue teams were trying to get the dead out. Any moment now the signal would be given for the machinery to turn and bring up the bodies. This information gave hope in many hearts devoured by uncertainty. María de los Angeles, leaning against the barrier, felt the vise which had gripped her innards relax a little. She no longer needed to hope; she was now certain it could not be Copperhead. And with that fierce egocentrism of mothers, she listened almost indifferently to the hysterical cries of the other women as they expressed their anguish and despair.

Suddenly the crying of the women ceased: a single bell followed by three rings resonated slowly and vibrantly: it was the signal to raise the elevator. A shudder moved through the multitude who avidly followed the vibrations of the rising cable, knowing that at the other end of the wire was the terrible unknown which all feared and hoped to decipher.

A grim silence, interrupted by one or two sobs, reigned on the platform. The cries slowly rolled over the plain and into the air, wounding hearts as a presage

15.11: The Devil's Tunnel

of death. Some minutes passed, and soon the great iron ring which connected the elevator cage to the cable appeared. The elevator shuddered for an instant and then came to a halt. Inside the cage a small group of bareheaded workers surrounded a black cart dirty with mud and coal dust. An immense cry greeted the appearance of this funeral car, and the multitude desperately rushing the pit entrance made it difficult to move the bodies off. The first body they saw was covered with blankets and they could only see bare feet, stiff and covered with mud.

The second body, which followed immediately, was bareheaded: he was an old man with gray beard and hair. Then the third and last corpse appeared. Between the folds of the blanket which enveloped him could be seen some tufts of reddish hair which shone like recently melted copper in the golden sunlight. Several voices cried out in shock: "It's Copperhead!"

The body was lifted by the shoulders and feet and was laboriously placed in the waiting stretcher. María de los Angeles, upon seeing that ruddy face and that hair which now seemed drenched in blood, made a superhuman effort to throw herself on the body of her son. But pressed up against the barrier she could only move her arms as an inarticulate soundless cry burst from her throat. Then her muscles relaxed, her arms fell to her side and she stood motionless as if hit by a lightning bolt. The group parted and many faces turned toward the woman who, with her head on her chest, deep in an absolute trance, seemed absorbed in contemplating the abyss open at her feet.

No one ever understood how she managed to jump over the barrier or the retaining cables. But many saw her for an instant as her bare legs dangled over empty space and she disappeared, without a sound, into the abyss. A few seconds later, a low and distant sound, almost imperceptible, erupted from the hungry mouth of the pit along with a few puffs of thin vapor: it was the breath of the monster gorged with blood in the depths of his lair.

15.12: The Devil's Tunnel

16: Modernismo

Modernismo

As the 19th Century drew to a close, much of Latin America found itself transformed by the progress brought about by the foreign investors and their allies among the upper levels of their societies. The Positivists had encouraged immigration, especially from Europe, in their belief that this would make their nations more European. Behind this rationale was also the racist attitude that their Indigenous, Mestizo and Black populations had little to offer. These European immigrants flocked to the cities, adding their numbers to those of the less privileged who had left rural poverty in the hopes of finding a better life in an urban environment. The growth was impressive in cities such as Buenos Aires, where at one point every third inhabitant had been born in Europe (mainly Spain or Italy).

The fast-growing cities such as Mexico and Buenos Aires reflected the elites' imitation of French culture, and the buildings put up around the turn of the century show a strong French influence.

Political, social and economic life continued to be dominated by the old conservative order of landlord-politician, army officer and priest, although Positivism was changing their outlook. Their nation's dependency on the center-periphery economic model continued, and it was fair to say that the system was a neocolonial one because of the control the center exercised on the periphery.

16.1: Muse

Modernismo (Chapters 16, 17)

Cultural- historical framework:	**With national consolidation accomplished, there is a search for refinement in literature** **Modernismo: An original Latin American movement, although there are influences from France (Parnassianism, symbolism)** **Waves of immigration from Europe** **Latin concern over losing identity to Anglo-Saxon influences (Nordomania)**
Approximate dates:	**Late 19th Century, early 20th**
Historical landmarks	**Spanish-American War, 1898** **Teddy Roosevelt and the Panama Canal (1903)** **First Inter-American Conference (Washington, 1889)**
Literature	**Modernismo: A highly esthetic movement of renewal. Art for art's sake; form more important than content Emphasis on the beautiful, the musical, the exotic Great use of symbols, metaphors, poetic imagery. Has Classical influences, but is highly original. Reaction against Positivism, Naturalism. Ivory-tower escapism** **José Martí, 1853-1895 Rubén Darío, 1867-1916 José Enrique Rodó, 1871-1917**
The Arts	**There is no exact parallel, although impressionism and more abstract forms of art, with their emphasis color and form over content, are an analogue to literary Modernism** **Use of the photographic camera frees painting from its function of capturing reality. Photography as art** **An "anti-Academic" current which stresses simplicity Popular and folk art paid more attention. Mexican "calaveras" (skull and skeleton drawings)**

Meanwhile, the middle class, which had always been small in Latin America, was growing with the influx of large numbers of immigrants, many of them from Europe's lower middle class. Slavery had been formally abolished, but the economic and social system tended to keep the Black population at the bottom of the pyramid. The Indigenous population defended itself as best it could from the inroads of Positivism by retreating to its communities far from the Europeanized cities.

Art at the turn of the Century

The academies still exercised their influence, following French models, although some new currents in Europe, such as Impressionism, had their Latin American followers. But popular art grew in influence, and a movement which could be called "anti-academic" also became more prominent as the middle class increased its influence, and the old artistic models seemed increasingly tired and slavishly imitative of the European ones. The "anti-academic" current was especially strong in Mexico, where a type of popular painting which was later to be called "primitive" was becoming more and more widespread. This primitive painting was simple and direct, with little depth or perspective, and yet with a charm and warmth that appealed to unsophisticated eyes as well as the jaded connoisseur. Mexico also produced a unique category of wood-block carving used in inexpensive and popular newspapers: the *calaveras*, or skull and skeleton drawings.

Popular protest was growing in Mexico after the long years of the Positivist Díaz dictatorship, and the inexpensive broadsides illustrated by these caricatures were one way the people could let their feelings be known. Chief among the *calavera* artists was José Guadalupe Posada, whose work had an influence on the Mexican Revolution of 1910 as well as on the Mexican muralist school which grew out of that historic event.

16.2: Calavera

The new literature: Modernismo

Spanish America in particular was ready for a renewal of literary traditions as the reforming zeal of the realists and naturalists began to run its course. This renewal was the literary movement known as "Modernismo", and as it burst out in the last decade of the Century (and well into the 20th) it marked a coming of age of Latin American literature and the entry into the modern period. It was a powerful movement that dominated and defined much of what was written in the period and was quickly imitated in Spain, which was a considerable tribute to its attraction. Modernism thus became a watershed marker in the sense that Latin American literature, especially poetry, can be defined in terms of whether it was Modernist, or came before or after the Modernist period.

Modernism was new and escapist; it turned its back on the emotional excesses of Romanticism, the naiveté of Costumbrismo, the photographic representation of Realism, and the socio-political commitment of Naturalism that was influenced by Positivism. The impact of Modernism stemmed from its novelty, freshness, symbolism, and its unique images, color, and musical sounds. The Modernist lived in an ivory tower, and from those heights could ignore with disdain the ugly realities that existed below in the day to day existence of lesser people.

This is a complex movement, with many roots and manifestations. It had a strong Greco-Roman classical element, but the liveliest influences were French Parnassianism and symbolism. The name of French Parnassianism was derived from Mount Parnassus, the Greek mountain sacred to Apollo and the muses. The tendency emphasized the form of what was written over the social or political content, which was of little interest. Art was "for art's sake", and was frequently disconnected from the real world. Its symbols were the beautiful but cold statues of marble and the swan, an animal of great and pure physical beauty, but of little practical use. The other major root, French symbolism, used poetry to obtain musical effects through the sounds of words and the rhythm of the verse.

Modernism inaugurated a period which, despite its brevity, was called the "Golden Age" of Latin American literature. The principal authors were widely imitated by adulators in America and Spain. After the emphasis on the real, the ugly and the disagreeable which Realism and Naturalism brought, this new current was an escape from these unfortunate aspects of life by means of an art that was refined, perfectionist, cultured, precious and cosmopolitan.

Despite these escapist tendencies, Modernism, like Romanticism, also had a political side. This can be seen in some of the poetry of Rubén Darío (*Walt Whitman, To Roosevelt*) and especially in the essays of Rodó (*Ariel*). The principal political theme is the ambivalence of Latin America toward the United States, very evident after the Spanish-American War of 1898 and the Independence of Panama in 1903. There was great admiration for the energy, efficiency, work and dynamism of the powerful Anglo-Saxon neighbor to the north, but at the same time there was much concern over the growing US tendency toward imperialism, intervention, and excessive emphasis on material things.

16.3: Musicality of Modernism

The Master of Modernismo: Rubén Darío

The chief figure of Modernism was the Nicaraguan poet Rubén Darío (a name he adopted, perhaps to suggest a link to the exotic and distant empire of Darius). Darío crammed a lot of living (and considerable excesses) into his half-century (1867-1916), working as a journalist, diplomat and writer, often in places far removed from his homeland.

16.4: Darío

Darío is also responsible for giving Modernism its chief symbol: the swan, selected because of its great beauty and grace, and also because its main asset was its beauty (without any significant function). There was also mythological symbolism involved, since the Greek god Zeus had taken the form of a swan when he seduced Leda. Helen of Troy was the fruit of that union, and she became immortal, a symbol of the imperishable nature of true beauty inherited from her father-God. Darío's poem that follows ("The Swan") brings together these various elements of Modernism.

Darío knew the United States through travel and the careful reading of its literature. He admired the energy of the country, and we can see that admiration in the verses he wrote to honor Walt Whitman. But after the Spanish American War and Teddy Roosevelt's intervention in Panama in 1903, Darío began to be concerned over the danger which US dynamism and expansionism represented for the weaker and less organized nations to the south.

The Swan by Rubén Darío

It was a divine hour for humankind.
Before, the Swan sung only at the moment of death.
But when the accent of the Wagnerian Swan was heard
it was in the midst of a dawn's aurora, it was revival.

Over the tempests of the human ocean
was heard the song of the Swan, unceasing,
dominating the hammering of the old Germanic Thor
or the trumpets that sing of the sword of Argantir.

O Swan! O sacred bird! If before, the pale Helena
blossomed full of grace from Leda's blue egg,
becoming the immortal princess of Beauty,

under your snow-white wings the new Poetry
conceives in the glory of light and harmony
eternal and pure Helen, incarnation of the ideal.

16.5: Leda and the swan

Walt Whitman (1890) by Rubén Darío

The grand old man lives in his country of iron,
A beautiful patriarch, serene and saintly.
With an olympic crease between his eyebrows
that dominates and conquers with noble charm.

His infinite soul seems like a mirror;
with his tired shoulders that merit a cloak;
and with his harp carved from seasoned oak
he sings his song like a new prophet.

Priest, whose breath is divine inspiration,
he announces better times in the future.
To the eagle he says: "Fly!",
and to the sailor: "Row!"

And "Work!" to the hardy laborer.
Thus goes the poet on his way
with his splendid imperial countenance.

16.6: Walt Whitman

To Roosevelt by Rubén Darío

(Note: this poem makes a number of mythological and literary references.
Among them:
    Nimrod was a legendary hunter and the earth's first great Imperialist. See
Genesis. Leo Tolstoy (1828-1910), the great Russian novelist, preached a life of
abnegation, pacifism, and non-resistance. Netzahualcoyotl was an Aztec emperor and the first Mexican poet known by name (1403-1470). Bacchus, god of
wine, was reputed to have learned Pan's alphabet from the Muses. Cuauhtémoc
was the nephew of Moctezuma and the last emperor of the Aztecs. He died at
the hands of the Spaniards in 1525.)

The voice of the Bible, or Walt Whitman's poetry
is needed to reach you, Hunter!
Primitive and modern, simple and complex,
with one part Washington and four part Nimrod!

You are the United States
you are the future invader
of innocent America which still has Indian blood,
still prays to Jesus Christ and still speaks Spanish.

You are a proud and strong example of your race;
you are cultured; you are able; you oppose Tolstoy.
And breaking wild horses, or assassinating tigers
you are Alexander Nebuchadnezzar.
(You are a professor of Energy,
as today's lunatics would put it).

　　　You believe that life is a fire,
and that progress is an eruption;
that where you aim your bullet
is where progress will also strike.

　　　No.

The United States is powerful and great.
When it shakes there is a deep shudder
Through the enormous vertebrae of the Andes.
If you shout, it sounds like the roar of a lion.
Hugo has already said to Grant: "The stars are yours".
(The slowly dawning Argentine sun barely shines
and the Chilean star rises...) You are rich.
You join the cult of Hercules with that of Mammon;
and Liberty, with her lamp in New York
lights the path to easy conquest.

16.7: Roosevelt and Colombia
(This cartoon is dated 1903, before Panama achieved independence, with U.S. help. Roosevelt is angry at Colombia because its government would not accept U.S. terms for a canal through Panama, then a Colombian province).

　　　But our America which had poets
since the old times of Netzahualcoyotl,
and has preserved the footsteps of the great Bacchus;
who once learned Pan's alphabet;
who consulted the stars, who knew Atlantis;
whose name resonates to us through Plato;
who in the remote moments of his life
lived in light, in fire, in perfume, in love;
the America of the great Moctezuma, of the Inca,
the fragrant America of Christopher Columbus,
Catholic America, Spanish America,
the America in which the noble Cuauhtémoc said:
"I am not lying in a bed of roses"; that America
that trembles with hurricanes and lives off of love;
that America lives, oh men of Saxon eyes and barbaric souls.

It dreams. And loves, and resonates;
she is the daughter of the Sun.
Be careful. Long live Spanish America!

A thousand cubs of the Spanish lion are loose.
You would need, Roosevelt, to be by God Himself,
the terrible Rifleman and the strong Hunter
to be able to keep us in your steel claws.

And, although you have everything,
one thing is missing: God!

Queen Mab's Veil by **Rubén Darío**

16.8: Queen Mab

Queen Mab, in her chariot made from a single pearl, pulled by four coleopters with golden shells and jeweled wings, treading on a ray of the sun, slipped through the window of a garret where the four men were: thin, bearded and impertinent, complaining as if they were unfortunate.

In those days, the fairies had distributed their gifts to mortals. Some had received mysterious rods which filled the heavy merchant's boxes with gold; others were given marvelous ears of grain which, when shaken out filled the granaries to overflowing with their riches; others received glasses which let them peer into the innards of mother earth and see gold and precious stones; others were given the thick hair and muscles of Goliath, and enormous maces to beat burning iron; and some were given strong talons and agile legs to mount their swift steeds who drink the wind and spread out their manes as they speed down the roads.

The four men were complaining. Fortune had given one of the men a sculptor's chisel, one the iris of a painter's eye, one the gift of rhythm, and the last the blue sky.

Queen Mab heard their words. The first one said:

"And just look at this! Here I am in a great struggle with my life's dreams in marble! I have cut the block loose and I have my chisel. You fellows have: one of you gold, one harmony, one light. I think of the white and divine Venus who shows her nudity under the sky-colored ceiling. I want to give the mass of marble a line and plastic beauty; and may a colorless blood like that of the gods flow through the statue's veins. I have the spirit of Greece in my brain, and I love the nudes in which the nymph flees and the faun unfolds its arms. Oh Fidas! You are for me proud and august as a semi-god, in your niche of tender beauty, a king facing armies of beauties who, in front of your eyes, strip off their magnificent tunics to show the splendor of the shape of their rosy, snowy bodies.

You beat, you wound and you tame the marble, and the blows have a harmonic sound like verse, and the cicada admires you, lover of the sun hidden among the young grape arbors with virgin vines. Yours are the blond and luminous Apollos, the severe and sovereign Minervas. You, like a magician, convert rock into image and the elephant's tusk into festive cup. And when I see your greatness I feel the martyrdom of my smallness. Because the glorious times have passed. Because I tremble when facing the stares of today. Because I contemplate the immense ideal and exhausted energies. Because as I chisel the block I am overcome by discouragement."

16.9: The complainers

And the second one said: "Today I will break my paint brushes. What need do I have for the iris of a painter's eye and this great palette of colors of the flowers of the fields if in the end my painting won't be allowed into the gallery? What will I have accomplished? I have gone to all the schools, to all the artistic inspirations. I have painted the torso of Diana and the face of the Madonna. I have asked the fields for their colors, their shades, and I have adored the light as if she were a lover, I have embraced her as a mistress. I have been an adorer of the nude, with all its magnificences, with all the carnation-shades and fleeting half-tones. I have drawn on my canvasses the halos of saints and the wings of cherubs. But always the terrible disenchantment! The future! To sell a Cleopatra for two pesetas and be able to buy lunch! And I am the one who could, in the trembling of my inspiration, sketch out the great painting I have within me!"

And the third one said: "My soul is lost in the great illusion of my symphonies, I fear all disillusionments. I listen to all the harmonies, from Terpandro's lyre to the orchestral fantasies of Wagner. My ideals shine brightly in midst of the daring of my inspirations. I have the perception of the philosopher who heard the music of the spheres. All noises can create passion, all echoes can have combinations. Everything fits in the lines of my chromatic scale.

Vibrant light is a hymn, and at noontime the jungle finds an echo in my heart. From the noise of the tempest to the song of a bird, everything merges and links together in the infinite cadence. But at the same time, I see only the crowd that scoffs, and the cell of the madhouse."

And the last one said: "We all drink the clear water from the fountain of Jonia. But the ideal floats in the blue; and in order for the spirits to enjoy the supreme light it is necessary for them to climb the heights. I have the verse which is honey, and the one that is gold, and the one that is red-hot iron. I am the vase of celestial perfume; I have the perfume: I have love. Dove, star, nest, lily, you know my dwelling-place. For the immeasurable flights I have wings of eagles which open up the magical blows of the hurricane. And to find consonants, I seek them in the mouths that join; and the kiss bursts forth, and I write the verse, and then if you see my soul, you will know my muse. I love the epic poems because from them springs the heroic breeze that stirs the flags that wave on the lances and the pennants that tremble over the helmets. I love the lyrical songs because they speak of goddesses and of loves. I love the pastoral poems because they smell of vervain and thyme, and the sacred breath of the ox crowned with flowers. I would write something immortal, but I am overcome by a future of misery and hunger."

Then Queen Mab, from the depths of her chariot made from a single pearl, took a blue veil, almost imperceptible to the touch, as if shaped by sighs, or of the gaze of blond and pensive angels. And that veil was the veil of dreams, of sweet dreams, which make life rose-colored. And with it she wrapped the four thin, bearded and impertinent men. And they stopped being sad, because hope entered their bosoms, and the joyful sun entered their heads, with the little devil of vanity, which comforts poor artists in their profound disillusionments.

And since that time, in the garrets of the unhappy brilliant ones, where the blue dream floats, they think of the future as if it were a new dawn, and we hear the laughter which wipes away sadness, and we see them dancing strange happy dances around a white Apollo, around a pretty landscape, around an old violin, and around a yellowing manuscript.

Sonatina by Rubén Darío

The princess is sad... What ails the princess?
Her sighs escape that strawberry mouth
which has lost its laughter, which has lost its color.
The princess is pale on her throne of gold,
the keyboard of her sonorous clavichord is silent
and in a vase a forgotten flower faints.

The garden is full of triumphant peacocks;
the chatty dueña says banalities,
and the red-clothed buffoon pirouettes.
The princess laughs not, the princess feels not;
the princess pursues over the eastern sky

16.10: The Princess

the vague dragonfly of a vague illusion.

Is she thinking perhaps of the prince of Golconda or China,
or in the one who has stopped his silver chariot
to look into her eyes and see the sweetness of light?

Or the king of the islands of fragrant roses,
or the one who is sovereign of clear diamonds,
or the proud owner of the pearls of Hormuz?

Oh!, the poor princess of the strawberry mouth
who wants to be a swallow, who wants to be a butterfly.
to have light wings, to fly under the sky,
to go to the sun on the luminous ladder of a light ray,
to greet the lilies with the verses of May,
or lose herself in the wind over the thunderous sea.

She no longer wants the palace, nor the silver distaff,
nor the enchanted falcon, nor the scarlet buffoon,
nor the unanimous swans on the lake of azure.

And the flowers are sad for the flower of the court;
the jasmines of orient, the lotuses of the north,
the dahlias of the west, and the roses of the south.

Poor little princess of the blue eyes!
She is imprisoned in her gold,
imprisoned in her veils
in the jail of marble in the palace royal;
the arrogant palace surrounded by guards,
and the hundred Black custodians
with their hundred halberds,
awide-awake greyhound and colossal dragon.

Of if she were just a butterfly
who left the chrysalis!
(The princess is sad. The princess is pale)

16.11: The Knight

Of adored vision of gold, rose and ivory!
Who would fly to the land where the prince exists
(The princess is pale. The princess is sad)
more brilliant than the dawn, more beautiful than April!

"Hush, hush, princess", says the fairy godmother
he is coming this way on a winged horse
a sword on his waist and on his hand a falcon,
the happy knight who adores you before seeing you,
who comes from afar, victor over Death,
to ignite your lips with his kiss of love.

16.12: Modernismo

17: The U.S. Emerges

The emergence of the United States

The turn of the century saw the emergence of the United States as a dynamic and even aggressive regional and world power after over a century of relative indifference to Latin America (outside of Mexico). This new U.S. role profoundly affected Latin America, its literature and its art.

The earliest significant expression of a Latin American policy toward Latin America was, as we have noted previously, the Monroe Doctrine of 1823, which because of United States weakness and distraction by other problems was not enforced for most of the 19th

17.1: Uncle Sam

Century. Thus, the British taking of the Falkland/Malvinas Islands (1833), Spanish raids on the Pacific Coast of South America (1850's and 60's) and French intervention in Mexico in the mid 1860's were not countered by any effective U.S. action.

By the 1840's the Latin American perception of the U.S. was shaped not by the Monroe Doctrine so much as by U.S. expansion to the West at the expense of Mexico. During the Mexican-American War Mexico lost substantial portions of its national territory to its northern neighbor, a fact that Mexicans will never forget, although many in the United States relegate that episode to ancient history and tend to forget that most of the Southwest was Spanish and Mexican long before it was American.

Latin fears over U.S. expansion were calmed somewhat during the U.S. Civil War and Reconstruction, when internal problems distracted the United States and kept it from taking a more active role in Hemispheric affairs. This was the period when French Emperor Napoleon III, acting in concert with

Mexican conservatives, seized upon the excuse of unpaid debts to install the Hapsburgh Maximilian and his Empress Carlotta on the "throne" of Mexico. The brief interlude of Mexico under a foreign emperor was accompanied by bitter fighting between liberals and conservatives until the French withdrew their troops and Maximilian was executed. The U.S., in the middle of its Civil War, did not act.

After Reconstruction and economic recovery the U.S. sought markets for its expanding industrial production and began to look southward. In 1889 the first Inter-American Conference was held in Washington, primarily responding to the U.S. agenda of stimulating trade and commerce. Fittingly, the permanent secretariat set up after the meeting was called "The Commercial Bureau of the American Republics".

Towards the end of the Century there was a strong current of thought in the U.S. that stressed social Darwinian ideas of the survival of the fittest, and Spencerian notions of superiority of the Anglo-Saxon and European races of the mid-latitudes. Building upon the earlier notions of the U.S. as a chosen people with a manifest destiny to become a great power, they were to provide the ideological basis for U.S. policies in Latin America and the Caribbean for an extended period. These ideas were coupled to the geopolitical theories of Admiral Alfred Thayer Mahan to justify the expansion of a superior nation into the weaker and inferior nations of Latin America (and especially the Caribbean Basin). To be taken seriously as a major actor on the world stage, the argument went, it was essential that the U.S. control its own "back yard" of the Caribbean, which was frequently called "the American (U.S.) Mediterranean". This in turn meant controlling the proposed inter-oceanic canal and several key islands of the Caribbean.

The decline of Spain as world power and the continuing struggle by Cuban and Puerto Rican patriots for independence provided the opportunity to make these ideas operational. The explosion of the battleship USS Maine in Havana harbor in early 1898 was the excuse the U.S. needed to launch into the "splendid little war" which brought Puerto Rico, Cuba and the Philippines into the U.S. orbit.

Art in this period includes two increasingly powerful media: the camera and the cartoon. Photography had been invented in the 1840's, but its use as a tool for recording historical events did not come into its own until the U.S. Civil War. The Spanish-American War of 1898 was the first major event in Latin American history in which photography, as historical document as well as expression of esthetic creativity, was a significant instrument. Cartoons, of course, had been around for a long time, but technological progress in mass printing techniques made it an increasingly useful and effective tool in this period. Adding to the impact of both photography and the cartoon in this period was the fact . that the publishing giants William Randolph Hearst and Joseph Pulitzer saw in the 1898 War an opportunity to expand their circulation, using both the photograph and the cartoon to do so.

José Martí, poet of Cuban Independence

José Martí has a richly deserved place as both writer and hero of the Cuban independence movement. As an author he was extraordinarily versatile: he produced some of the best lyric poetry of the late-romantic and early-modernist period, and he was also a skilled essayist and translator. Because of his political activities in favor of Cuban independence from Spain, he was jailed and forced into exile for long periods of time. Most of his exile was spent in the United States (mainly New York), and in this

17.2: Martí

period he became a keen observer of his host country. He earned his living by translating and writing about the United States for several major Latin American newspapers. He also held diplomatic posts (consul, conference representative) for various Latin American nations, and left the best insider's description of what went on at the First International Conference of the American Republics (which founded the Inter-American System) in Washington, 1889-1890.

Martí was in many ways the ideal "bridge" person between the Latin American and U.S. political and cultural worlds of his day. Like Rodó and many others before him, he admired much of what the United States had to offer, but he also warned his Latin compatriots of the seductive and less attractive side of U.S. materialism (see his essay, *Nuestra America-Our America*). He was especially concerned that the United States would seek to force Spain out of Cuba and Puerto Rico for its own political and economic benefit.

As a poet Martí took many of the finer elements of the late romantic period in Latin American literature and re-fused them into the foundations of the emerging modernist movement. His poetry is thus simpler, more emotional and less aloof than Darío's. His *Simple Verses* are still very popular, and have been adapted to become the lyrics of the song *Guantanamera*.

Because of his anti-imperialist writings, Martí has been warmly embraced by the Castro regime in Cuba. But he is equally beloved by Cuban exiles living outside Cuba as the symbol of their homeland. He died in combat against the Spanish while leading a landing in Cuba in 1895.

17.3: U.S. devours Cuba

Simple Verses by José Martí

I am a sincere man
born where the palm trees grow;
and before dying, I want
to release these verses from my soul.

I come from all places,
and to all places I go;
art I am among the arts;
and in the hills I am hill.

I know all the strange names
of the herbs and the flowers,
of mortal trickery,
and sublime pain.

I have seen the dark night
rain upon my head
and the rays of pure light
coming from divine beauty.

17.4: Lover

I have seen wings born on shoulders
of beautiful women,
and butterflies flying up
out of the debris.

I have seen a man
with a dagger in his side,
who never spoke the name
of the woman who killed him.

Quick, like a reflection,
twice I have seen a soul, twice:
first when the old man died
and then when she said goodbye to me.

I trembled once - at the grating,
at the entrance of my vineyard -,
when the savage bee
stung my little girl's forehead.

I felt pleasure, of a sort
that I never felt before: when
the warden, crying
read my death sentence.

I hear a sigh over
land and the seas,
yet it is not a sigh, it is
my son about to awaken.

If they say take from the jeweler
the best of his jewels,
I take a sincere friend
and set aside love.

I have seen the wounded eagle
fly the serene blue sky,
and I've seen the lair
where the poisonous viper dies.

I know full well that when the world
surrenders, tired, to rest,
that over the deep silence
the quiet stream murmurs.

I have put a daring hand,
stiff with horror and joy,
to touch the burned-out star
that fell at my front door.

I hide in my wild chest
the pain that wounds me:
the son of an enslaved people
lives for it, is quiet, and dies.

All is beautiful and constant,
all is music and reason,
and all, just like the diamond
is coal before light comes.

I know that the stupid man is buried
with great pomp and many tears,
and that there is no fruit on earth
quite like the cemetery's.

17.5: Woman

I am silent, and I remove
the pomp of the verse-maker;
I hang up on a withered tree
my academic gown.

My Little Horseman by José Martí

Mornings
my little one
would wake me
with a big kiss.

Astride
my chest
he made bridles
of my hair.

Giggly he with pleasure
giggly I with pleasure
he spurred me,
my little horseman.

What a gentle spur
his two fresh little feet.
How he laughed,
my little horseman!

17.6: Martí's son

And I kissed
his little feet,
two feet that fit
in a single kiss!

Our América (fragment) by José Martí

...   But our America faces, perhaps, another danger. Not one from within, but rather from the United States. It stems from the different origins, methods and interests of the two major continental elements. And the moment is approaching when this hard-driving and enterprising nation, which scorns us and does not know us, will approach us, demanding intimate relations...

This formidable neighbor's scorn and lack of knowledge is the greatest threat to our America. Because the moment of closer contact is upon us, it is urgent that our neighbor get to know us, and soon, so that they will not scorn us. Ignorance may lead her, perhaps, to greed with regard to us. But respect, through getting to know us, would preclude this from happening. We have to have faith in the good side of man and be careful of man's bad side. We must allow the better side to emerge and prevail over the worse. If not, the bad will prevail. Nations should have a pillory for those who provoke useless hate, and another for those who do not tell the truth soon enough. ...

Nor should we assume, through some parochial antipathy, that the blond people of the continent are inherently and fatally evil because they do not speak our language, because they do not live as we do, because their political scars are different from ours, or because they do not highly regard men who are quick-tempered or swarthier. Nor should we think less of them because they, from their lofty but still unsure eminence, may look down on those who, less favored by History, are still struggling to establish republics; nor should we hide the facts surrounding the problems that must be solved for peace; we must study them in order to reach the urgently required tacit union of the continental soul. The unanimous anthem is already heard; the present generation is now carrying striving America forward along the path shown by our founding fathers; from the Rio Bravo to the Strait of Magellan, the Great Sower has scattered from the wings of the condor the seeds of the new America!

José Enrique Rodó: Ariel and Caliban

The Uruguayan José Enrique Rodó (1871-1917) is the principal prose writer of the modernist movement. He is best known for his extended essay, Ariel, named after the airy spirit in Shakespeare's The Tempest. Ariel has often been interpreted simplistically as symbolizing the struggle between the spiritual and cultural values of Latin America (represented by Ariel) and the crass materialistic and utilitarian values of the United States (represented by Caliban, that less attractive character from The Tempest).

17.7: Rodó

Although this first-level interpretation is not necessarily contrary to Rodó's thinking (as well as that of many other Latin Americans then and since), it misses much of the rest of his message. Rodó's voice is that of the nobler values of Latin culture speaking out against the mechanistic and deterministic dictates of Positivism, which were so prevalent in his period around the turn of the Century. Rodó notes the many contributions of both cultures, summarized in his statement that the Anglo-Saxon gift to mankind was liberty while the Greco-Roman (Latin) gift was culture. However, neither is the exclusive preserve of one group, and each must learn from the other.

Rodó was not criticizing the United States as much as warning the Latins that their "Latinity" was endangered by an excessive and unquestioning acceptance of foreign values, especially those he labeled as "nordomania". Rodó felt that Latin America had a tendency to drift toward chaos, and that an excessive emphasis on unbridled liberty would exacerbate this trend. Caliban's materialism, he said, posed grave dangers to Ariel's core values of spirituality, idealism, free will and beauty, with the end result being a "de-Latinization" of Latin America. We must understand that Rodó was part of the esthetic reaction against Positivism and that many of his arguments were phrased in the rhetoric of the Parnassian and Modernist movement of his period. Nevertheless, his ideas have had a profound influence on how Latin Americans view the United States and the dangers (as well as opportunities) it presents to their core values.

In effect, Rodó's advice to the Latin youth of his day is balanced: grow, and develop all your possibilities as human beings, avoiding early specializations in your career which would close doors. Be careful not to separate ethics from aesthetics, for the good is better if it is also beautiful; admire and respect the United States, and borrow from that great country those things which can enhance your own worth, but be wary of the materialism that can corrode the spirit that makes you what you are. In recent years Rodó has been criticized for presenting his cultural arguments in bi-polar terms, focusing on Anglo-Saxon and Latin currents without regard for the contributions of the Indigenous, the Blacks, or the Mestizos. Despite these defects, his "Arielismo" is important to our understanding of how the Latin Americans view the United States.

Ariel by José Enrique Rodó

That afternoon the old and venerated teacher brought his young disciples together for the last session of the year's studies. They called him "Prospero", alluding to the wise magician of Shakespeare's The Tempest. They had already arrived in their spacious study room, in which a delicate but severe taste was evident, emanating from the noble presence of books, Prospero's faithful companions. An elegant bronze statue of The Tempest's Ariel dominated the room, as the deity of its serene environment. The old teacher usually sat next to this bust, and so they gave him the name of the magician who in the play had served and favored the fantastic personage who was the object of the sculptor's

17.8: Ariel

work. But perhaps he had intended, in his teachings and character, a deeper reason and sense.

In Shakespeare's work Ariel, genius of the air, represented the noble and winged part of the human spirit. Ariel is the domination of reason and sentiment over the gross stimuli of irrationality. It is generous enthusiasm, the high and disinterested motives for action, the spirituality of culture, the vivacity and grace of intelligence, the ideal toward which human selection climbs, correcting in superior man the tenacious vestiges of Caliban, symbol of sensuality and crudeness, chiseled by the persevering reality of life.

The statue, a true piece of art, showed the aerial genius at the instant when, liberated by the magic of Prospero, he hurls himself into the void. His wings are unfolded, and his light garments are loose and floating, with the caressing light falling like gold on bronzed silk. His face is uplifted, lips parted in a calm smile. All of this as Ariel reaches the smooth and graceful moment of takeoff. With great inspiration, the sculptor's art had managed to keep, at the same time, an angelic and idealistic appearance. Prospero, meditating, touched the statue's face, and arranged the affectionate and attentive young group around him. Then with his firm and magisterial voice, which he used to fix an idea and penetrate the inner depths of the soul like the clear illumination of a shaft of light, or the incisive blow of chisel on marble, or the pregnant stroke of brush on canvas, or wave on sand, began to speak:

The utilitarian conception as an idea of human destiny, and the mediocrity of equality as a social norm, are intimately related and make up what is called in Europe the spirit of Americanism. It is impossible to meditate on both inspirations of conduct and sociability, and compare them with others, without insistently bringing forth the image of that formidable and fertile democracy of the North. That democracy of the North shows off the manifestations of its prosperity and power, like an overwhelming proof of the value of its institutions and the direction of its ideas. If one can say that utilitarianism is the basic definition of the English spirit, then the United States can be considered the incarnation of that word "utilitarian". And the gospel of this word is scattered all over as it is linked to the material miracles of its triumph. And Spanish America is not exactly characterized as a land of unbelievers in the face of this triumph. The powerful Federation is carrying out in our midst a sort of moral conquest. The admiration for her greatness and her strength is a sentiment which advances with great strides in the spirit of our leaders, and even more perhaps in the spirit of our masses, who are fascinated by the stamp of victory. And from admiring it one moves, with an easy transition, to imitating it. Admiration and belief are, for the psychologist, passive forms of imitation....

One imitates that which one believes to be superior and prestigious. And thus there floats through the dreams of many of our people who are concerned with our future, a sort of vision of a "de-latinized" America imitating the image of the archetype from the North. This happens without the extortion of conquest, but rather through our own free will. We are inspired by the desire to bring to fruition the most suggestive of parallels with the North, which show up in constant proposals for renewal and reform. We have our nordomania. It is necessary to confront this consumption of nordomania with the limits which reason and sentiment indicate.

Any severe judgment made of the North Americans must begin by extending to them, as one would do with high adversaries, the chivalrous formality of a greeting. It is easy for my spirit to do this. To deny good qualities is just as bad as to ignore defects. They are born (to use Baudelaire's paradox) with the innate experience of liberty. They have kept the faith with their original laws, and have carried out, with mathematical precision and assurance, the fundamental principles of their organization. They have thus given their history a unity which, even if it excluded the possibility of acquiring other aptitudes and merits, has the intellectual beauty of logic. The trail of their footsteps shall never be erased in the annals of human law, because they were the first who embodied our modern concept of liberty. Moving from the first shaky attempts, and despite all the utopian imagining, they converted it into an imperishable bronze and a living reality. Because they have demonstrated through their example that it is possible to extend to a vast national organism the firm authority of a republic. Because, through their federative form of government they have revealed, using de Tocqueville's fortunate phrase, the way in which it is possible to reconcile the brilliance and power of large States with the happiness and peace of small ones. ...

Their culture, which is a long way from being refined or spiritual, nevertheless has an admirable efficiency which is always directed in a practical manner toward the achievement of an immediate goal. They have not fixed on a single general scientific law or principle. Rather, they have made magic with the wonders of applied principles, and have become giants of utility. They have given the world the steam engine and the electric dynamo, billions of invisible slaves who have multiplied man's power a hundredfold, like Aladdin's lamp. The growth of their greatness and strength shall be the object of enduring astonishment in the future...Puritan liberty, which gave it light from the past, united this light with a faith which still endures. Next to factories and schools, their strong hands have also built houses of worship where many millions of free consciences pray. They have been able to salvage, in the shipwreck of all ideals, the highest ideal, keeping alive a religious tradition. This religious tradition, which might not soar on the wings of a deep and sensitive spiritualism, but at least sustains among the raw utilitarian tumult the strong reins of morality. ...

Deprived like an orphan of deep traditions which would give it direction, this nation has not learned how to move from the inspired ideals of the past to a high and disinterested conception of the future. They live for the immediate reality, for the present, and because of that they subordinate all their activity to the selfishness of personal and collective well-being. Prodigious in their wealth, the North Americans have been able to acquire the satisfaction and vanity of sumptuous magnificence; but they have not been able to acquire the carefully selected note of good taste.

17.9: U.S. sells flag

18: The Mexican Revolution

The Mexican Revolution

The Mexican Revolution which broke out in 1910 was the most profound and far-reaching revolution Latin America had known up to the middle of the 20th Century. It made deep and irreversible changes in many aspects of Mexican life: political, social, economic and cultural. It broke the old colonial and neo-colonial patterns of foreign penetration and ruptured the historical ties between landowner-politician, priest and army officer. Beyond Mexico, it provided an example for the rest of Latin America, even though the Mexicans never attempted to export their revolution or claim that what they did could be easily replicated in other countries.

The Mexican Revolution was also in a sense a continuation of the aborted popular revolt of 1810 led by the priests Hidalgo and Morelos, which had been coopted by the conservative elites. The 1910 Revolution broke the power of these elites, the Catholic Church, and the old-style military.

The stage for the Revolution was set by the long conservative rule of General Porfirio Díaz, who for 34 years had governed Mexico under the ideology of the Positivists. His regime boasted of many signs of material progress, but these favored the Mexican elites and the foreign investors, to the detriment of the large masses of lower class Mexicans. The economy was neocolonial, since it was based on control of Mexico's extractive industries (especially oil and minerals), by American, British and other European investors. Inter-

18.1: Fighter

nally Díaz controlled Mexico through a tight alliance of the large landowners, the Church, and the military and police forces directly under his command. Each of these legs of his three-legged stool of conservative power supported each other, and the system endured, providing the stability so cherished by the Positivists and so attractive to the foreign investor.

Table 18.1: Early 20th Century Movements, Chapters 18-20

	The Mexican Revolution
Cultural-historical framework:	**Many social, political, economic, cultural changes.** **Growing influence of the United States; interventions** **Slow increase in size and influence of the middle class**
Approximate dates:	**Early 20th Century**
Historical landmarks	**Mexican Revolution, 1910-?**
Literature	**Fragmentation, and a multitude of tendencies:** **1. Escapism: form is everything, content nothing** **2. Anti-modernist (post-modernist) current: simplicity and sincerity.** **3. Literature of fantasy and imagination, including surrealism and psychological themes.** **4. Literature of the Mexican Revolution** **5. Social protest literature** **6. Feminist literature** **7. Many other currents**
The Arts	**Fragmentation, and a multitude of tendencies:** **1. Abstractionism: form is everything, content nothing** **2. Primitivism: simplicity, sincerity** **3. Surrealism, cubism** **4. Mexican muralism** **5. Social protest art** **6. Feminism** **7. Many other currents**

But by the beginning of the new century things were starting to change. The rural masses and urban labor were chafing under their exploited status, and a growing middle class, mainly mestizo and city-dwelling, was becoming politicized and increasingly resentful at being excluded from the superficial material progress being made in their nation.

The spark that set off the Revolution was the 1910 re-election campaign of Porfirio Díaz (for his eight term). In a 1908 interview with a foreign journalist, the aging Díaz let it be known that he might not choose to run in 1910. This led an intellectual member of an upper-class family by the name of Francisco Madero to announce his candidacy. Running on a campaign of "no-re-election and effective suffrage", Madero was able to gather considerable support among the middle class, and the possibility that he might win stirred hope among the lower classes. Díaz

18.2: Porfirio Díaz

promptly arrested Madero and proceeded to win a rigged election. But he miscalculated the degree of unrest in Mexico and shortly after the election, when his police fired on a demonstration in Mexico City, he went into exile himself. The first stage of the Revolution had ended with the departure of the old dictator.

Madero, returned from exile in Texas, was declared President and took the reins of power. But Madero was essentially a 19th Century liberal, and his program was a "constitutionalist" one based on clean elections and limits on the re-election of the president. He was well-meaning, but had no real program for the profound social, economic and political changes that Mexicans were clamoring for. He had also made the critical mistake of allowing many of the senior generals of Díaz' old army to remain in place.

When it became clear that Madero's reform program would be a very limited one, unrest and violence broke out in numerous places in Mexico. One of the most significant movements was the cry for land reform led by Emilano Zapata, whose cry of "land and liberty" mobilized thousands of followers who began invading the large land holdings (the haciendas) and taking them over. The landowners appealed to their allies among the senior military officers, who under the leadership of the reactionary general Victoriano Huerta moved to put down the revolt, take Madero and his Vice President prisoner, and then execute them "as they tried to escape".

By 1913 Huerta and the counter-revolutionary "federales" were in control of Mexico City, the port city of Veracruz, and not much else. The rest of Mexico was in chaos, with local leaders fighting for the increasingly radical goals of the

Revolution under the broad banner of the "Constitutionalists". Zapata continued his land seizures, Pancho Villa in northern Mexico ran his own war, and Venustiano Carranza attempted to take over the leadership of the remaining factions.

Huerta was finally defeated in 1914, and Carranza became president at the head of the coalition of Constitutionalists. For the first time since Independence radical mestizos, at the head of large numbers of Indigenous, had wrested power away from the creole elite. Carranza was able to consolidate his power by accepting some of the more radical proposals made by Zapata and others. These were institutionalized in the revolutionary constitution of 1917, which included such far-reaching provisions as land reform, social security protection for workers, restrictions on the power and wealth of the Church, and nationalization of oil

The Mexican Revolution was also a cultural revolution. The European cultural values of the Positivists and the elites were

18.3: Emiliano Zapata

swept aside in favor of local and native traditions. Respect for Indigenous values became a major part of Mexico's official government cultural programs after centuries in which these values had been considered inferior. Because Mexico had very high levels of illiteracy, murals were used as educational and propagandistic tools to gain support for the Revolution's goals. The ubiquitous and inexpensive broadside woodcuts of José Guadalupe Posada and others had mobilized the Revolution's supporters in their protests against Díaz, and after the revolution had consolidated its power they too were used to propagate and support its goals.

Mexican literature in this period was dominated by the theme of the Revolution. Sometimes this took the form of biographies of the leaders and fighters, with very mixed quality. The most successful examples of the literature of the Mexican Revolution were produced by writers and journalists who participated or closely observed the fighting phase, bringing to these writings a reality and sense of vividness that those sitting in comfort far from the battle field could not hope to duplicate. Novels and short stories written by these observers and fighters of the Revolution joined the murals of Rivera, Orozco and Siqueiros ("the Big Three") to become the best cultural witnesses to this key turning point of Mexican history.

A story from the fighting phase:
Guzmán's *Pancho Villa on the Cross*

Because the Mexican Revolution had this cultural dimension as well as political, social and economic ones, there were important manifestations in literature as well as art (the muralists). There is a whole genre of novels, memoirs and stories surrounding the period of greatest fighting between 1910 and 1920. One of the best writers of the Mexican Revolution from the unique perspective of the eye witness was Martín Luis Guzmán, who came from a prominent Mexico City family and was with Pancho Villa during many of the key moments of the revolutionary struggle. Guzman's major work is the book The Eagle and the Serpent, a title chosen because it is the ancient Aztec icon of Mexican nationhood, as well as for its contemporary significance as the symbol of the struggle between good and evil, between the forces for change and the forces of reaction and counter-revolution. Not exactly a novel, The Eagle and the Serpent is a loosely connected series of anecdotes and stories, sometimes embellished, of Pancho Villa and his army as they fought their way across the Northern part of Mexico during the violent stage of the Mexican Revolution.

18.4: Pancho Villa

Guzmán's relationship to the central figure of Pancho Villa bears some similarities to the relationship between Sarmiento and Facundo, with the added value that Guzmán knew Villa well and was able to observe him closely over an extended period of time. There is tension between the earthy, crude, macho, animal-like *caudillo* that is Villa and the educated, citified writer-journalist that is Guzmán. Villa was not above mocking and even humiliating Guzmán, but as the story which follows indicates, he was also capable of listening to his advice.

In one of the more bizarre incidents of the Mexican Revolution, in March 1916 Pancho Villa ordered his men to cross the border and attack the small town of Columbus, New Mexico, killing several Americans and destroying parts of the town and the small military outpost. The reasons for the raid were unclear, but apparently Villa hoped that his brazen act and the expected US response would appeal to Mexican nationalism and result in greater support for his group. The raid was, technically, the last time the continental United States was invaded by a hostile foreign force. U.S. public opinion was outraged, and President Woodrow Wilson ordered General John Pershing to mount a Punitive Expedition to catch Villa. This proved to be a frustrating and difficult task, and after a year of marching around the deserts of northern Mexico the Expedition gave up.

Pancho Villa on the Cross
by Martín Luis Guzmán

The Aguas Calientes Convention had barely ended when the fighting began again. That is to say, the conciliatory efforts failed at the practical level before the theoretical one. And the efforts failed, after all, because that is what most of the members wanted. If there were armies available and at hand, how could one resist the urgent temptation to use them? Maclovio Herrera, in Chihuahua, was one of the first to take to the field, challenging Pancho Villa's authority.

"That big-eared SOB" said Villa of his one-time ally Herrera, "I am the one who made him what he is! He is my son in arms! How can that deaf and ungrateful traitor dare to abandon me?" So great was Villa's ire that only a few days after Herrera rebelled he was under attack from the troops Villa sent to get him. The encounters were bloody and terrible: it was Villistas against Villistas, hurricane against hurricane. He who did not kill, died.

One of those mornings Llorente and I went to visit Villa, and we found him so somber that we felt panic just looking at him. The burning fire in his eyes made me think that we humans belong to several different species, and that between these species there are unbridgeable distances, worlds that

18.5: Villistas

have no common denominator. And if one of us penetrated into the world of an opponent we would feel a certain vertigo over the chasm that divides us. A reflex shudder swept through my soul that morning as I faced Villa, in the framework of terror and horror.

In response to our "good morning, general", he responded in a grim tone: "Not good, my friends. We have too many empty sombreros". I did not fully understand the meaning of that phrase, and I don't think Llorente did either. But while he kept the silence of true wisdom, I, with stupid haste, almost inciting a crime, said, "We have too many what, General?"

He took a step towards me and replied with a careful and slow tone that showed that he was barely containing his rage: "Too many empty sombreros, Licenciado. Don't you understand man talk? Or don't you realize that because of the Long-eared one (wait till I catch that bastard!) my boys are killing each other? Do you understand now why we have too many empty sombreros? Am I speaking clearly enough?"

I froze and said nothing. Villa was pacing back and forth in the rail car to the interior rhythm of his anger. Every couple of steps he swore between clenched teeth: "That deaf SOB...   ...   That deaf SOB". Several times Llorente and I looked at each other, and then, not knowing what to do or say, we sat down next to each other. Outside the morning was bright, interrupted only by the distant sounds and voice of the bivouacked camp. In the train car the only sound besides the raging in Villa's soul was the tic-track of the telegraph.

The telegrapher sat facing us, leaning over his table, his movements precise, and his face as expressionless as his equipment. Several minutes passed this way. Then the telegrapher, who had been busy transmitting, turned to his chief and said: "It looks like it's here, General".

He took the pencil from behind his ear and slowly began to write. Villa moved over to the

18.6: Revolutionaries

telegraph table with an air that at the same time was agitated and glacial, impatient and calm, vengeful and disdaining. He was between us and the telegrapher, and I could see his profile leaning over the equipment.... The telegrapher peeled off the top sheet of the pink pad where he had been writing the message and handed it to Villa. Villa took it, but then handed it back to him, saying: "You read it to me, my friend. But read it carefully, because now I think we're getting down to business".

Villa's voice carried echoes of somber emotion, echoes so deep and threatening that they were reflected in the voice of the telegrapher, who separating each word carefully, scanning each syllable, began to read the message with a flat voice: "I have the honor of communicating to you..." Then the tone of his words became more elevated as the reading continued. The message, laconic and bloody, was the report of the defeat that Villa's troops had just inflicted on Maclovio Herrera's forces.

As he listened, Villa's face seemed for an instant to move from the shadows to the light. But then, as he heard the final phrases, his eyes blazed and once again his face burned with the fire of his maximum fury, his overwhelming and uncontrollable rage. What set him off was the closing phrase in the message in which the commander of his victorious forces, after listing his dead and wounded, asked Villa what he should do with the one hundred and sixty of Herrera's men who had laid down their arms and surrendered.

"What to do with them?" yelled Villa. "Well, what else but shoot them! What a stupid question! Why do even my best men, my most loyal and sure ones, let me down? What do I need these generals for if they don't even know what to do with traitors they get a hold of?"

18.7: Villista

He said all of this without taking his eyes off the poor telegrapher, and through his eyes, and then the wires of the telegraph, Villa could perhaps feel how his anger reached the battlefield where his men lay dead. Turning to us, he continued: "And what do you think, sir lawyers?" "What do you think about them asking me what to do with prisoners?"

But Llorente and I, barely looking at him, stared out the window to the vague infinity beyond. We were Villa's least concern. Turning back to the operator he ordered him: "OK, friend. Tell that so-and-so to stop wasting my time and the telegraph's. Tell him to shoot the hundred and sixty right now, and if he doesn't tell me within the hour that he has carried out the order I'll go there and shoot them myself so he'll learn how to handle things. Did you understand me?"

"Yes, general". The telegrapher started to write the message out first before transmitting it. Villa interrupted him after the first word: "Hey, what are you doing? Why aren't you obeying my order?" "I'm drafting the message, General"

"Don't give me any of that drafting crap. Just tell him what I said and that's it. Time was not made to be wasted on papers." And so the operator put his right hand on the transmitting apparatus, placed his index finger on the Morse key, and began to call the distant station: <tic-tic; trick-tic; tic-trick-tic>.

Between the pile of papers and Villa's arm I could see the operator's knuckles, pale and vibrating under the contraction of his tendons as he produced the little homicidal sounds. Villa never took his eyes off the movements which were transmitting his orders two hundred leagues North, nor did we. For reasons I could not understand, as stupid as those in dreams, I was trying to guess the exact instant in which the vibrations of the operator's fingers spelled out the words "shoot at once". For five minutes it was a terrible obsession which swept from my conscience every other immediate reality, every other sense of being.

When the operator finished his transmission, Villa, now calmer, sat down in the chair next to his desk. There he was silent for a brief moment. Then he shifted his hat to the back of his head, pushed the fingers of his hand through his reddish hair and scratched his skull as if trying to rip out something that was eating at his brain, at his soul. Then he was still. We sat watching him, silent, still.

Perhaps ten minutes passed. Suddenly Villa turned toward me and said: "And what do you think of all this, my friend?"

"Me, General?" "Yes, you, my friend".

Then, cornered, but determined to use men's language, I answered ambiguously: "Well, there are going to be a lot of empty sombreros, General".

"Bah. Who are you telling that to! But that's not what I am asking about. What about the consequences? Do you think this business of the execution is good or bad?" Llorente, more daring, got ahead of me: "To be frank, General, I don't think the order was a good idea".

I closed my eyes. I was sure that Villa, rising up from his seat, or even sitting down, would whip out his pistol to punish such a colossal reproach of his conduct in something so close to his soul. But a few seconds passed, and after that Villa asked in a calm voice which contrasted extraordinarily with the tempest that had come before: "Well, tell me why you don't think the order was a good idea".

Llorente was so pale that his skin looked just like his starched white collar. But he answered firmly: "Because the report said, General, that the hundred and sixty men surrendered".

"Yes. So what?"

"Well, taken in battle like that, they should not be executed"

"Why not?"

"Because of that, General: because they surrendered".

"That really is hilarious. Where did they teach you these things?"

The shame of my silence overwhelmed me. I couldn't take it any longer. I broke in: "I think the same thing, General. I think Llorente is right."

Villa took us both in with a single glance: "and why do you think that, my friend?"

"Llorente already explained it: because the men surrendered"

"And I'll repeat what I said: SO WHAT?" The WHAT was pronounced like a final and absolute interrogation. This last time, as he said it, he revealed a certain unease that led him to open his eyes even wider to wrap us in his now less focused gaze. From outside inwards I felt the weight of that cold and cruel stare, and from inside outwards I felt an impulse spurred on by the vision of remote mass executions. It was urgent that I come up with a sure and intelligible formula. I tried, explaining: "When a man surrenders, General, he grants life to others by giving up his career of killing. And as a result, he who accepts the surrender is obliged not to kill him".

Villa looked at me carefully and slowly. Then he jumped up and yelled at the telegraph operator: "Hey, friend, call them again, call them again..." The operator obeyed: <tic-trick-tic; trick-trick>. A few seconds went by. Villa inquired impatiently: "Are they answering?"

"I'm calling, General".

Llorente and I could not contain ourselves and we went over to the equipment table. Villa asked again: "Do they answer?"

"Not yet, general"

"Call harder"

The operator could neither call harder or softer. But we could see, in the contraction of his fingers, that he was trying to make the shape of each letter clearer and more precise. There was a brief silence, and then there broke out, dry and distant, the <trick-tic> of the receiver.

"They're answering" said the operator.

"OK, friend, OK. Transmit this, and don't waste any time. Listen closely: 'Delay execution prisoners until further order. General Francisco Villa'..."

<tic-trick-tic; trick-trick>   "Done?"

18.8: Villista prisioner

<tic-tic-trick-tic; trick-trick>
"Yes, General".

"Now tell the operator at the other end that I am standing here next to the equipment waiting for an answer, and I am holding him personally responsible for the slightest delay."

<tic-trick-tic; trick-trick>
"Done?"
"Yes, General"

The receiver rang out: <tic-trick-tic; trick-trick>
"What's he saying?"
"That he's going to deliver the telegram and bring back an answer..."

The three of us stood next to the telegraph table: Villa strangely uneasy; Llorente and I spellbound by anxiety.
Ten minutes went by.
<trick-tic-trick-tic; trick-trick>
"Is he answering?"
"That's not him, General. It's another station."
Villa took out his watch and asked: "How long has it been since we telegraphed the first order?"
"About twenty-five minutes, General".
Turning then towards me, Villa said, and I don't know why he picked me: "Will the counter-order get there in time? What do you think?"
"I hope so, General"
<tic-trick-tic; trick-trick>
"Are they answering, friend?"
"No, General, it's a different one".
As the minutes passed, we could hear in Villa's voice a vibration which we had never heard before: harmonics, veiled by emotion, deeper each time he asked if the <tic-tricks> were an acknowledgment of the counter-order. He had his eyes fixed on the little lever of the receiver, and whenever it showed the slightest movement he would say, as if he could influence the electricity running through the wires: "Is it him?"
"No, General, it's someone else".
Twenty minutes had passed since the sending of the counter-order when the operator finally said, picking up his pencil:
"They're calling now". <tic-trick-tic; trick-trick>
Villa leaned further over the table. Llorente, however, stood up straight. I went over and sat next to the operator to read the message as he was writing it.
<tic-trick-tic; trick-trick>
By the third line Villa could not contain his impatience and asked: "Did the counter-order get there in time?" Without taking my eyes of what the operator was writing, I nodded my head affirmatively. Villa took out his handkerchief and wiped the sweat from his brow.

****

That evening we ate with him; but during the whole time we sat together he did not talk about the morning's events. Only when we said goodbye, well after nightfall, Villa said to us, without any explanations: "Thanks, friends, many thanks, for the business with the telegrams and the prisoners..."

Azuela: A story from the consolidation phase

Mariano Azuela (1873-1952) was one of the great novelists of the Mexican Revolution. Like Guzmán, he too had accompanied Villa and other leaders on numerous campaigns. But his viewpoint is not so much biographical as Guzman's was, and he attempts to present the viewpoint of the common man, of the people themselves.

He had studied medicine, although he had always wanted to be a writer. His works cover the Revolution from the period of Madero (1910-13) through the presidency of Cárdenas in the 1940's. When the Revolution broke out he joined the Maderista faction, and then later the Villa group as a doctor. He wrote the greater part of his principal novel, *Los de Abajo* (*The Underdogs*) during the period with Villa. When Villa was defeated in 1915, Azuela went into exile in El Paso, Texas, and the novel was first published there. The title clearly reveals Azuela's attitude: he wanted to tell the story of the people who had always been Mexico's "underdogs", even after the changes brought about by the Revolution.

This theme is the basis for the story which follows: Juan Pablo is a humble representative of the masses who, due to circumstances and personal courage, becomes a revolutionary general and leader. But the corrupt politicians who began to control the Revolution after the fighting phase was over betrayed him and finally executed him because they could not tolerate his honesty and his firm loyalty to the ideals of the Revolution.

Azuela's story corresponds to the phase when the Revolution was becoming consolidated and beaurocratized. A series of official revolutionary political parties were organized, culminating in the "PRI - *Partido Revolucionario Institucional*" (translated as "Party of the Institutionalized Revolution " or "Party of the Revolutionary Institutions"). The PRI was finally voted out of the presidency

18.9: Revolutionaries by José Guadalupe Posada

in 2006, but remains a major political force, and maintains that it is the legitimate heir to the 1910 Revolution.

How, finally, Juan Pablo cried by M. Azuela

Juan Pablo is locked up in the chapel the night before his execution. The next morning, at the crack of dawn, he will be taken from his cell amidst the sound of bugles and the beating of drums to the far end of the barracks blocks. And there, with his back to a narrow adobe wall, in front of the whole regiment, the squad will be formed and he will be executed.

18.10: Juan Pablo by Posada

Thus one pays with one's life for the ugly crime of treason.

Treason! Treason!

The harsh word spoken yesterday during the Extraordinary Court Martial has been stabbed into the center of Juan Pablo's heart like a scorpion's stinger.

"Treason". Thus spoke the handsome little officer, who blinked his eyes and moved his hands like a comic actor's. Thus spoke the corseted officer, affected, perfumed like the women of the streets; a little officer with three shiny insignia ... virgin insignia.

And the word bounces around Juan Pablo's skull like a fixed idea in the Ferris-wheel of a typhoid victim's brain. "Treason! Treason! But treason against whom?"

Juan Pablo roars, but without raising his head, shifting in his chair and making his iron-trimmed boots creak on the tile floor.

The guard awakens: "Sentry aleeeeert!..." "Sentry aleeeeert!..."

The call is repeated and moves into the distance, losing itself from patio to patio, until it fades fearfully and with a shudder in a whimper of wind. Then a dog barks in the street. A sharp bark, mournful, with a tearful, almost human melancholy.

One day the Mexico City newspaper arrived in Hostotipaquillo with the lies telling of the feats of the drunkard Huerta and his savages. Pascual Bailón, skillful barber and sure druggist, called his intimate friends together. "It would be good to get rid of the tyrants now", replied Juan Pablo, who never spoke.

Then Pascual Bailón, a personage of some note, full of the readings of Juan A. Mateos and Don Ireneo Paz and other famous writers, with an epic gesture, and with his words reaching the heights of condors, spoke thusly:

"Friends, it is cowardly to speak in tongues, when our brothers to the North are speaking with gun powder".

Juan Pablo was the first to go out into the street.

The conspirators, numbering seven, did not speak with powder because they didn't even have flintlock pistols. But they did speak with iron, and they permanently silenced the tyrants of the village, the mayor and the guards of the municipal jail, to say nothing of setting fire to the La Simpatía store (odds and ends) belonging to Don Telésforo, the local political boss.

Pascual Bailón and his men went up to the ravines of Tequila. After their first skirmish with the Federals, there occurred a radical move which realigned the hierarchy. Pascual Bailón had always tried to place himself at a respectable distance from the line of fire, which he called, based on his readings of history, "prudence". But the others, who didn't even know how to read, said that this was simply called "fear". Then, by unanimity, Juan Pablo assumed the leadership of the group. This was Juan Pablo who in the village had been known only for his rough withdrawal, or by his very limited ability to put an edge on a plow, whet a workman's bar, or sharpen a machete. Fearless valor and serenity were for Juan Pablo the same thing as an eaglet's ability to spread its wings and fly through the sky. When the Revolution triumphed he was able to proudly wear, without any shame or false modesty, his insignias of the rank of general.

The pairs of lovers who liked to see the foliage of Mexico City's Santiago Tlatelolco garden tinted in the golden vapors of the morning sun would frequently run across a rough-looking man, carelessly leaning back on a park bench, in shirt-sleeves, his shirtfront open to show a hairy chest; sometimes he would drunkenly contemplate the moldy and eroded side of the church, its old and uneven rose-colored towers cutting into the sapphire-blue sky; other times he would be with a copy of El Pueblo, painfully spelling out each word as he read.

18.11: Lovers

Juan Pablo, on garrison duty in the capital, knows little about newspapers, now that Pascual Bailón, the new Cincinattus, having saved the motherland, has retired to private life to look after his interests (an *hacienda* in Michoacán and a rather nicely equipped little railroad). But when the newspaper's headline is printed in red for the nth time with the news the "Doroteo Arango has been killed" or that "the Government has refused the offer of five hundred million dollars made by US bankers", or perhaps "the people are beginning to feel the immense benefits of the Revolution", then he buys the newspaper. It is unnecessary to say that Juan Pablo adopts the daily opinion of El Pueblo: his jacket is unbuttoned because it no longer closes; the point of his nose has become purple and it has begun to sprout rather large little veins which wind through it like a snake; at his side a pretty adolescent dressed in flowery white plays, with a bright ribbon at her neck, and another, larger and opened up like a butterfly tied to the end of the braid which lies, heavily, in the midst of hips which have only just begun to broaden.

Juan Pablo had just finished rendering the reading of "the Immense Benefits which the Revolution have brought to the People", when his eyes happen to fix upon a hundred or so filthy, flea-bitten and cadaverous individuals who are standing in line along the Twelfth Factor street, waiting for the opening of the doors of the corn meal mill. Juan Pablo scrunches his left nostril and leans over to scratch his ankle. It is not that Juan Pablo, stung by the coincidence, has reflected. No. Juan Pablo does not ordinarily think. What happens in the depths of his subconsciouses usually emerges to the surface this way: the scrunching of a nostril, and a silent sharp snap, as if a flea had walked across his calf. That is all.

18.12: Prisioner by José Guadalupe Posada

And well, this is the third time Juan Pablo has been locked up waiting for his execution. The first time was for having rearranged the face of an effeminate emissary of the Secretary of War; the second for having lodged a bullet in the head of a paymaster. These were not major events, just the minutiae of service. Because in the simple dense mesquite-like logic of Juan Pablo there was no room for this business about the people continuing to be enslaved by others after the triumph of the Revolution. In effect, in his regiment the only line of action that was followed was "Don't ever turn your back to the enemy". The rest would be sorted out by each individual as best suited him. One can understand the kind of men Juan Pablo would take with him. One can understand why they adored him. And one can understand the valid reasons why the Government, concerned about his people, would twice set him free.

But the second time he came out of jail he found something new: his regiment had been dissolved, and his men broken up and sent to remote units; some in Sonora, others in Chihuahua, others in Tampico. Juan Pablo, a warehoused general with no more capital than the Colt at his left side, then felt the nostalgia for his little plot of homeland, and his old fighting buddies, with his freedom more limited now than when he was a blacksmith, and when the only tyrants he had on his head were the poor devil of the *La Simpatia* village store, (odds and ends), and the three or four "cats" holstered by the municipal guards, good fellows generally, if one did not mess around with them. Juan Pablo recognized this now, sighing and turning his nostrils to the west.

One evening, a certain individual who a few days before had been occupying the place in front of Juan him in the restaurant scratches his head, sighs, and mumbles: "Those '*civilistas*' are robbing us". Juan Pablo, brows furrowed, looks at the man who spoke, and is quiet. The next day: "The '*civilistas*' have grabbed our crops; after we have sowed the earth and watered it with our own blood". Juan Pablo leaves his plate for a second, touches the left half of his nose, and scratches his ankle. Then he eats and is quiet.

Another day: "The '*civilistas*' are not just annoying flies any more. Now they have sat down and taken over the table and they throw us, as if we were dogs, the leftovers from their meal". Juan Pablo, finally impatient, asks: "But, who are those sons of ..., who are those '*civilistas*'?"

"Those who have stolen our land, those lazy bastards".

The light went on in Juan Pablo's head.

18.13: Government "civilistas"

The next day it is he who speaks: "It would be good to get rid of those tyrants".

His friend takes him that night to a secret meeting in the sinister suburbs. There the conspirators are meeting. One, more respectable, speaks with sober tones on the theme that it is time to give the people their motherland.

Absorbed and unaware, Juan Pablo does not realize that the doors and windows are gradually filling up with shiny rifle barrels.

A harsh voice: "Hands up!"

Everyone puts them up. Juan Pablo also puts his hands up: or better said he raises his right hand vigorously, his fist wrapped around his Colt.

"Surrender or we shoot!" roars out a voice so close to him that it makes him leap backward violently. And Juan Pablo replies by emptying the chambers of his revolver.

In the midst of the white smoke, between the flash of the firing, under the dim light of the greasy lantern, Juan Pablo, his hair twitching, his teeth showing white, smiles in his apotheosis.

When the firing ends and there is no human figure left in the dim corners of the doors and windows, the conspirators themselves fall on him like a bolt of lightning. Hands and feet tied, Juan Pablo keeps smiling. And so there is no idle mocking when Juan Pablo says that he has been face to face with death so often that he is used to seeing her head-on without having his legs tremble.

If for the last six hours he has been rooted in his fabric chair, with his vigorous head sunk in his strong and sunburned hands, it is because something more cruel than death is destroying him. Juan Pablo still hears: "Treason! ...

18.14: Fighting by José Guadalupe Posada

treason!", as one by one the slow and steady ringing of the bells announce the coming of the dawn. "But treason against whom, Holy Mother of the Refugio?" Without opening his eyes he is looking at the little altar mounted on one of the walls of his little room; a religious figure of Our Lady of Refugio, two handfuls of withered flowers and a little oil lamp that sheds its yellow and funeral light. Then two large tears come to his eyes.

"Impossible!" Juan Pablo leaps with the energy of a wounded lion... "Impossible". But the clear insight of those facing death takes him back to a vivid scene of his infancy, in a noisy hut, black with soot, a great fire, and a little boy with unsure hands who cannot hold the tongs and drops the red-hot iron... Then a cry of pain and his eyes fill with tears... On the other side of the forge an old, barechested man stands tall, dried out like the bark of an oak tree, bearded with great hanks of hair like burned ixtle plant fibers. "What is this, Juan Pablo? Men don't cry!"

In hollow phrases wrapped in journalistic hypocrisy, the press said that the executed prisoner died with great serenity. The reporters added that the last words of the culprit were these: "Don't fire at my face", and that he pronounced these words with such authority that they seemed more like an order than a plea. It seemed that the executioner's squad did their job well. Juan Pablo jerked forward, slipped, and fell with his face to the stars, without crumpling, lying straight out. That's all the reporters saw. I saw more. I saw how in the glassy eyes of Juan Pablo two little diamond drops timidly grew and grew, and spread, as if they wanted to climb to the sky ... yes, two stars...

18.15: Execution of Juan Pablo

19: Early 20C. Nationalism, Ethnic relationships, the Role of Women

20th Century Cultural Fragmentation

With the coming of the new century it became more and more difficult to see clear patterns between historical trends, major cultural movements, and their manifestation in the arts and literature. The Mexican Revolution gives us a clear-cut case in which this is still possible, but that phenomenon was limited to one country even if it was closely watched in many others. Looking at Latin America as a whole in the 20th Century, we find that there is no single movement, such as Modernism or Romanticism, that permeates the cultural life of almost all the nations and which has a clear pattern of influence in the arts as well as the history of the period.

In a very general sense, one can identify some of the major elements of this fragmentation as follows:

1. An escapist literature (also present in the arts), which is a sort of heir to the Modernist trend to emphasize the esthetic element over content, to such a point that in its extreme manifestation the form is all and content nothing. In painting this current is represented by abstract art, especially in its more radical forms.

2. A post-modernist, or anti-modernist current, which is a reaction to the excessive estheticism of Modernism, and in which simplicity and sincerity are dominant. In painting, primitive or naive art provides a parallel.

3. Literature of fantasy and imagination, including themes that are psychological and surrealistic. Sometimes authors use historical myths, including pre-Columbian ones. In the arts, surrealism closely parallels this literary current.

4. The literature of the Mexican Revolution (examined previously), which is closely associated with Mexican muralism.

5. Social protest and revolutionary literature in various forms, accompanied by a similar current in painting, including Mexican muralism.

6. Feminist literature.

7. Many other currents.

The world of art continued to be influenced by various European currents which sometimes had relationships to the fragmented trends listed above and sometimes did not. France continued to be the principal source of these movements, which included traditional academic painting, Impressionism, Expressionism, Cubism, and Surrealism. Many (if not most) major Latin American painters spent time in Europe (mainly France), and would return to their native Latin American country inspired by the latest European movement. At times these fresh infusions died out, and at times they caught on or became modified by local movements. So it should not surprise us that a major Mexican Muralist like Diego Rivera should have gone through a Cubist phase, and another in which Surrealism is evident.

The Impact of Latin American Nationalism

A major force in Latin America had always been nationalism. It grew out of regional pride in things local or American, in contrast to those ideas and things brought over from the Old World. In the Colonial period there was a distinct current of local pride among the *criollos* which set them apart from the authorities sent from Spain or Portugal. This nativism, as we have seen, was a factor in creating the split which led to Independence. The Independence struggle created national symbols and myths in the form of the military heroes, their exploits, paintings of these heroes and their battles, flags, anthems, national crests and seals, and literature that exalted all of these things.

The Mexican Revolution, although limited in its impact to one country, permitted an outpouring of this nationalist spirit and its expression in both art and literature. Parallel movements sprung up in other countries, especially those where pride in things Indigenous or Pre-Columbian was allowed to break through the veneer imposed by the elites who continued to focus their primary attention on Europe.

19.1: The U.S. looks South

Economic nationalism was also present in the form of resentment over foreign exploitation of national resources, most notably those non-renewable ones for which it seemed the powerful international "centers" of trade could set the price paid to the "peripheries". Oil in particular was closely linked to economic nationalism, and one of the major goals of the Mexican Revolution was to wrest control of Mexico's oil away from the US and British companies which had extracted it for so many years under the Díaz dictatorship. Economic nationalism surrounding oil was also present in Venezuela, Brazil and Argentina at various

labor, survive in the latifundium. The judge, the subprefect, the constable, the teacher, the tax collector, are vassals to the feudalism of large landownership. The law cannot prevail against the *gamonales*. The official who insists on imposing the law, will be abandoned and sacrificed by the central power structure, around which the influences of *gamonalismo* are always omnipotent, whether they act directly, or through the parliament, and are equally efficient whichever path they take. ...

19.4: Gamonal

The oldest and most evident defeat is, without a doubt, that which reduces the protection of the Indigenous peoples to a matter of ordinary administration. From the days of Spanish colonial legislation, the wise and tidy ordinances, drafted after conscientious surveys, show themselves to be totally fruitless. The prolific output of the Republic, from the days of Independence, in matters of decrees, laws, and other measures seeking to protect the Indians against exploitation and abuse, is at least large and considerable. But today's *gamonal*, just the like *encomendero* of yesterday, has nevertheless very little to fear from administrative theory. He knows that things are different in practice.

The individualistic nature of the legislation of the Republic has favored, without a doubt, the absorption of Indigenous property by the latifundium system. The Indians' situation, in this sense, was more realistically addressed by Spanish legislation. But legal reforms have no greater practical value than administrative reforms, when faced with a feudalism which is intact in its economic structure. ...

The assumption that the Indigenous problem is an ethnical problem is fed by the oldest repertoire of imperialistic ideas. The concept of inferior races served the white West well in its task of expansion and conquest. To hope for the emancipation of the Indigenous on the basis of the mixing of the aboriginal race with that of white immigrants, is an anti-sociological naiveté... The Asian peoples, who are not one bit superior to the Indigenous peoples, have assimilated Western culture, insofar as its dynamic and creative aspects are concerned, in an admirable way, without transfusions of European blood. ...

The tendency to consider the Indigenous problem as a moral problem, embodies a conception that is liberal, humanitarian, nineteenth centuryish, enlightened, which in the political order of the West animates and motivates the "leagues of the Rights of Man". The antislavery conferences and societies, which in Europe have denounced more or less fruitlessly the crimes of the colonizers, are born from this tendency, which has always relied too much on the calls to civilization's moral sense... The humanitarian preaching has neither stopped nor impeded imperialism in Europe, nor has it modified its methods.

The struggle against imperialism no longer relies on anything but solidarity and the strength of the movements for emancipation of the colonial masses ...

In the field of reason and morality some centuries ago one could locate, with greater energy, or at least with greater authority, religious action. This crusade did not create, nevertheless, anything but laws and other measures which were very wisely inspired. The fate of the Indians did not vary substantially ... Despite this, religious preaching had more evident possibilities for success than liberal preaching. Religious preaching appealed to the exalted and operational Spanish Catholicism, while the former attempted to gain the ear of the insufficient and formal local American liberalism.

But today the hope for an ecclesiastical solution is undoubtedly the most obsolete and anti-historical of all. Those who represent it are not even concerned with their distant (so distant!) teachers in obtaining a new declaration of the rights of the Indians, with adequate authorities and ordinances, but rather they are concerned with charging the missionary with the function of mediating between the Indian and the gamonal. This task the Church could not accomplish in a medieval order, when its spiritual and intellectual capacity could be measured in churchmen like Father Las Casas. So with what instruments can it count on to prosper now? In this sense, the Adventist evangelistic missions have moved ahead of the Catholic clergy ...

The notion that the problem of the Indian is an educational one, does not seem to be supported by a strictly and authentically pedagogical criterion. Pedagogy today must take into consideration, more than ever before, the social and economic factors. The modern pedagogue knows perfectly well that education is not simply a matter of schools and didactic methods. The social and economic environment inexorably conditions the work of the teacher. *Gamonalism* is fundamentally adverse to the education of the Indian; his survival requires maintaining the ignorance

19.5: Indigenous

of the Indian as much as the cultivation of alcoholism. The modern school is incompatible with the feudal latifundium. The mechanics of serfdom would totally annul the actions of the school, even if the school through some miracle inconceivable within the existing social reality and the feudal atmosphere, might be able to conserve its purely pedagogical mission. Even the most efficient and grandiose moral teaching would not be able to create those miracles ...

The pedagogical solution, proposed by many in perfect good faith, is not officially discarded. The educationalists are, I repeat, those who can least think of making it independent of socio-economic reality. At the present moment such a solution does not exist, except as a vague and unformed suggestion, for which. no institution or doctrine assumes responsibility.

The new analysis consists of seeking the Indian problem in the problem of land.

The Land problem

Those of us who from the socialist viewpoint study and define the problem of the Indian, begin by stating that the humanitarian and philanthropic viewpoints are obsolete in that, as a prolongation of the apostolic battle of Father Las Casas, they are based on an ancient pro-Indian campaign. Our first effort attempts to establish the basically economic nature of the problem. We rebel, basically, against the instinctive (and defensive) tendency of the *criollo* to reduce it to an exclusively administrative, pedagogical, ethnic or moral problem, in order to avoid at all costs the plane of economics. For this reason, the most absolutely incorrect of the reproaches which can be leveled against us is that of lyricism or literaturism. By placing the socio-economic issues in center-stage, we assume an attitude that is as far removed from lyricism and literaturism as possible. We are not content with restoring the Indians' right to education, culture, progress, love and heaven. We begin by restoring, categorically, the Indians' right to land. This restoration is a totally materialistic one, and should be enough to keep anyone from confusing us with the inheritors or imitators of the evangelistical preaching of the great Spanish priest who, for our part, we greatly and feverously admire despite our materialism.

Nor does this problem of land, whose solidarity with the problem of the Indian is all too evident, cause us to diminish, reconcile or attenuate it opportunistically. Quite the opposite. For my part, I try to lay out the problem in terms that are absolutely unequivocal and unadulterated.

The agrarian problem can be presented, above all, as the problem of the liquidation of feudalism in Peru. This liquidation should have been carried out by the demo-bourgeois regime which was formally established by the independence revolution. But in Peru in the last hundred years we have not really had a true middle class or a true capitalistic class. The ancient feudal class, camouflaged or disguised as the republican middle class, has kept its strength ... And the fact is that during the century of the republic, the large agrarian land holdings have been strengthened and increased despite the theoretical liberalism of our Constitution, and of the practical requirements of the development of our capitalist economy.

The surviving expressions of feudalism are two: latifundium and serfdom ... We cannot liquidate the serfdom that burdens the Indigenous race without liquidating the latifundium.

Once we lay out the agrarian problem in Peru this way, there is no room for erroneous deformations. The economic-social (and therefore political) problem emerges in all its magnitude from the domain of those men who act in that plane of actions

19.6: Latifundium

and ideas. And it is fruitless to try and convert it, for example, into a technical-agricultural problem in the domain of the agronomists.

No one denies that the liberal solution to this problem would, in accordance with the individualist ideology, be the breaking up of the latifundiums in favor of small landownership. And this approach is not utopian, or heretical, or revolutionary, or Bolshevik, or vanguardist, but rather constitutionally orthodox, democratic, capitalist, and middle-class ... It has its origin in the liberal ideas which inspire the constitutional Statues of all the demo-middle class States...

Consistent with my ideological position, I think that the time for attempting in the liberal method, the individualistic formula in Peru has now passed. Leaving aside doctrinal reasons, I fundamentally consider the following incontestable and concrete factor to give a special nature to our agricultural problem: the survival of the community and of practical socialism in the lives and agriculture of the Indigenous peoples.

The Changing role of women

In a manner parallel to ethnic relationships, the role of women in Latin America has also changed, with an acceleration of this change in recent years. Through the Colonial period and much of the National period, relationships between the sexes were defined mainly by the concept of *machismo*, and the related idea of *marianismo*.

Machismo is the exaggerated predominance taken by the male in Latin American society. The term is derived from the word *macho*, which is literally "a male animal". It is a celebration of man's social and sexual predominance, power and virility. It has its roots in medieval notions of chivalry and honor and in the need for males to give special protection to women. In its less benevolent aspects it can become male aggressiveness and the felt need to control women. Tellingly, a romantic affair is frequently described by a Latin male as a "conquest" of the female. The Iberian Colonial systems had legal, religious and economic provisions which insured that women were kept in a subordinate status. It was common for women to have to get the permission of their fathers or husbands to acquire real estate or to travel abroad.

Marianismo is a related term derived from the Virgin Mary, and it portrays women as sexually pure, spiritually superior, and morally above men. Women are thus seen as the guardians of values and propriety, especially in the family circle. As good mothers and wives they are required to be tolerant and forgiving of the strayings of their sons, fathers, brothers and husbands, who are the bearers of the *macho* tradition.

19.7: Marianismo

These two inter-related cultural traditions for centuries worked to keep women in their assigned place. For upper class women this meant the home (as daughter or mother), with very few professional alternatives, the convent being the principal one. Middle and lower class women had somewhat greater social and economic freedom, but their activities were usually linked to their husband's profession in an assisting capacity (farm worker, small landowner, shopkeeper, craftsman, etc).

Gradually certain professions opened up to women, with teaching and the health professions being the first. The entry into the world of the office and factory was slow, as was the political arena. Despite these obstacles, extraordinary women have had great impact in Latin America. We can cite as an example the influence of Evita Perón in Argentina, who was a key factor in the rise to power of her husband Juan Perón in 1943, and who played an important role in transforming Argentina until her early death in 1952 at age 33. Among other things, she was responsible for the woman's vote and for initiating social legislation which greatly benefited the urban worker and marginalized groups in Argentina.

In the world of letters women have always played a role, going back as far as Sor Juana in the Colonial era, although the small number of women authors up until the 20th Century suggests that it was difficult for women to break through society's restrictions in order to find the freedom to express themselves through the arts. The first Latin American winner of a Nobel Prize for literature was the Chilean Gabriela Mistral, and poetry of high esthetic and sensual quality has been written by authors such as Delmira Agustini.

Gabriela Mistral (Chile, 1889-1957)

The first Nobel Literature prize-winner in Latin America, Mistral was a poet of chaste love and sadness. Her early poems dealing with love and tragedy were the product of her first love, a young man who killed himself, apparently over a financial problem. This great tragedy in Mistral's life, at the age of twenty, was the inspiration for *Sonnets of Death*. She never married, and eventually the tragic love of her youth slowly slipped into the mists of time until Mistral admitted she no longer could remember the face of her lover.

19.8: Mistral

Her love then becomes focused on children, sometimes her imaginary babies, sometimes the children of friends, and sometimes her students. Love becomes maternal, but with a tinge of sadness over not ever being able to have her own children. But religion was always present to console her. She was a school teacher for many years, first in the rural environment in which she grew up (she started to teach at age thirteen), and then later in the Ministry of Education, where her imaginative ideas (including the use of visual aids) influenced several generations of Chilean teachers. The tenderness, the beauty and the simplicity of her poems won her worldwide acclaim, and in 1945 she received the Nobel Prize. She carried out various diplomatic and cultural assignments for her government and various international organizations. She taught and lectured in various US universities, and died in New York in 1957.

Because of the simplicity and directness of her poetry, Mistral fits within the "post-modernist" (or "anti-modernist") current of 20th Century Latin American literature.

Rocking by Gabriela Mistral

The sea with its thousands of waves
  rocks, divine.
Listening to the loving seas,
  I rock my baby.

The errant wind in the night
  rocks the wheat.
Listening to the loving winds,
  I rock my baby.

God the Father his thousands of worlds
  rocks without a sound.
Feeling his hand in the shadow
  I rock my baby.

19.9: Rocking

Great Dream by Gabriela Mistral

Like a child sleeping
don't make me think of it.
He slept thus in my inner self
with much lassitude.

  I took him out of the dream
and all his wishes,
and now he has gone back
to sleep again.

  His forehead is upright
and his temples too.
His feet are two mussels
and his sides are fish.

  I can hear his breathing
like running water;
his eyelashes flutter
like leaves of the maiten tree.

I tell them to leave him
well alone just as he is
until he wakes
by his own desire...

His sleep is aided
by the roof and the door frame.
the Earth who is Cybele,
the mother who is woman.

I wish I could learn
to sleep since I have forgotten
and one learns so many
unfaithful things when awake.

And we go on sleeping
as a gift from him,
this dream is a great one
until the dawning...

19.10: Lovers

The Sonnets of Death by Gabriela Mistral

From the cold niche in which men placed you,
I will bring you down to the warm and humble earth.
They did not know that I will sleep there
and that we will dream on the same pillow.

I will lay you down in the sunny earth with a
mother's sweetness for her sleeping child,
and the earth will be the cradle's softness
when it receives your pained child's body.

Later I will sprinkle soft dust and rose powder,
and in the light blue dust of the moon,
the airy remains will become imprisoned.

I will leave singing my beautiful revenges
because in that hidden depth no one's hand
will enter to dispute with me your handful of bones!

This long fatigue grows greater each day,
and the soul will tell the body that it will not go on
dragging its mass along the rosy path,
where humans walk, happy with living...

You will sense their brisk digging next to you,
when another sleeping one comes to the quiet city.
I will wait until they have covered me fully...
and then we will talk for an eternity!

Only then you will understand why, young
your still strong flesh and bones
had to go down, untired, to sleep.

Light will shine on your destiny, now dark;
you will know that our alliance was made in the stars
and, the enormous covenant broken, you had to die...

Evil hands took your life since the day
when, at a signal of the stars, you left the nursery
covered with lilies. All flourished in delight.
But evil hands tragically entered it...

I said to the Lord: "By all the mortal paths they take him.
Beloved shadow which they know not how to guide!
Pull him away, Lord, from those fatal hands
or sink him in that long sleep you know how to bestow!

I cannot shout out, I cannot follow him!
His ship is pushed along by the dark wind of storm.
Return him to my arms or cut him down in the flower of youth."

The rosy ship of his life halted...
Who says that I do not know of love, that I had no pity?
You, who will judge me, will understand, Lord!

I have no solitude by **Gabriela Mistral**

The night is desolation
from the mountains to the sea.
But I, who rock you,
I have no solitude!

The sky is desolation
if the moon falls into the sea.
But I, who hold you,
I have no solitude!

19.11: Solitude

The world is desolation
and the flesh sadly goes.
But I, who hug you,
I have no solitude!

Bread by **Gabriela Mistral**

They left bread on the table,
half burned, half white,
squeezed on top and opened
with brilliant white crumbs.

It seems new or never seen to me,
and something else that he has not fed me,
but turning over the crust, as if asleep,
I have forgotten its feel and smell.

It smells of my mother as she breast-fed me,
it smells of three valleys I have traveled:
Aconcagua, Pátzcuaro, Elqui,
and of my inner soul when I sing.

There are no other smells in the farm
and that is why it has called me thus;
nor is there anyone in the house
but that bread opened up on the plate,
who with its body recognizes me
and I with mine recognize it.

It has been eaten in all climates
the same bread in a hundred brothers;
bread of Coquimbo, bread of Oaxaca,
bread of Santa Ana and of Santiago.

In my infancy I knew
the shape of the sun, the fish, or the halo,
and my hand knew its crumb
and the warmth of the feathered chick...

19.12: Children

Then I forgot it until this day
in which the two of us found each other,
I with my body of old Sara
and he with his of five years.

Dead friends with whom I have eaten it
in other valleys feel the vapor
of a bread milled in September
and in a Castilian August reaped.

It is another, the one we ate
in lands where they laid down.
I open the bread and give them its warmth;
I turn it over and I give them its breath.

My hand is full with it
and I look upon my hand;
I let out a repentant cry
for forgetting so many years,
and my face becomes aged
or is reborn with this discovery.

Since the house is empty
let us, the re-found ones, be together,
on this table without meat or fruit,
the two in this human silence,
until we shall once again be one
and our day has reached its end...

The sleepless one by Gabriela Mistral

As the night thickens
and the standing lie down,
and the surrendered straighten out,
I hear him climb the stairs.

It matters not that they do not hear him
and only I sense him.
Why should he be heard
by the sleeplessness of another servant!

In a breath of mine he climbs
and I suffer until he arrives
a crazy cascade which his destiny
sometimes drops and others climbs
and a crazy feverish thorn
knocks like castanets against my door.

I don't get up, I don't open my eyes,
and I follow his whole form.

19.13: The sleepless one

An instant, like the damned,
under the night we have a truce;
but I hear him go down again
as if in an eternal tide.

He comes and goes all night long
an absurd gift, given and returned,
a medusa lifted by the waves
who now goes away, and now comes near.
From my bed I help him
with the breath I still have left,
to keep him from searching aimlessly
or hurting himself in the shadows.

The steps of silent wood
echo like glass to me.
I know on which ones he rests,
and asks himself, and answers himself.
I hear where the faithful wood,
like my soul, creaks for him,
and I know his mature and final step
which was going to come and never comes...

My house suffers his body
like a flame that toasts him dark.
I feel the warmth of his face
-burning brick- against my door.
I test an unknown saying:
I suffer life, I die alert,
and in this trance of death's agony
my strengths ebb with his strengths!

The next day I rest in vain
with his cheeks and my tongue
tracing the fogged glass
in the mirror of the stairs.
And my soul is calmed a few hours
until the blind night falls.

The vagabond who crosses it
tells it to me like a fable.
He only barely carries his flesh,
he is only a little of what once was,
and the look in his eyes

sometimes chills and sometimes burns.

If you see him, don't question him;
just tell him not to return,
that his memory should not ascend,
so that he may sleep and I may sleep.
Kill the name which like the wind
In its routes darkens
And not look upon my door,
erect and red like a bonfire!

Delmira Agustini (Uruguay, 1886-1914)

She too was a poet of love, but of a very different tone from Mistral's. Agustini grew up in a well-to-do Uruguayan family and was educated at home by tutors. She could read and write by age four, and by ten was writing verses. Her short life was tragic: she married young and divorced almost immediately (she returned from her honeymoon with the remark that she found the experience extremely boring). But she continued to see her former husband, and in one of their secret meetings in a hotel her husband killed her and then himself.

19.14: Agustini

Agustini's poetry is frankly and openly erotic, although it is always accompanied by expressions of spiritual love. She dedicated some of her work to Eros, the god of love, but the depth of her feeling has suggested a comparison with mystical poets such as Saint Teresa of Avila. The intensity of her spiritual and physical love is clearly evident in her poetry and finds form in the esthetic nature of her work.

Wings by Delmira Agustini

I had...two wings!...
Two wings
That in Azure lived like two sidereal roots...
Two wings,
with all the miracles of life, of death
and of illusion. Two wings,
thundering
like ships sails in a fugitive star;
two wings,
like two firmaments
with storms, with calm and with stars...

Do you remember the glory of my wings?
The golden ringing of the bells
the rhythm, the unspeakable
shades of stored-up treasure
all Iris, but a new Iris
obscuring and divine,
who will be adored by the plain pupils of the Future
(The pupils matured in full light!)... the flight...

The burning flight, devouring and unique,
which for a long time tormented the skies,
and awoke suns, meteors, storms,
gave brilliance to the rays and the stars;
and the amplitude: had
warmth and shade for all the World,
and even could incubate a beyond.

19.15: Wings

One rare day
fainting to earth,
I slept in the plush depths of this forest...
I dreamed divine things!...
A smile of yours awoke me, I think...
And I could not feel my wings!...
My wings?...
I saw them fall apart between my arms...
It was like a thaw!

Nocturne by **Delmira Agustini**

Linked in the night to the lake of your soul,
one could say a weaving of glass and of calm
knitted by the great spiders of sleeplessness.

Cream of sacrificial water in vases of alabaster;
mirror of purity which gives brilliance to the stars
and reflects the chasm of Life in a sky...

I am the errant swan of the bloody trails
and I go staining the lakes and soaring into flight.

19.16: Nocturne

Your Love by **Delmira Agustini**

Your love, slave, is like a very strong sun:
golden gardener of life,
fiery gardener of death,
and the prolific poem of my life.

Crow's beak with odor of roses,
sweet stinger of delight
your tongue is. Your mysterious hands
are claws gloved with caresses.

Your eyes are cruel midnights,
black honeycombs of cursed sweetness
which exhaust themselves in my harshness;

chrysalis of a future flight
in your magnificent and dark embrace
bewitched tower of my solitude.

19.17: Lovers

20: Guatemalan Reform/Revolution

Guatemala's Reform/Revolution

The Mexican Revolution, although never intended for export, had echoes in much of Latin America, and its immediate neighbor Guatemala, provides us with a good example.

There were certainly enough parallels: Guatemala had been ruled for many years by a caudillo who had favored foreign investors (mainly U.S.). Like Mexico, Guatemala has a large Indigenous population which was kept marginalized from active participation in the economic benefits of Guatemala's export economy. There were also numerous *Mestizos*, some of whom made up a small but restive middle class.

20.1: United Fruit Co.

The old caudillo, General Jorge Ubico, was overthrown in 1944 by a coalition of the middle class, students, and junior military officers who were disgusted with the corruption of the old regime. This coalition was united by a desire for reform and to limit the privileges given to the principal foreign investor, United Fruit Company, which owned much of the banana-producing land in the country.

20.2: Bananas

The first president in Guatemala's Revolution was Juan José Arévalo, a reformist and university professor who derived much of his inspiration from the Mexican model, although the Guatemalan case was never to go to the lengths that the Mexican Revolution did. In light of the Mexican Revolution (and the Cuban and Nicaraguan Revolutions which came later), it almost seems more appropriate to label the Guatemalan case "reform" rather than "revolution".

To break the hold of United Fruit Company and other foreign investors, the Arévalo government set in motion a land reform program which would nationalize unused land and turn it over to landless groups at the bottom of the socioeconomic pyramid; the owners of the land would be compensated by the government based on the value they had placed on the land for tax purposes. United Fruit had considerable unused land which they argued was needed as a reserve for future expansion and also in case their banana trees came down with disease and had to be replaced. As was typical in such cases, United Fruit had undervalued their land for tax purposes, and stood to take a significant loss if the land reform program went through. The Arévalo regime also proposed social and labor legislation which would have increased taxation and labor costs to large landowners.

Arévalo was succeeded by Jacobo Arbenz, a retired army officer who continued and intensified the Revolution's programs. Arbenz was something of an anomaly, a military man who believed in the need for significant change and who made many enemies within the military as well as the Guatemalan elite.

20.3: Arbenz

The United Fruit Company had friends in high places, including the Dulles brothers in the Eisenhower administration. John Foster Dulles at the time was Secretary of State, and Allen was Director of the Central Intelligence Agency. Company officials lobbied hard, and they persuaded the Eisenhower administration that Arbenz was a dangerous leftist who was threatening U.S. interests in Central America and the Caribbean. The U.S. Government cut off military assistance to Guatemala and imposed an arms embargo. In response, Arbenz asked for help from the Soviet bloc and received shipments of arms from Poland.

To the Eisenhower people this was the final provocative act which confirmed their suspicions that the Revolution was becoming a Soviet beachhead in the Hemisphere. The President then authorized the Central Intelligence Agency, supported by the U.S. military, to work with dissident Guatemalan officers to bring down the Arbenz Government. With support from the Somoza regime in Nicaragua the CIA armed a group of exiled Guatemalan military men led by Colonel Castillo Armas, who entered Guatemala at the head of a small group. The Guatemalan army refused to repel the force of exiles, or give weapons to workers and peasants who were willing to fight for Arbenz. Under an intense propaganda and psychological warfare effort (headed by E. Howard Hunt, later of Watergate fame), the Arbenz government collapsed in 1954.

Colonel Castillo Armas was installed as president, and launched a counter-revolution which quickly returned nationalized lands to the United Fruit Company and other large landowners. The Guatemalan attempt at Mexican-style Revolution, or even a more modest reform, was over. Guatemala began a long

20.4: J. F. Dulles

period of conservative presidents under direct or indirect military influence, a pattern which has continued to this day.

Like the Mexican Revolution, the Guatemalan had an element of cultural nationalism, although it never had a chance to develop fully. As we shall see below, part of this cultural nationalism focused on the Mayan roots of most of Guatemala's population and on the long period when they were under either Spanish or Creole control and exploitation.

Art: Surrealism and the Fantastic

In this period Latin American art and literature was strongly influenced by European Surrealism, which was blended with local currents of the fantastic and the imaginatively "real but unreal". Surrealism stressed the world of dreams, of imagination, and of the hidden psychological currents in each person's inner self. These features appealed to many writers and painters in Latin America who saw it as an outlet for their creativity. This emphasis on surrealism and the fantastic was the basis for the "magic realism" which has been so influential in recent years.

In many cases the surrealists drew on local myths and legends as the basis for their exploration of the world of fantasy and psychology. One fruitful source of these myths was pre-Columbian history and the oral traditions still to be found among the Indigenous peoples, especially in the areas of the old Aztec, Maya and Inca empires.

This Surrealist-Indigenous current was also linked to *Indigenismo*, which was an attempt by socially conscious writers and painters to focus attention on the Indigenous peoples after over three centuries of cultural neglect by the European-oriented elites. Indigenismo was a major element in the Mexican muralist movement and also shows up in the writings of the Guatemalan Miguel Angel Asturias.

Asturias: Maya Magic and Surrealism

Miguel Angel Asturias (Guatemala, 1899-1974) was a politically committed writer who used the rich Maya cultural heritage, with its myths and legends, to give a magical and surrealistic touch to his novels and stories. As a boy he had to move from Guatemala City to the countryside because of political problems his father was having with Guatemala's military dictator of the day. Living in a small village among the Maya, he had close contact with them, and they shared with him their oral traditions, especially the *Popol Vuh* and *Chilam Balam*.

After obtaining his law degree (with a thesis on the social problems of the Indians), he lived in Paris where he studied Maya ethnography with the best European experts. Working with them, he prepared a Spanish translation of the Popol Vuh. He used his scientific and linguistic research to accumulate the information on the Maya which appears in much of his later work, such as *Legends of Guatemala* and *Men of Corn*. In this latter work corn plays a dual role: it provides profits for the foreign exploiters and their upper-class local collaborators in Guatemala, but corn is also the focus of religious ceremonies and a basic source of food for the Indian masses of the country.

In the Paris of the 1920's Asturias had many contacts with the new intellectual currents then in vogue, especially Surrealism, and this too influenced his later work. He knew André Breton, one of the founders of the Surrealist movement, as well as Pablo Picasso.

In 1945 he published his novel *Señor Presidente*, which is one of the sharpest literary criticisms of Latin American militarism ever written. The Guatemalan reformist presidents Arévalo and Arbenz gave him support and diplomatic posts.

20.5: Asturias

But he was forced to go into exile when Arbenz fell, and these circumstances provided him with additional themes: foreign meddling in his country, and the exploitation of the banana workers. Asturias' writings, based on his special blend of scholarly research, imagination and political commitment, won him the Nobel Prize for Literature in 1967; this was the first for a Latin American novelist.

The story which follows, *The Legend of La Tatuana*, is from the book *Legends of Guatemala*, and takes place in a world that is part dreamland, part reality, and part magical universe of Asturias' surrealistic imagination and fantasy.

The Legend of la Tatuana by Miguel Angel Asturias

The Almond Master has a red beard, and he was one of those priests the white men would touch, believing them to be made of gold because of the rich clothes they wore. He knows the secret of the plants that cure all illness, and the vocabulary of obsidian (the stone that talks), and he can read the hieroglyphics of the constellations.

He is the tree that showed up one dawn in the forest where it grows, without it ever having been planted by anyone, as if it had been carried by ghosts. The tree that walks... The tree that counts the years of four hundred days by the moons it has seen, and he has seen many moons, like all trees, and he came, already ancient, from the Place of Abundance.

When the moon of the Owl-Fisherman was full (this was the name of one of the twenty months of the year of four hundred days), the Almond Master divided up his soul between the roads. The roads were four in number, and they went in different directions toward the four distant corners of the sky. The black corner:

night of sorcery. The green corner: spring storms. The red corner: Guacamayo, or tropical ecstasy. The white corner: promise of new lands. Four roads.

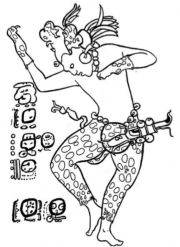

20.6: **Almond Master**

"Little Road, Little Road!..." said a white dove to the White Road, but the White Road did not hear the dove. The dove wanted the road to give up the Master's soul, the soul that cured one of dreams. Doves and children have that disease.

"Little Road, Little Road!..." said a red heart to the Red Road; but the Red Road did not hear the heart. The heart wanted to distract the road so it would forget the Master's soul. Hearts, like thieves, do not return things that are forgotten.

"Little Road, Little Road!..." said a green vine to the Green Road, but the Green Road did not hear the vine. The vine wanted the soul of the Master to recover some of the debt it owed of leaves and shade.

How many moons did the roads spend wandering?

The speediest, the Black Road, the road no one spoke to, stopped in the city, crossed the plaza, and in the merchants' quarter, in exchange for a short rest, he gave the Master's soul to the Merchant of Jewels without price.

It was the hour of the white cats. They wandered from one place to the next. The clouds seemed like clothes on the clothesline of the sky.

When the Master found out what the Black Road had done, he once again took human form, stripping himself of his vegetable form in a creek which bubbled forth under the blushing moon like the almond flower, and he walked to the city.

He reached the valley after a day's travel, in the first hours of the evening, at a time when the flocks were coming in, conversing with the shepherds, who answered his questions with monosyllables, astonished as if seeing an apparition, at his green tunic and his red beard.

In the city he headed west. Men and women surrounded the public fountains. The water sounded like kisses as it filled the jars. And guided by the shadows, in the merchants' quarter he found the part of his soul which the Black Road had sold to the Merchant, who was smoking in a corner, and he offered a hundred bushels of pearls for his soul.

The Merchant smiled at the madness of the Master. A hundred bushels of. pearls? No, his jewels had no price.

20.7: The Merchant

The Master increased the offer. Merchants always say no until their level is reached. He would give him emeralds, as large as corn ears, by the hundreds of measures, until he would have a lake of emeralds.

The Merchant smiled at the madness of the Master. A lake of emeralds? No, his jewels had no price.

He would give him amulets, deer eyes to call the water, feathers for protection against the tempests, marihuana for his tobacco...

The Merchant said no. His jewels had no price, and besides, why keep talking? He wanted that little piece of soul to trade, in a slave market, for the most beautiful slave he could find.

And it was all useless, useless for the Master to offer and talk, despite all he said, of his desire to recover his soul. Merchants have no heart.

A thread of tobacco smoke separates reality from dreams, black cats from white cats, and the Merchant from the strange buyer, who as the left shook his sandals on the hinge of the door. Dust has curses.

After a year of four hundred days (according to the legend) the Merchant was crossing the roads of the mountains. He was returning from distant lands, accompanied by a slave bought with the soul of the Master, and by the bird in flower, whose beak sought drops of honey in the hyacinths, and by a retinue of thirty mounted servants.

"You have no idea" said the Merchant to the slave, bridling his horse, "how you are going to live in the city! Your house will be a palace and all my servants will be at your orders, and I will be the last servant, if you order it!"

"There" he continued with his face half bathed in sunlight, "everything will be yours. You are a jewel, and I am the Merchant of Jewels without price! You are worth the little piece of a soul which I did not exchange for a lake of emeralds!... Together in a hammock we will watch the sun set and rise, we will do nothing, listening to the stories of a cunning old lady who knows my destiny. My destiny, she says, is in the fingers of a giant hand, and she will know your destiny also, if you ask her for it."

The slave was naked. Over her breasts, down to her legs, wound her black hair wrapped into a single braid, like a snake. The Merchant was dressed in gold, his shoulders warmed by a cloak of goats' wool. He had malaria and he was in love, and to the coldness of his disease was linked the trembling of his heart. And the thirty mounted servants reached his retina like the figures in a dream.

Suddenly, large isolated drops of rain began to spray the road, and he could hear, far off in the distance, on the slopes of the hills, the cries of the shepherds who were gathering up their flocks, fearful of the tempest. The riders stepped up their pace to reach shelter, but they had no time: behind the first large drops, the wind whipped the clouds, bringing violence to the jungle until they reached the valley, and sped down and threw themselves on the wet blankets of haze. The first lightning flashes illuminated the landscape, as if they were the explosions of a mad photographer who was taking snapshots of the storm.

20.8: Maya Gods

In the midst of the horses which ran with fright, their reins broken, their legs agile, their unruly manes into the wind, and their ears pinned back, the Merchant's horse stumbled, and threw him rolling to the base of a tree. At that instant a bolt of lightning hit the tree, and its roots grabbed him like a hand grabs a stone, and threw him into the abyss

Meanwhile, the Almond Master, who had stayed lost in the city, wandered through the streets like a madman, scaring the children, picking up trash, and talking to the donkeys, the oxen and the ownerless dogs, who in his eyes formed with mankind a collection of beasts with sad looks.

How many moons did the Roads spend wandering?...

The sun, who was sticking his head out of the white shirt of daylight, was erasing on the door, decorated in gold and silver, the Master's shoulder, and the brown face of she who was a piece of his soul, a jewel that he could not buy with a lake of emeralds.

How many moons did the Roads spend wandering?...

The answer was muffled in the lips of the slave and she stiffened like her teeth. The Master grew silent with the insistence of a mysterious stone. The moon of the Owl-Fisherman was growing full. In silence each washed the other's face with their eyes, like two lovers who have been separated and suddenly find each other.

The scene was disturbed by insolent sounds. They had come to arrest them in the name of God and the king: he for being a warlock, she for being possessed by the devil. Between crosses and swords they took them down to the jail, the Master with the red beard and the green tunic, and the slave with her flesh so firm that it was like gold.

Seven months later, they were condemned to die burned at the stake in the Plaza Mayor. On the eve of the execution, the Master drew near to the slave and with his fingernail he tattooed on her arm a little boat, telling her:

"By means of this tattoo, Tatuana, you will always flee when you find yourself in danger, as you will flee today. My will is that you should be as free as my thoughts; draw this little boat on the wall, on the ground, in the air, anywhere you like, close your eyes, jump in and go..."

"Go, because my thought is stronger than the clay idol strengthened with onion!"

"And my thought is sweeter than the honey of the bees that suck the flower of the suqinay tree"

"And my thought is the one that turns invisible!"

Without losing a second La Tatuana did what the Master said: she drew the boat, she closed her eyes and climbed in, the boat began to move, and she escaped from the prison and from death.

And the next day, the morning of the execution, the constables found in the jail cell a dried tree that had in its branches two or three almond flowers, still pink.

20.9: Maya sarcophagus

21: The Cuban Revolution; Che Guevara

The Revolution

The Cuban Revolution which brought Fidel Castro to power in early 1959 has been one of the historic landmarks of 20th Century Latin America. It brought more profound and enduring changes than even the Mexican Revolution, involved the two superpowers (at one point bringing them to the verge of nuclear war) and because it set itself up as an exportable example, had considerable impact on a number of other Latin American nations.

Although there were surface similarities with the Mexican case, such as heavy foreign

21.1: Marx and the flag

investments and a long dictatorship which established the conditions for revolt, the Cuban situation was quite different. For one, Cuba historically has been under the strong influence of an outside nation against which it struggled to gain its full independence. First it was Spain, which maintained control of Cuba until the Spanish-American War of 1898. After the War the US ran Cuba under a military administration for some time before giving Cuba a limited independence in which the US retained the right to intervene and to control certain foreign policies under the Platt Amendment.

21.2: Platt Amendment

Beyond that, US economic ties to Cuba were so strong that it was a classic case of a dependent neocolonial economy. US companies controlled Cuba's principal crop, sugar, as well as the major hotels and gambling casinos that attracted large numbers of US tourists across the ninety miles to Florida.

For many years before Castro's rise to power Cuba's politics had been under the direct or indirect control of Fulgencio Batista, a one-time Army sergeant who staged a successful coup in 1933, promoted himself to General, and ruled the country with a tight grip from then on.

Fidel Castro was an energetic, articulate and charismatic student leader, offended at the corruption of the Batista regime, and, typical of many revolutionaries, was an alienated and educated member of the middle class. He had been very active in student politics, and had been present in Colombia during the 1948 riots and revolutionary violence known as the *Bogotazo*. In 1953 he led a gang of some 160 student revels in a quixotic and suicidal frontal attack on an army barracks in Santiago,

21.3: Castro

Cuba (the date, 26 July 1953, still serves as the official title for Castro's movement). Most of the group were captured or killed. Castro was fortunate to have been spared and put on a show trial, where his defense (*History will absolve me*) became one of the basic documents of his revolution. Batista felt secure enough to release Castro (and his brother Raul) and send them into exile in Mexico on the promise that they would not engage in any future political activities.

Once in Mexico, Castro proceeded to do just that, attracting a number of Cuban exiles as well as revolutionaries who had just left Guatemala with the fall of the Arbenz government. An Argentine medical student by the name of Ernesto "Che" Guevara was among them.

Castro had promised his followers that the end of the year 1956 would find him either dead or back in Cuba fighting against Batista. True to his word, in the last days of December of that year he and 81 followers made the passage from Mexico to southern Cuba on the small (normal capacity 16) and aging yacht *Granma*. The landing was disastrous; they were quickly spotted by Batista's troops and almost wiped out before the twelve survivors could make it to the sanctuary of the Sierra Maestra mountains.

From there he waged a two-year hit-and-run guerrilla war against Batista, enlisting the support of peasants and finally city-dwellers who had been abused by Batista's repressive security forces. In the end the outcome was as much due to Batista's errors as it was to Castro's successes. Batista's troops had little luck pinning down the elusive guerrillas, and took out their frustrations on opposition leaders, student groups, labor organizers, and anyone else

21.4: Castro's guerrilla warfare

they thought might be collaborating with Castro. The end result was to create more recruits for the guerrillas, and reduce international support for Batista until toward the end of 1958 even the US cut off military assistance. On the last day of December 1958 Batista and a small group of family and friends flew off into exile, leaving the way clear for Fidel Castro and his increasingly large group of guerrillas and supporters to take over.

In January 1959 there was almost universal adulation for Castro in Cuba, and much admiration for him in Latin America and the United States. Predictably, however, when he moved to put a land reform and social welfare program into place he ran into increasing opposition from the Cuban upper class and from American firms with investments in Cuba. The US government position under the Eisenhower administration quickly turned to opposition and then hostility as Castro's reforms led to increasing amounts of confiscated and nationalized US investment, and as Castro turned to the Soviet Union and its allies for support. The final break came when Castro nationalized US oil firms after they refused to refine Soviet oil. The Soviet Union was all too happy to quickly step up its level of support to include weapons and the implicit guarantee that it would help defend Cuba against attacks from the US.

By the time of the 1960 break with the United States the general outlines of Castro's program had become clear. The Revolution would involve nationalization of almost all sectors of the economy under a centralized collective arrangement. Leadership would be in the hands of a small number of Party officials, with Fidel at the head. The political system would be authoritarian, and intolerant of internal opposition. There would be a leveling and redistribution of wealth, with a broad medical and welfare program that would cover all for free. Internationally there would be hostility to the United States and a corresponding swing towards the Soviet Union and its allies.

The Cuban Revolution, like the Mexican before it, also involved a cultural element. Instead of murals, the emphasis was on film, art, literature and sports. An apt symbol of the Revolution's interest in culture is the painter Wilfredo Lam, of mixed Chinese, African and European descent. His political views made him unwelcome in pre-Castro Cuba, and he spent time in France and Spain (until the collapse of the Republic); he was closely associated with Picasso and the Surrealists. Castro's Revolution welcomed him back to Cuba, where he became one of its warmest supporters.

Castro's charisma and disdain for professional politicians led to what he called "direct democracy" in which the principal decisions were made by a small group at the top and then ratified by public acclaim in his dramatic and emotional speeches to the gathered thousands. By 1960 the reforms were

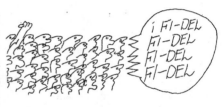

21.5: Direct democracy

beginning to threaten the interests of the middle class, many of whom went into exile in Florida.

In its last months the Eisenhower administration had begun to plan covert operations to eliminate Castro. Some of these involved bizarre assassination plots, but the most significant was a greatly amplified version of what had "worked" against the Guatemalan government of Arbenz in 1954. This would involve training, arming and using Cuban exiles to launch an invasion of Cuba in the expectation that there would be an internal uprising that would finally bring Castro down. Incoming President John F. Kennedy, who had talked a tough anti-Castro line in the 1960 presidential campaign against Richard Nixon, reluctantly allowed the plan to go forward, although he cut back the commitment of US combat aircraft, a decision that was to prove fatal. The invasion force, operating from bases in Florida and Nicaragua, sailed into the Cuban Bay of Pigs in April 1961, and encountered a strong and well-trained Castro-led force that quickly defeated it. The uprising within Cuba never materialized, Castro's forces were prepared for the invasion, and without a heavy commitment of US power (denied by Kennedy) there was no chance of success.

21.6: Soviet missile

The US turned next to commercial and political sanctions, including an economic blockade that continues to the present. This did not bring Castro down either, and in the long run only increased his links and dependence on the Soviet Union and its allies. In October 1962 Soviet Premier Nikita Kruschev placed nuclear-tipped missiles in Cuba, an act that brought a naval blockade and almost led to all-out war between the United States and the Soviet Union.

Castro's links to the Soviet Union led him to act as the Russian's surrogate in conflicts in Angola, Ethiopia and other parts of Africa, sending large numbers of Cuban troops to support Marxist regimes against opposition guerrillas and the Government of South Africa.

In 1980 Castro surprised the United States (and his own people) by briefly allowing Cubans to freely leave for the U.S.. The resulting flow, known as the "Mariel boatlift" for its port of exit, reached 125,000 before it was cut off. The Mariel exiles were different from the first wave of upper and middle class Cubans who had left in 1959-61; they were poorer, less educated, and included in their number were a small but troublesome, and potentially dangerous, group of criminals and mental institution inmates.

With the collapse of the Soviet Union and disappearance of the Warsaw Pact Castro lost his chief patron. Trade with his former supporters in Eastern Europe and Russia was still possible, but only in terms of hard currencies which were in extremely short supply in Cuba.

The balance sheet on the Cuban Revolution is a mixed one, with the final results still not in. Assessments of the Revolution by Cubans themselves tend to be partisan and sometimes extreme, depending on whether one has gained or lost from the process.

On the positive side Castro can point with pride to the fact that the Revolution removed the class and social barriers that had been maintained since colonial days. Education, health and welfare benefits were for the first time available to all Cubans, and were basically free. The corruption symbolized by the casinos, bars and houses of prostitution had disappeared. Cuba was a military power to be respected in the Caribbean, and for a considerable period of time its alliance with the Warsaw Pact checkmated US military attempts to bring his regime down. Finally, Latin Americans of all political stripes acknowledged, and many admired, the way he had stood up to US pressures ranging from plots to invasions to blockades.

21.7: Castro

On the negative side there had been a loss of freedoms and human rights under a regime whose control is far more totalitarian than the dictatorship that preceded it. Shortages and long waits for basic necessities abound. The average Cuban may not see extremes of rich and poor, but the overall feeling is one of hardship and sacrifice for an ideology which has been abandoned by most of the formerly Marxist states in the world. The respect that many Latin Americans have for Fidel is tinged by bitterness over the attempts that the Cuban government made to export its revolution to other nations via subversion and guerrilla warfare. There is also the reality that many of Cuba's most intelligent, educated and promising citizens have been forced to live outside their own country in a long and seemingly permanent exile.

Ernesto "Che" Guevara, Argentina, 1928-1967

Ernesto Guevara de la Serna was born the 14th of June 1928 in Rosario, a port on the River Plate north of Buenos Aires. Che's family had once belonged to Argentina's oligarchy but a series of financial misfortunes had reduced them to a modest middle-class status. Che's father Ernesto was an educated, easygoing aristocrat who had led a soft life and had failed in a number of business enterprises. He never was very close to his son and let his wife take care of his upbringing.

There is little doubt that Che's mother Celia de la Serna de Guevara, had the key role in his formative years. She was a remarkable woman, strong, outspoken, and rebellious. Her family once had been rich and was aristocratic, and one of her ancestors was viceroy of Peru in the colonial period. She went out of her way to scandalize Argentine society and was one of the first women to drive a car and smoke in public. Celia developed an extremely close relationship with her son, molding his ideas on life, politics and humanity to fit her increasingly leftist views.

When little Ernesto was almost two he developed chronic asthma, a condition which was to plague him to the end of his life. The circumstances are interesting: his mother took him swimming one day in early fall; the weather was cool and Ernesto got chilled. The chill grew worse and was eventually diagnosed as asthma. No one blamed his mother but she did blame herself, and, perhaps to compensate, showered attention on Ernesto to the irritation of her husband and the other children. Concern for Ernestito became the center of the Guevara family's activities. They moved to Alta Gracia, Córdoba province, in 1932 to give him the benefit of a drier climate. Since he could not attend primary school with the other children, his mother tutored him at home.

Despite his mother's spoiling, Che developed a strong and stubborn character and grew up determined not to let his asthmatic condition limit his activities. He had tremendous drive to prove himself better than anyone else, another characteristic which followed him to his death in Bolivia. Che always pushed himself to his physical limits and as a boy plunged into the most rugged of sports. As a teenager he played rugby, although he frequently had to leave the field to use his asthma inhaler. Although he had inherited his mother's intelligence and his father's love of books, he was only a mediocre student. Friends have noted that he seemed frankly bored with academics, and was rebellious and undisciplined.

Che grew up in an Argentina convulsed in political chaos. He witnessed the failure of a fraudulent and corrupt civilian government which gave way to a series of military presidents and finally to the dictatorial and semi-fascistic General Juan Perón. Under Celia's tutelage he developed contempt for society and authority and a strong hatred for the military, for a capitalistic economy, and for Anglo-Saxon influence in Latin America.

In this period Che fell in love with the daughter of one of the richest oligarchs in Argentina. Her family strongly opposed the girl's relationship with the bohemian and rebellious Guevara and eventually forced her to stop seeing him. This experience might have contributed to Che's hatred for the oligarchy.

In 1947 he entered the Medical College of the University of Buenos Aires, prompted perhaps by a desire to find out more about his own asthma or perhaps to help his mother, who was suffering from a slow but relentless cancer. As happened in high school, he was bored, but managed to cram enough to pass his final exams.

21.8: Che Guevara

Che always had a wanderlust, a passion for travel. As a boy he frequently took long trips on his bicycle, getting away from the cities he seemed to hate so much. In 1949 he went by bicycle to northeast Argentina, just across the border from the jungles and mountains of Bolivia. This feat was considered noteworthy enough to merit a commercial in a sports magazine. In 1951 it was a 3,500-mile odyssey by motorcycle across the Andes to Chile, by tramp steamer to Peru and Colombia, then by raft down the Amazon. While in medical school he shipped out on a freighter to Patagonia as a ship's doctor. And in 1953 came his final departure from Argentina on the longest trip of all: one that would take him to revolutionary Bolivia, to the leftist Guatemala of Arbenz, and the turning point in his life, the meeting with the exiled Fidel Castro in Mexico.

In Guatemala Che made friends with a group of Latin American Communists, exiled in the increasingly leftist regime of Jacobo Arbenz. In the process he further developed his Marxist ideology. One of these exiles was the Peruvian Hilda Gadea, who helped him take the final steps leftward and who was to become the third of five key women in his life. Although physically unattractive and four years older than Che, she was "simpática" and a strong willed radical like his mother Celia. She was a veteran revolutionary, experienced, bohemian and proletarian. They lived together, were married in 1955, with Raúl Castro as best man. She presented him with his first child Hildita in 1956. Che was in Guatemala long enough to see the government of Arbenz fall in the face of a right-wing army revolt. The new government forced Che to leave Guatemala for Mexico.

In Mexico he renewed this friendship with the exiles and through them made contact with members of Fidel Castro's "26 of July movement." Che met Fidel in July 1955 and in his first meeting talked for 12 straight hours with Castro; Che says that when that talk was over at dawn, " I was a revolutionary". Che was with Fidel and his group on the *Granma*.

In the campaign Che quickly showed his ability, was promoted to *comandante* and given his own column of about 150 men. With this column he led the decisive attack against the city of Santa Clara in Las Villas Province. This, the biggest battle of the Cuban campaign, included the ambush of a four hundred-man troop

21.9: The Granma

train. The city fell on the first day of January 1959. That same day Batista fled to Santo Domingo and 26 of July guerrillas entered the city of Havana opposed. Che emerged from the campaign a mature, tested individual. His wanderlust was temporarily sated as he settled down to help Castro consolidate power and build a new society.

His role was that of a tropical Robespierre as he supervised the hurried trials and executions of hundreds, perhaps thousands, of Batista's officers, policemen and supporters. Che was also one of the key figures who turned the 26 of July Movement from a patriotic, liberal, revolution to communism. One source has noted that if Fidel Castro was the heart, soul, voice and bearded image of the Cuban revolution, Che was its brain. He supervised the agrarian reform program and later as president of Cuba's National Bank controlled the rapid nationalization of the U.S. investments in Cuba. Relations with the United States steadily deteriorated as Castro moved closer to economic, military and political dependence on Moscow.

During the Cuban campaign he met the fourth woman in his life: Aleida March, a pretty and intelligent revolutionary who served as his secretary during the campaign. They married in June 1959 and she bore him four children before he left for Bolivia. Shortly after the victory over Batista Che began working on his first book, *Guerra de Guerrillas (Guerrilla Warfare)*, in which he proposed to present the lessons of the Cuban campaign applied to Latin America as a whole. Much of the book, especially the tactical portion, is not new. What are original are the three fundamental lessons that Che derived from Cuba as being valid for all of Latin America:

1st. Popular forces can win a war against the army.

2nd. It is not always necessary to wait for all the conditions for revolution to be present; the insurrectional "foco" can create them.

3rd. In underdeveloped South America, the armed struggle should basically be carried out in the countryside.

But Che and Fidel were not about to limit themselves to writing books and make speeches about how "the Andes will be the Sierra Maestra of the Americas". In 1959 four separate attempts were made in the Caribbean and Central America to export revolution; all failed. Later attempts were made in Venezuela and other South

21.10: Che and Fidel

American countries with varying degrees of success. One of Che's biographers says that in 1961 he noticed a large map of Argentina hanging in his private bathroom in Havana's La Cabañas fortress. When he asked about it, Che replied: I do a lot of my thinking here and I think a lot about a guerrilla "foco" in Argentina.

In 1964 Che helped his friend Jorge Ricardo Masetti set up a guerrilla band in northwest Argentina, not far from the Bolivian border. Masetti was not able to get popular support, lacked political ties, and was finally chewed up by the Argentine army and the environment, a forewarning of things to come. In April

1965 Che Guevara disappeared from public view after returning from a short trip to Africa. There was intense speculation over his activities: he was dead; he was in the Dominican Republic; he was in Colombia; he was in Vietnam. (81)

Actually, Che spent about six months in 1965 with the Kinshasa rebels in the Democratic Republic of Congo. He had taken about 125 Cubans with him in an attempt to export revolution to Africa under the auspices of the Havana-based Organization of African, Asian and Latin American Solidarity. We don't know much about this period - there are no pictures or diaries, but we do know that Che felt it was a failure. Che himself blamed the rebels, saying that they had no will to fight. From a more objective viewpoint we can see some of the reasons for the failure: Che's group were foreigners; they could not speak the language and could not get popular support. Again, a preview of Bolivia.

So Che returned to Cuba, frustrated, approaching middle age, his previously close friendship with Castro strained, looking more like a Rasputin than a dashing revolutionary. He immediately went into seclusion, to rest and to think. As it turns out, what he was thinking about was nothing less than the initiation of a Latin American revolution with a base in Bolivia. And why Bolivia? Guevara never fully explained his choice, but we can speculate. The export of revolution had pretty much failed in the Caribbean, in Central America, and in Venezuela, Peru and Colombia. Brazil, Chile and Argentina were too powerful, with large and well-organized armies. That left little choice: Bolivia or Ecuador.

His choice of Bolivia on the surface seemed logical, for it is a country with profound social problems and a history of violence and chaos. Further, the specific area he selected in Bolivia, the southeastern slope of the Andes, indicates that he was still thinking of eventually returning to Argentina. As we shall see later on, his misreading of the realities of the Bolivian situation was his fatal error. Guevara's probable strategic objective was to expand his guerrilla "foco" so as to create a strong base area and hopefully provoke United States intervention and thus create "one, two, many Vietnams" in Latin America.

The preparations for the Bolivian campaign began in early 1966 when Cuban agents began making contacts in Bolivia at the same time as Bolivian and Cuban guerrillas started intensive training in Cuba. In June the agents purchased a farm in Nancahuasú; this was to be the base camp for launching his revolution. Che himself arrived in Bo-

21.15: Che's group in Bolivia

livia the 3rd of November 1966 via Prague and Sao Paolo, Brazil. He used a forged Uruguayan passport and was disguised as a clean-shaven, balding, middle-aged businessman. In a few days he was in Nancahuasú. Nancahuasú lies in a transitional area between the barren high Andes and the lush Amazonian rain-forest. The environment is extremely hostile and relatively unpopulated – the Bolivians pretty much leave it alone. Deep river valleys are thickly forested but the hills above them are bare except for scrub brush.

The first months are spent preparing the base area; digging caves for hiding supplies, and sending out short patrols for familiarization. (87) Che's group initially consists of 12 men; by the end of December the group has grown to 24, 15 of them Cubans. The Cubans are a carefully selected elite: all are veteran guerrillas and most had been with Che in the Cuban campaign or in the Congo. Five of the Cubans hold the rank of comandante (the highest rank in the Cuban army) and five belong to the Central Committee of the Cuban Communist Party.

In December 1966 the first sign of trouble emerges for the guerrillas: in a long discussion with the head of the Moscow-line Communist Party of Bolivia, Che refuses to subordinate his group to the Party in La Paz, insisting that the military phase of revolution, under Che, should override the political. This dis-agreement ends any chance for political support from the Bolivian Communists. In January 1967 the group begins a 48-day conditioning march in which other problems become apparent: the environment takes its toll; two men drown, and the rest suffer from hunger, exposure and exhaustion; Che loses 15 pounds in the march. Che hopes that they will convince many peasants to join them, but they find few people in the area and those they do meet are uninterested in revolution.

By March the Bolivian Government begins to hear rumors of a guerrilla group wandering around the southeastern jungles, captures two deserters and sends a patrol out to search the base camp at Nancahuasú. (91) But the Bolivian ambush on 23 March in which a lieutenant and seven men die. (92) At the time of the ambush Che has 47 men; this is the largest his group will ever be in Bo-livia. Of these, 20 are foreigners.

21.16: Che in Bolivia

Facing Che's guerrillas is an under strength and poorly armed Bolivian army that numbers on paper about 8000 men. But three-quarters of these are recruits conscripted for six months of basic training. Although weak and ineffective from a military viewpoint, the Bolivian army has hidden strengths: it is a people's Army, closely identified with the peasants in a way which Batista's corrupt and aloof military in Cuba never was.

The initial reaction of the Bolivian government to the March ambush was to request large quantities of U.S. military aid including tanks and aircraft. Despite these requests, United State's assistance was very carefully limited to small quantities of equipment, and most importantly to the intensive training of an elite 650 man Bolivian Ranger battalion. This training was handled by a 16 man mobile training team and took four months. In the end it was that Bolivian unit which captured Che with no direct U.S. military involvement on the operational side, although a CIA agent was with the Rangers when they captured and killed Che.

During the month of March a fascinating figure joins the guerrillas: Heidi Tamara Bunke, a.k.a. Tania. There is some confusion about her role and whom she really worked for. She was born in Argentina of German communist parents, refugees from Hitler's Germany. As a girl she returned to East Germany where she was educated and where she met Che in 1959. The exact nature of their relationship is not clear, but she did keep in contact with Che for the next five years and went to Bolivia to prepare the way for Che's group. Tania was the last of the key women in Che's life. She combined Aleida's physical attractions with the intellect and revolutionary fervor of Celia and Hilda. Another foreigner in Che's group was the French intellectual Regis Debray, the author of an ideological treatise on Castro's brand of communism. He had been with the group from the start but soon realized he lacked the endurance to stay with the guerrillas in the field. The Bolivians captured him as he tried to work his way out of the combat area. Despite his cover as a journalist he was tried by the Bolivian army and sentenced to 30 years in jail.

In mid-April, the guerrillas were further weakened by an accidental split into two groups. But this time the radios had failed and for the rest of the period in Bolivia the two groups spent a great deal of time and energy in trying to link up. They never did and the Army was able to pick them off individually. By midsummer, despite a few small successful encounters with the Army, the principal enemy of the guerrillas is not the Army but the environment. The two groups are frequently lost and food and water are scarce. At one point, Che notes in his diary that the only food he has had in two days is a greasy soup made from lard. Discipline and morale begin to break down. Che has frequent asthma attacks and begins to show signs of physical deterioration and mental strain. He mentions in his diary one incident in which he stabs his mule in the neck out of frustration.

Meanwhile the Army begins to gather considerable information on the group from deserters and cooperative peasants. Using this information it raids the guerrillas' carefully prepared supply caves, depriving them of medicines, food, ammunition and weapons. In late August the group that split off from Che's main group falls into an ambush while crossing the Masicuri River. There is only one survivor. Among the dead are Tania and Joaquín, his second-in-

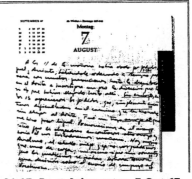

21.17: Last dairy entry, 7 Oct 67

command. By late September 1967 the end is near. Che's group is reduced to a handful of tattered and hungry men wandering almost aimlessly inside a steadily shrinking circle of Rangers. The night of 7 October the guerrillas make camp in the steep and wooded ravine of the Turo River. When they wake they find Rangers on the high ground above. The guerrillas try to escape by dropping downstream but Rangers have sealed off that exit. The firefight begins shortly after noon and lasts about two hours.

At the end Che is wounded and cannot walk. His carbine is shot through the upper hand guard and is useless. As the Rangers close in Che raises his hands, stumbles out from behind a rock and says: "Don't shoot... I am Che Guevara and I am worth more to you alive than dead." A few hours later he is shot by a Bolivian sergeant, and his body is displayed and photographed in a local school-house. The Bolivian soldiers bury Che in a secret and unmarked grave to avoid making a shrine out of his burial site. In July 1997 the remains are found, identified, and returned to Cuba for a hero's burial.

21.18: Followers of Che

22: Central America: Conflict and Peace

The decade of the 1980's saw unusual amounts of attention being paid to events in Central America, normally an area of secondary concern in the Hemisphere. The events involved another potentially major revolutionary process, covert and overt U.S. efforts to counter it, a civil war in a second country, and a sense that the region as a whole was drifting toward a war that might involve not only all of the Central American regions, but also the U.S. and possibly surrogates of the Soviet Union. In response to this range of serious threats to stability, a group of Latin American nations launched a painfully slow peace process which eventually appeared to have resolved two of the most serious conflict situations in the region.

22.1: Dominoes

Nicaragua: Revolution and Counter-revolution

The story of the Nicaraguan Revolution bears more than passing similarity to the Cuban, although the outcome has been quite different. Like Cuba, Nicaragua had been under heavy U.S. influence for much of its history, at first because of its favorable geographic location for a possible Isthmian canal. When in 1903 the chosen route turned out to be Panama, Nicaragua's importance to U.S. policy-makers diminished considerably, although the proximity to the Panama Canal and U.S. business investments in Nicaragua continued to give it a certain priority in U.S. Central American concerns.

22.2: Sandino

Political instability in Nicaragua led to a long series of U.S. military interventions in the period from 1907 to 1933. The U.S. presence was welcomed by some Nicaraguan politicians and strongly resisted by others. One of those who resisted was General Agusto C. Sandino, who in the late 1920's led an effective guerrilla campaign against the U.S. Marines and their Nicaraguan allies. Toward the end of the Hoover administration, with the U.S. in the depths of the Depression, the U.S. government decided that a protracted campaign against Sandino and his insurgents was politically damaging and militarily unwinnable without a major commitment of U.S. forces.

To extricate U.S. troops from Nicaragua, a professional military force trained by the U.S. was established. The plan was that this force would stay out of politics and act as a stabilizer between the two main political camps, the liberals and the conservatives. The first commander of this Nicaraguan National Guard (Guardia Nacional) was General Anastasio Somoza Sr., who rather quickly converted the Guard into his personal force and became deeply involved in the politics the Guard was supposed to abstain from. Somoza had been educated in the United States and knew how to manipulate U.S. emissaries and policy-makers in Washington by assuring them of Nicaraguan support and guaranteeing U.S. businesses that they would find Nicaragua to be a stable country for their investments. Internally, Somoza was ruthless in his political activities and his use of the Guard to defend his family interests. In 1934 he had Sandino assassinated, thus eliminating a potential rival for power (and in the process making him a national martyr). In 1937 Somoza assumed the presidency and began the forty-year period that could fairly be called the Somoza family's dynastic rule of Nicaragua.

Somoza senior died by an assassin's bullet in 1956, and over the next two decades was succeeded in the presidency by two sons and a close family friend. Anastasio Somoza junior, who had been trained at the U.S. Military Academy at West Point, had been National Guard Commander for much of this time and became President in 1967, governing directly or indirectly until overthrown by the Sandinistas in 1979.

22.3: Somoza

The Sandinista Front for National Liberation (FSLN for *Frente Sandinista de Liberación Nacional*) was begun as a Cuban-style revolutionary "foco" in 1960, and was almost wiped out several times by Somoza's forces. Although there was no direct connection to the Sandino of the 1920's, the group took his name as a symbol of the continuing struggle against U.S. intervention and against the kleptocracy of the Somoza family. By the mid-1970's the Sandinistas were in something of a stalemate, strong enough to survive, but unable to win a decisive victory against Somoza. They were handicapped by their division into three main factions, which made coordinated action difficult. Acting on the persuasive advice of Fidel Castro, the three factions united and stepped up both their campaign for international support (from Cuba as well as other nations in Latin America and Europe) and their internal effort to broaden their appeal to wide sectors of the lower and middle classes.

Like Batista in Cuba before him, Somoza helped the insurgents through his ruthless pursuit of anyone believed to be a guerrilla sympathizer. A turning point in the struggle for the hearts and minds of average Nicaraguans was a devastating earthquake in Managua in 1972. Somoza and the National Guard, in charge of the relief effort, stole many of the international relief supplies and sold them to their countrymen for personal profit. Wholesale violations of the human rights of ordinary Nicaraguans alienated large sectors of the public, and caused Somoza increasing problems with the Carter administration. By 1978 wide-spread fighting had damaged or destroyed important parts of many of Nicaragua's cities, since Somoza did not hesitate to use his combat aircraft to bomb neighborhoods in which the FSLN were present. Toward the end of the fighting period in mid 1979, Somoza and the Guardia Nacional were almost totally isolated, and the FSLN was supported by large sectors of the Nicaraguan people, including the Church, most labor and student organizations, and large numbers of lower and middle-class citizens.

The end came in July 1979. Despite a last-minute U.S. effort to send an OAS peacekeeping presence to save what was left of the Somoza regime, the insurgents pushed into Managua and all the other principal cities. Somoza escaped into exile in Miami, and the Guard disintegrated, with many of the officers and senior noncommissioned officers making it across the border into Honduras with their weapons.

The triumphant FSLN, at the head of the broad coalition of anti-Somoza forces, found an economy in shambles, a severely damaged infrastructure, and an international community that was waiting to see if the Nicaraguan Revolution would turn out to be like the Cuban one twenty years before. There was an attempt to create a coalition government with representatives of the many groups which had supported the FSLN at the end

22.4: Guerrilla

of the struggle, but it soon became clear that real power lay in the hands of those with the weapons, namely the fighters of the FSLN. Within the FSLN the leadership was in the hands of the nine-man "Directorate", made up of three members from each of the three main factions; the Ortega brothers (Humberto and Daniel) were the more significant members of this Directorate. Ministerial posts were more widely distributed, to include several Catholic priests as cabinet members. There was also a commitment to a mixed economy which would allow significant private holdings of lands and businesses, thus departing from the Cuban model.

In one respect the FSLN was fortunate to have had the Somoza dynasty as their enemy: the Somozas owned many business enterprises and about 20% of the country's agricultural land. This was immediately confiscated and distributed to both cooperatives and individuals in a rapidly implemented land reform program.

Like the Cuban Revolution, and with the help of several thousand advisors and technicians from Cuba, the Soviet Block, and other countries, the Nicaraguan Revolution set out on a sweeping reform program. One of their first priorities was a crash literacy drive, and in a few months they were able to teach basic writing and reading skills to most Nicaraguans (critics noted that the literacy training also included a heavy dose of FSLN propaganda). The Revolutionary government made free health care and social services available to all Nicaraguans, and cooperatives were set up under FSLN supervision to make these services available. There was also a cultural renaissance, with an emphasis on popular involvement in the arts, music, and literature (especially poetry). Although many of these features were based on the Cuban model, the Nicaraguan Revolution always had a distinctive touch, especially the way it blended socialism, nationalism and Christianity.

The initial U.S. reaction under the Carter administration was cautious but helpful. Despite hostility by some members of the FSLN, who could never forget the long years of U.S. support to the Somozas, there seemed to be a willingness on both sides to work out differences. The initial aid package from Washington, although not all the FSLN had asked for, was generous and helped a great deal in the early days of the new revolutionary government. There was concern in Washington over the large numbers of Cuban (and other Soviet-bloc) advisers, especially in the areas of intelligence and security, but this was explained as logical since the Cuban model was the most relevant.

The U.S.-Nicaraguan relationship changed abruptly when the Reagan administration took office in January 1981. Hard-line anti-communist ideologues in Washington could not accept the links between the FSLN and Cuba, to say nothing of the Soviet Union. The U.S. aid programs to Nicaragua were cut off or severely curtailed. More ominously, the Reagan administration chose as one of its principal vehicles to influence Nicaragua the same device that had been used against leftist regimes in Guatemala (1954) and Cuba (1959-   ): anti-Communist exiles. There were a significant number of ex-members of the Guardia Nacional in makeshift camps in Honduras, and by working with a compliant Honduran military, it was possible for the CIA to organize and support these former members of the Guardia into what became known as the "Contras" (Spanish for counter-revolutionaries). There were other covert and overt actions: sabotage, mining of Nicaraguan harbors, diplomatic pressures, and an economic embargo.

22.5: Reagan

Although the Contras never had a realistic chance of bringing down the Sandinista government, they were able to wreak considerable damage in northern Nicaragua, and forced the FSLN regime to divert a large percentage of its national budget to defense. In a short period of time the Nicaraguan military, with support from Cuba, the Soviet Union and its allies, became the strongest military force in Central America, and there were fears that an FSLN-Contra confrontation could spill over into a wider regional war involving all the Central

American nations. Inevitably, this would also have involved the United States and the allies of Nicaragua.

By the late 1980's there was a war-weariness in Nicaragua (as well as much of the rest of Central America). Economic conditions in Nicaragua, aggravated by the Contra war and the economic embargo, were bad and getting worse. Sandinista promises for reform could only be partially fulfilled, and the revolutionary fervor of the first few years was wearing thin. Further, there was no single charismatic leader (such as Fidel Castro) who could rouse the passions of Nicaraguans. Although Daniel Ortega was president, he was still beholden to the nine-man FSLN Directorate and the FSLN party bureaucracy. Externally, the crisis in the Soviet Union and the Eastern European allies meant that the large amounts of military and economic aid to Nicaragua were about to end. Furthermore, the Central American peace process (described below) was well under way and seemed to suggest that the Contra war was about to have a peaceful resolution.

In these circumstances Nicaraguans went to the polls in February 1990 in a remarkable election that was undoubtedly the most carefully watched ever in Latin America (there were several thousand outside observers, including Jimmy Carter and large numbers of UN and OAS poll-watchers). The results were a surprise to just about everyone: the FSLN and Daniel Ortega could get only 41% of the vote and lost to a coalition of center and right parties (55%) led by Violeta Chamorro, the widow of an assassinated staunchly anti-Somoza journalist. Perhaps even more amazing than the elections was the peaceful way in which power was transferred from the FSLN regime to the Chamorro administration. A second election in 1996 saw another peaceful transfer of power and a second electoral defeat for the FSLN.

But governing was not easy for Violeta Chamorro. Her coalition had quarreling factions, and the Sandinistas controlled the labor unions, much of the economic life of the country through their cooperatives, and the security forces under Humberto Ortega. Nevertheless, the remarkable outcome in Nicaragua was that a revolution that came to power with a socialist program and a Marxist orientation was given the opportunity to implement its programs, and then peacefully gave up power through a democratic process. The democratic process in 2007 returned Ortega to power, part of a populist "pink tide" which has emerged as an important political force in Latin America, led by President Hugo Chávez of Venezuela.

22.6: Ortega

El Salvador: Civil War

22.7: Farabundo Martí

The other source of concern in the 1980's was the civil war in El Salvador. Here a government with strong links to the U.S., supported by a military which had historically been associated with land-owning elites, was fighting a popular insurgency with some parallels to the FSLN in Nicaragua. The Salvadoran insurgency had a similar name: FMLN - Farabundo Martí Front for National Liberation. Farabundo Martí was a Marxist who had been a close associate of Sandino, and had led a popular uprising against a conservative government in 1932, demanding land reform and social justice. The army brutally put down the revolt in an event known as *La Matanza* ('The Massacre"), in which perhaps 20,000 Salvadorans died, including Farabundo Martí.

Like the FSLN, the FMLN received outside support from various nations sympathetic to their cause, including Cuba. When the FSLN came to power in Nicaragua in 1979 they were able to provide moral and material support to their Salvadoran counterparts, although the degree and significance of this support remains arguable. There seems no doubt that the aid was significant, but it is also true that the FMLN had broad support within El Salvador, and would have been capable of continuing their guerrilla struggle indefinitely by means of peasant support and weapons and supplies captured from the Salvadoran Army.

The year 1979 was a key one in El Salvador: a coalition of reformist middle-rank officers, centrist politicians, and businessmen staged a bloodless coup which removed a general-president and ended a long history of rule by retired military officers beholden to the conservative elites (mainly landowners). There was hope that the 1979 reformist Junta could make peaceful changes which might avoid the bloodshed that Nicaragua had experienced. Mild land reforms and other changes were indeed launched by the 1979 Junta, but opposition by the landowners and conservative senior military officers was too great, and the Junta was pushed aside. Also significant were the actions of covert "death squads", linked to the conservative forces in the military and the landowners, who did not hesitate to intimidate and kill peasants or politicians who proposed reforms they considered too radical.

When the government shifted to the right after the reformists were removed from the Junta, full-scale civil war broke out between the military and a revitalized FMLN, which had won over important sectors of the political left. Thousands of

22.8: Guerrilla

ordinary Salvadorans died in this period, and the death squads also assassinated Archbishop Oscar Romero and American missionary nuns.

With the Reagan administration, the U.S. role greatly increased in El Salvador, especially in terms of military assistance. Although efforts were made to include respect for human rights in the training of the Salvadoran military, the activities of the death squads did not fundamentally change. El Salvador's economy increasingly became a war economy, heavily dependent on U.S. aid for survival, and as the military became stronger their role in running the nation increased accordingly.

As the struggle intensified, the fight in El Salvador was seen as closely linked to the situation in Nicaragua, especially if either conflict (the Contra War in Nicaragua or the civil war in El Salvador) should cross borders and lead to regional conflict. For the Reagan administration the Nicaraguan-Cuban role in supporting the FMLN was ominous, and suggested a Central American version of the "domino theory": "yesterday Nicaragua, today El Salvador, tomorrow the rest of Central America". There were echoes of the Vietnam experience as well. Liberals in the U.S. framed the argument in terms of "never again": never again should the U.S. get itself involved, as it did in Vietnam, defending a conservative and corrupt old order in fighting against a revolutionary guerrilla movement. (A sample bumper sticker from the period read: "El Salvador is Spanish for Vietnam"). Conservatives in the U.S. agreed that there was an analogy with Vietnam, but that the appropriate lesson should be to "do it right this time" (i.e., to go in with superior U.S. force to decisively crush the guerrillas).

By the end of the 1980's, the war-weariness that led to elections in Nicaragua was having its effect in El Salvador as well. Both sides seemed to realize

22.9: The international players

that they were strong enough to continue the fighting indefinitely, but were not strong enough to win a clear-cut victory. The Bush administration in Washington, less ideological than Reagan's, was anxious to disengage from a situation that it saw as costly and with little prospects of victory. Aided by outsiders, including the United Nations, the FMLN and the Salvadoran government in late 1991 signed a peace agreement that finally brought an end to the long and painful civil war.

The Central American Peace Process

The slow and difficult path to peace in Central America was an historical turning point, and a remarkable achievement. For one, it was organized by a group of Latin American nations themselves, often in the face of opposition from a U.S. government that believed a military solution was not only preferable, but also possible. Secondly, it for the first time brought the United Nations into a serious conflict situation in the Hemisphere (in the past conflict resolution had either been handled by the U.S., or the Organization of American States under strong U.S. influence). Ultimately the peace process accomplished its goals in terms of ending the Contra War in Nicaragua and the civil war in El Salvador, and eventually winding down the 30-year insurgency in Guatemala. This is not to say that the Central American peace process has solved all of the region's problems. Economies are still weak, recovery from many years of conflict is slow, ecological and infrastructure damage is severe, democracy is fragile, and new conflicts may break out in the future. But the importance of the process merits a look at how it operated and achieved its objectives.

The process began in early 1983, when a group of four concerned Latin American nations met on the Panamanian island of Contadora to discuss ways in which they might launch a new peace initiative. It is noteworthy that the four countries were the four immediate geographic neighbors of Central America: Mexico to the north, and Panama, Colombia and Venezuela to the south. Over the next few years they met numerous times and drafted several proposed peace treaties for consideration by the various parties involved. (See the Contadora September 1983 *21 Objectives* document, which follows, for a summary of the main ideas proposed by the Contadora group). The Reagan administration's position was clear: although never directly attacking the so-called Contadora process, the U.S. made it known that it regarded such efforts as well-meaning meddling at best, and as helping the FSLN and FMLN at worst. The hard-liners in the Reagan administration argued that the Contras could defeat the FSLN regime, and that

22.10: Arias

U.S. support for the Salvadoran military would defeat the FMLN insurgency.

The peace process seemed to be stalled in early 1987, mainly over U.S. opposition and the fact that the five Central American nations were reacting somewhat negatively to peace proposals written up by outside (albeit neighboring) nations. In mid 1987 the process was revitalized when Costa Rican president Oscar Arias proposed a new (although similar) peace plan which enlisted the help of the United Nations to verify and support the peace agreements. This proposal, which won the Nobel peace prize for Arias, became the definitive Esquipulas agreement under which the Central American peace process achieved significant results in Nicaragua, El Salvador and eventually Guatemala. Under United Nations sponsorship, four countries committed themselves to a major effort in the peacekeeping and verification aspects of the agreement: Canada, Germany, Venezuela, and Spain. Although Canada had long experience with United Nations peacekeeping, the other three did not, and their involvement in the Central American peace process was an important development.

In early 1989 the new Bush administration took over from Reagan's, and this permitted an agreement between the White House and the democratically-controlled Congress to support the peace process, end U.S. support for the Contras, and lower the U.S. profile in Central America. Coupled with the crisis in the Soviet Union and the Warsaw Pact, this meant that the Central American crisis no longer was likely to lead to a superpower confrontation and thus could be resolved on the basis of local interests.

The United Nations peacekeeping mission, ONUCA (for the Spanish letters  for UN Observers in Central America) moved into the five Central American nations and, with OAS support, began supervising the fulfillment of the Esquipulas peace plan. For a few short months things were tense as some of the Contras resisted being demobilized, as they were required to do under the peace plan. The UN responded by bringing in a battalion of 800 Venezuelan paratroopers to supervise the demobilization and to persuade the Contras that they should cooperate. With the Contras demobilized, the size of the

22.11: UN peacekeeping Nicaraguan armed forces shrank dramatically as the Sandinista government peacefully turned power over to Violeta Chamorro after the February 1990 elections.

With the Contra war over, the peace process shifted its attention to El Salvador. ONUCA became ONUSAL (UN Observers in El Salvador), and in a similar process supervised the demobilization of the FMLN at the same time as it verified that the Salvadoran Armed Forces were being cut back. An important difference with Nicaragua was that in El Salvador the old police organizations, which had been under military control and had a reputation for brutality and human rights violations, were disbanded, and the new police forces created in their place were structured so as to include personnel from both the FMLN and the previous military and police groups.

In theory the Esquipulas Central American peace process was supposed to apply to all five Central American nations, and by 1993 it was reasonably successful in Nicaragua and El Salvador, as described above. Costa Rica was not directly involved in the conflict, and Honduras' role was mainly to provide the bases from which the

22.12: Salvadorian democracy

Contras could move into Nicaragua; with the Contras demobilized Honduras too was at peace. This left only Guatemala with a continuing conflict between the Marxist guerrillas in the hills and the Guatemalan military. Talks to resolve this conflict on a basis similar to the others had yielded few results until a final agreement between the parties was reached in 1996 with considerable United Nations involvement.

The Contadora Objectives Document
(9 September 1983) Considering:

The situation prevailing in Central America, which is characterized by an atmosphere of tension that threatens security and peaceful coexistence in the region, and which requires, for its solution, observance of the principles of international law governing the actions of States. ...

Declare Their Intention of Achieving the Following :

To promote detente and put an end to situations of conflict in the area, restraining from taking any action that might jeopardize political confidence or obstruct the achievement of peace, security and stability in the region;

To ensure strict compliance with the aforementioned principles of international law, whose violators will be held accountable;

To respect and ensure the exercise of human, political, civil, economic, social, religious and cultural rights;

To adopt measures conducive to the establishment and, where appropriate, improvement of democratic, representative, and pluralistic systems that will guarantee effective popular participation in the decision-making process and ensure that the various currents of opinion have free access to fair and regular elections based on the full observance of citizens' rights;

To promote national reconciliation efforts wherever deep divisions have taken place within society, with a view to fostering participation in democratic political processes in accordance with the law;

To create political conditions intended to ensure the international security, integrity and sovereignty of the States of the region;

To stop the arms race in all its forms and begin negotiations for the control and reduction of current stocks of weapons and on the number of armed troops;

To prevent the installation on their territory of foreign military bases or any other type of foreign military interference;

To conclude agreements to reduce the presence of foreign military advisers and other foreign elements involved in military and security activities, with a view to their elimination;

To establish internal control machinery to prevent the traffic in arms from the territory of any country in the region to the territory of another;

To eliminate the traffic in arms, whether within the region or from outside it, intended for persons, organizations or groups seeking to destabilize the Governments of Central American countries;

To prevent the use on their own territory by persons, organizations or groups seeking to destabilize the Governments of Central American countries and to refuse to provide them with or permit them to receive military or logistical support;

To refrain from inciting or supporting acts of terrorism, subversion or sabotage in the countries in the area;

22.13: Wounded soldier

To establish and coordinate direct communication systems with a view to preventing or, where appropriate, settling incidents between States of the region;

To continue humanitarian aid aimed at helping Central American refugees who have been displaced from their countries of origin and to create suitable conditions for the voluntary repatriation of such refugees, in consultation with or with the cooperation of the United Nations High Commissioner for Refugees (UNHCR) and other international agencies deemed appropriate;

To undertake economic and social development programs with the aim of promoting well being and an equitable distribution of wealth;

To revitalize and restore economic integration machinery in order to attain sustained development on the basis of solidarity and mutual advance;

To negotiate the provision of external monetary resources, which will provide additional means of financing the resumption of intra-regional trade, meet the serious balance-of-payments problems, attract funds for working capital,

support programs to extend and restructure production and promote medium-
and long-term investment projects;

To negotiate better and broader access to international markets in order to
increase the volume of trade between the countries of Central America and the
rest of the world, particularly the industrialized countries; by means of a revision
of trade practices, the elimination of tariff and other barriers, and the achievement of the price stability at a profitable and fair level for the products exported
by the countries of the region;

To establish technical cooperation machinery for the planning, program-
ming, and implementation of investment and trade promotion projects.

The Ministers for Foreign Affairs of the Central American countries, with
the participation of the countries in the Contadora Group, have begun negotiations with the aim of preparing for the conclusion of the agreements and the
establishment of machinery necessary to formalize and develop the objectives
contained in this document, and to bring about the establishment of appropriate
verification or monitoring systems. To that end, account will be taken of the
initiatives put forward at the meetings convened by the Contadora Group.

[Adopted on September 9, 1983, by the Contadora countries of Mexico, Panama, Colombia, and Venezuela and the Central American nations of Guatemala,
Honduras, El Salvador, Nicaragua, and Costa Rica].

22.14: The players: U.S., Priest, guerrilla, soldier, landowner, peasant

Index

academic art, 134, 150
academies, 111-2, 173
adelantados, 47
African slaves, 71
Afro-Latins, 3
Age of Discovery, 40
Agriculture of the Torrid Zone,
    by Andrés Bello, 117-120
Aguilar, Jerónimo, 49
Agustini, Delmira, 226
Almagro, Diego de, 59-61
Alvarado, Pedro de, 50
Amazon Basin, 6, 7, 9
Anáhuac, Valley of, 23, 30
Andes, 6, 8
Antarctica, 4, 9-10
    and Line of Tordesillas, 43-4
APRA, 213-4
Aragon, Kingdom of, 41
Araucana, La,
    by Alonso de Ercilla, 62-5
araucanians, 61-5
Arbenz, Jacobo, 230-1
Arévalo, Juan José, 229-30
Argentina, Antarctic claim, 10
    as seen as Bolívar, 107-8
Arias, Oscar, 256-7
Ariel, 189-92
Art
    in Colonial period, 81
    in early 20C, 212
    in Neoclassical period, 112
    in the Romantic period, 134

of Encounter, 44
of Independence period, 104
late 19C, 173
Maya, 18
surrealism, 231
Asturias, Miguel Angel, 231-6
Atahualpa, 33, 58-61
Avellaneda, Gertrudis 141-5
Ayacucho, battle of, 113
Ayllu (Incas), 31
Aztecs
    art, 24
    ideograms, 24
    literature, 25-30
    poetry, anonymous, 29-30
    view of the Conquest, 67-9
Azuela, Mariano, 204-18
Balbuena, Bernardo de, 89
ball game, Pre-Columbian, 22
Barbarism, and Civilization,
    Ch 12, 121-132
Barber, The, by Luis C. López,
    158-9
Baroque, Ch 9, 81-92
Batista, Fulgencio, 237-9
Bay of Pigs invasion, 240
Bello, Andrés, 115-120
Bernal Díaz del Castillo, 52-6
black Legend, 71
Bolívar, Simón, 102, 104-8
    and Bello, 115
    and Olmedo, 112-115

Bolivian campaign, Guevara in,
    245-8
Bonampak murals, 18
Brazilian Independence, 103-4
Brazilian positivism, 163-4
Bread by Gabriela Mistral, 223-4
*Brief Account of the Destruction of
    the Indies*, by las Casas, 71-6
Buenos Aires, 171
Bunke, Heidi Tamara, 247
Bush, George, and Central
    America, 257
Cabildo, 109
Cabral, Alvares, 40, 42
calaveras, 173
Caliban, 189-92
Canada and Central America, 257
Cape Horn, 4
capitalism, 163
Caribbean, 7, 8
Carranza, Venustiano, 196
Carter Administration and
    Nicaragua, 251-2
cartography in the Conquest, 48-9
Castille, Kingdom of, 41
Castillian language, 77
    in America by Bello, 116-7
Castillo Armas, Colonel, 230
Castro, Fidel, 237-41, 243
    and Nicaragua, 250
Catherwood, Frederick, 135
Catholic Church, 79
Catholic Monarchs, 41
cattle culture, 149
caudillos, 110, 120
Caviedes, Juan del Valle, 93
center-periphery, 163, 212
Central America,
    as seen as Bolívar, 107
Central America: Conflict and
    Peace, Ch 22, 249-60
Central American Confederation,
    110
Chamorro, Violeta, 253, 257

Charles I of Spain, 50, 57
Chilam Balam, book of, 21-2
Chile,
    and Bello, 116
    Antarctic claim, 10
    as seen as Bolívar, 108
    Conquest of, Ch 7, 61-5
Church-state linkage, 82
CIA, and Guatemala, 230
circular time, 17, 24
Civilization and Barbarism,
    Ch 12, 121-132
Classical Maya period, 17-18
Colloquium by Juan del Valle
    Caviedes, 95-6
Colombia, as seen as Bolívar, 107
Colonial boundaries, 80
Colonial centuries, Ch 9, 77, 79-92
Columbus, Christopher, 42-5
    describes the New World, 12
Columbus, New Mexico, 197-198
Comte, Auguste, 161
Conquest of Chile, 61-5
Conquest of Mexico, Ch 6
    art in, 48
    literature of, 49
Conquest of Peru, Ch 7
Conquest, Aztec view of, 67-9
conservatives vs liberals, 110
Constantinople, capture of, 40
Constitutionalists in
    Mexican Revolution, 196
Contadora Group, 256-60
    Objectives Document, 258-60
Contras, in Nicaragua, 252, 255
Cook, Captain James, 135
corbeled arch, 18
Cortés, Hernán, 49-56
Costumbrismo, Ch. 14; 136, 149
creation story, Maya, 19-20
crescents of Middle America, 8
criollos, 102
Cuauhtémoc, 176-7

Cuba, and Spanish-American
    War, 184
Cuban Independence, 185
Cuban Missile Crisis, 240
Cuban Revolution, Ch21, 237-41
    and Mexican Revolution, 237
    cultural aspects of , 239
cultural fragmentation, early
    20C, Ch 19, 211
cultural mestizaje, 83
culture-areas, 4
Cuzco, 30-1, 32, 36, 58
Darío, Rubén, 175
Darwin, Chales, 135-6, 161
    in South America, 112
Defender of the Indians, Ch 8, 63-8
democracy at Independence, 109
Departure, by Gertrudis Gómez
    de Avellaneda, 142
Devil's Tunnel, The,
    by Baldomero Lillo, 165-170
Dias, Bartolome, 40
Díaz, President Porfrio, 163, 193
direct democracy, in Cuba, 239
domino theory in Central
    America, 255
Dulles, Allen, 230
Dulles, John Foster, 230
early 20th Century Movements
    Table 18, 193, 194
Eastern Route, to Spice Islands, 40
Echeverría, Esteban, 121, 125-132,
    165
economic nationalism, 212-3
education in Colonial period, 86
Eisenhower Administraton,
    and Cuba, 239 240
    and Guatemala, 230
El Cid, 39
El Inca Garcilaso, 33-6, 150
El Salvador civil war, 254-60
elites, 163
empty sombreros, Mexican
    Revolution, 198-199

Encounter, art of, 44
    literature of, 44
Enlightenment, 100, 111-2, 161
Enriquillo rebellion, 72-6
Ercilla y Zúñiga, Alonso, 62-5
escapist literature, 211
Esquipulas agreement, 257-8
ethnic relationships, 213-4
Ex-voto, 150
Facundo Quiroga, 123-5
Facundo, by Domingo Sarmiento,
    123
Falklands, 4, 9-11
Falklands/Malvinas Islands, 183
    British take, 1933, 111
Far, Far South, 9-11
Farabundo Martí Front for National
    Liberation, 254-60
Federales in Mexican Revolution,
    195-196
Federales, in Argentina, 121-132
Felipe the interpreter, 60
feminism, 84
feminist literature, 211
Ferdinand of Aragon, King, 41
Ferdinand VII of Spain, 101-2
feudalism, 217-8
first Americans, 15
First Dream, by Sor Juana, 88
Foco, 244
    in Nicaragua, 250
folk art, 150
Frair Gomez' scorpion, 152-4
Frair Vicente, 60-1
France, 171
France, emphasis on "Latin"
    America, 3-4
French intervention in Mexico,
    3, 183-4
FSLN, 250
gamonales, 214-5
Garcilaso de la Vega, 30, 33-6
gaucho poetry, 154-8
glyphs, Maya, 20

Golden Age, 174
golden rod, 22-6
Gómara, Francisco López de, 52
Gómez de Avellaneda, Gertrudis,
      141-5
Gorki, Alexis, 165
grammar, first Spanish, 41
Granada, fall of, 39, 41
Granma (Castro boat), 238, 243
Great Dream,
      by Gabriela Mistral, 220-1
Greco-Roman roots of
      Neoclassicism, 111
Guantanamera, song, 185
Guatemalan Reform/Revolution,
      Ch 20, 229-236
Guatemalan Revolution, and Che
      Guevara, 243
Guerrilla Warfare by Che Guevara,
      209
Guevara, Che, 209, 238, 241-48
Guzmán, Martín Luis, 197-203,
      204
Haitian Independence, 103
Henry the Navigator, 40, 42
Heredia, José María, 136-141
Hernández, José, 154-8
Herrera, Maclovio, 198-200
Hidalgo, Father Miguel, 103, 193
high-density Indigenous, 15
Hispaniola, Island of, 72
History will Absolve Me
      by Fidel Castro, 238
Holy Alliance, 111
How to find your fortune in the
      palaces by Caviedes, 97
Huerta, General Victoriano, 195
Humboldt, Alexander, 112, 135
I have no solitude
      by Gabriela Mistral, 222-3
Iberia, Ch 5, 37
immigration, 171
In a storm, by José M. Heredia,
      138-140

Incas
      art, 32-3
      conquest of, 57-61
      literature, 33-6
Independence norm, 102
Independence of Mexico, 193
Independence, Ch 10, 93-108
Indigenous in Romantic
      period, 136
Indigenous values in Mexican
      Revolution, 196
Indigenous, 3, 7, 13, 214-8
Inter-American Conference, First,
      184, 185
Isaacs, Jorge, 145-8
Isabel of Castille, Queen, 41, 42
Jamaica Letter by Bolívar, 105-
Junín Victory: Bolivar's Anthem
      by José J. Olmedo, 113-5
juntas, and Independence, 101
just war, 75
La Perrichola, 152
Lake Texcoco, 23
Lake Titicaca,22
Lam, Wifredo, 239
land problem, 217-8
Las Casas, Bartolomé, 70-6, 165
latifundium, 214-5
Latin America,
      culture-areas, 4
      definition, Ch. 2, 3-4
Legend of la Tatuana
      by Miguel A. Asturias, 232-6
liberals vs. conservatives, 110
Lillo, Baldomero, 165-170
literature
      in Neoclassical period, 112
      of Encounter, 44
      Maya, 18-22
López, Luis Carlos, 158-60
L'Ouverture, Toussaint, 103
low-density Indigenous, 15
Luján, Micaela, 151-2
machismo, 218

Macuilxochitzin, 27-9
Madero, Francisco, 195, 204
Magellan, Ferdinand, 40
Mahan, Admiral Alfred Thayer,
    184
Maine, USS, 184
Mainland of Caribbean, 7-8
Malinche/Marina, 49, 53-5
Malvinas, 9-11
Malvinas/Falklands Islands, 183
María, by Jorge Isaacs, 145-8
marianismo, 218
Mariátegui, José Carlos, 214-8
Mariel boatlift, 240
Marina/Malinche, 49, 53-5
Martí, Farabundo, 254
Martí, José, 185-9
Martín Fierro, 154-8
Maximillian, Emperor, 184
Maya, 15, 16, 17-22
    and Asturias, 231
Mayor, The,
    by Luis C. López, 159
mestizo, 15-16, 59
Mexican Independence, 193, 103
Mexican Revolution, 173
    and Cuban Revolution, 237
    and Guatemalan, 229
    cultural impact, 212
Mexican-American War, 183
Mexico,
    as seen by Bolívar, 106-7
    Conquest of, Ch 6
Mexico's Grandeur
    by Bernardo Balbuena, 89-92
Miami, as "capital of Latin
    America", 6
Middle America, 7
military
    and democracy, 109-10
    in Latin America, 109-10
mining, 165-170
Mistral, Gabriela, 219-26
Moctezuma, 50, 51-2, 53

Modernismo, Ch. 16, 171-192
monarchy, 113
Monroe Doctrine, 183
Moors, in Spain, 39
Morelos, Father José, 103, 193
Muralism, Mexican, 173
My Little Horseman,
    by José Martí, 188
Nahuatl language, 25
Napoleon III, 183-4
Napoleon, invasion of Iberia, 101
nationalism, 212
nativism, 101
natural regions of Latin America,
    10-11
naturalism, Ch. 15, 161, 164-5
nature, in Romanticism, 133
Nebrija, Antonio, 41
Neoclassicism, Ch 11, 109-120
    and Romanticism, 133
New Laws of the Indies, 1542, 70
Nezahualcoyotl 25-7, 176-7
Niagra Falls, and Heredia, 136-8
Nimrod, 176
Noche Triste (tragic night), 51, 55
Nocturne by Delmira Agustini, 227
Nordomania, 189-92
oil, 212-3
Olmedo, José Joaquín de, 112-115
onomatopoeia, 113
ONUCA, 257-8
ONUSAL, 257
oral tradition, 16
order and progress, 164
Organization of American States
    (OAS), 5
Orinoco River, 7, 9
Ortega, Daniel, 251, 253
Our America, by José Martí, 188-9
Owen, Walter, 154
Palma, Ricardo, 151-4
Panama Canal, 249
Panama, U.S. intervention, 175
Paraguayan Independence, 103

Paraná-Plata river system, 7
Parnassianism, 174
peace process in Central America,
    256-60
Pedro I of Brazil, 104
periphery and center, 163, 212
Perón, Juan, and Echeverría, 126
Pershing, General John, 198
Peru,
    as seen as Bolívar, 108
    Conquest of, Ch 7
physical geography, 5-12
Pizarro, Francisco, 57-61
Plateresque, 81
Platt Amendment, 237
politics, in Romanticism, 134
Poma de Ayala, Guamán, 59-61
Popol Vuh, 19-20
popular art, 173
    in Colonial period, 83
    in the Neoclassical period, 112
    in the Romantic period, 136
population, 6
Portugal, and Europe, 37
Posada, José Guadalupe, 173, 196
Positivism, Ch. 15, 161, 163-4,
    171, 189, 190
Positivists in Mexico, 193
post-modernist literature, 211
Power structure in colonial
    centuries, 80
pre-Columbian literature, 16-22
PRI (Party of the Revolutionary
    Institutions), 204-205
Princess, The,
    by Rubén Darío, 180-2
Privileges of the Poor
    by Juan Caviedes, 96-7
Protest in Colonial years, 93
protest literature, 211
Puerto Rico, and Spanish-American
    War, 184
Punitive Expedition, 198
Quechua, 30-1, 33, 36, 59

Queen Mab, 178-80
Quetzalcoatl, 24, 30, 48, 49-50
Quiché, 19
Quipu, 32
railways, 163
Reagan Administration, and
    Nicaragua, 252
Realism, Ch. 15, 161, 164-5
Reconquest, the, 39, 41
    and Conquest, 77, 79
Redondilla, by Sor Juana, 84-5
regionalism, 149
Renaissance, 33, 39, 62, 81
Reply to Sor Filotea,
    by Sor Juana 85-8
republicanism, in Independence
    period, 113
Requirement, the, 60-1
retablos, 82
rimland of Caribbean, 7-8
Rivera, Diego, 196
rivers of Latin America, 6-7
Rocking, by Gabriela Mistral, 220
Rodó, José Enrique, 189-92
Romance, by Gertrudis Gómez de
    Avellaneda, 142-4
Romanticism, Ch 13, 133
Roosevelt, Theodore, 175-8
Rosas, Juan Manuel, 121, 123, 154
Royal Commentaries of the Incas,
    33-6
San Martín, José de, 102
Sandinista Front for National
    Liberation, 250
Sandino, Agusto C., 249
Santiago, 39
Sarmiento, Domingo F. , 121,
    123-5, 154
Scorpion of Fray Gomez, 152-4
Seven Essays on Interpretation of
    Peruvian Reality, 214-8
Shakespeare, 189-92
Simple Verses, by José Martí, 186

Slaughterhouse, The
by Echeverría, 126-132
slavery, 71, 77. 173
Sleepless One
by Gabriela Mistral, 224-6
smallpox, in Conquest, 48
Social Darwinism, 161, 184, 213
Somoza Jr., Anastasio, 250
Somoza Sr., Anastasio, 250
Sonatina, by Rubén Darío, 180-2
Sonnets of Death
by Gabriela Mistral, 221-2
Sor Juana, 83-8
South America, 8-9
South Georgia Island, 10
South Pole, 4, 1-10
Soviet Union,
and Central America, 249, 251
Spain, and Europe, 37
Spanish crown, 79
Spanish language, 77
Spanish-American War, 175, 237
Spencerianism, 161, 184, 213
Spinster Girls,
by Luis C.López159-160
state-centered approach, 5
stela, 22
Suárez, Inés de, 62
surrealism, 231
swan, Modernist symbol, 175
tapestry metaphor, 11
Tarik, 39
temperate area, 6
Tempest, The, by Shakespeare,
189-92
Tenochtitlán, 23-4
fall of, 68-9
terraces, 31
Texcoco, Lake, 23, 25
Tierra del Fuego, 4, 13
To Cuba's Star
by José Heredia, 140-1
To him, by Gertrudis Gómez de
Avellaneda, 144-5

To my wife, by José Heredia, 138
Tolstoy, Leo, 176-7
Tooth of Parnassus by Caviedes,
95-7
Tordesillas, Line of, 43
tradición, 151-4
travel painting in Romantic period,
135-6
trepanning, 31-32
tumi, 31, 36
Tupac Amaru I, 98
Tupac Amaru II, 97-100
Tupamaro guerrillas, Uruguay, 98
types, in Romanticism, 133
U.S., emergence, Ch. 17, 183
U.S., attitudes towards, 174-7, 183
Ubico, Jorge, 229
UN peacekeeping, 257-60
Unitarians, in Argentina, 121-132
United Fruit Company, 230
United Kingdom, in Antarctica, 10
Valdivia, Pedro de, 62-3
Valley of Anáhuac, 23
Velásquez, Diego, 49, 50
vertical climates, 9
Viceroyalties, 80
Vietnam, 245, 255
Villa, Pancho, 197-203, 204
Visigoths, 39
votive offerings, 150
war of the flowers (Aztec), 23-4, 48
warfare, Spanish in Conquest, 48
waves of population, 16
Whitman, Walt, 175-6
Wilson, Woodrow, 198
Wings by Delmira Agustini, 226-7
women, changing role, 218-9
Your love
by Delmira Agustini, 227-8
Zapata, Emiliano, 195
Zola, Emile, 165

About the author

Dr Child was born of American parents in Buenos Aires, Argentina, and lived in South America for 18 years before coming to the United States to attend Yale University. Following graduation from Yale he entered the U.S. Army, and served for 20 years as an Army Latin American Specialist until his retirement as a lieutenant colonel. In 1982 he joined the Department of Language and Foreign Studies, where he teaches a variety of courses (in both English and Spanish) dealing with translation and Latin American studies, with an emphasis on popular culture.

Dr. Jack Child by Daniel Silver

His research has focused on cultural studies and conflict resolution in Latin America. He has received several grants for research dealing with negotiations in Antarctica and the Falklands/Malvinas, and peace-keeping and confidence-building measures in Central and South America. His interest in high latitudes has taken him on twelve trips as staff lecturer and guide aboard expedition cruise vessels to Antarctica and sub-Antarctic islands, including South Georgia and the Malvinas/ Falklands. He has published numerous articles and books on all these research areas, including:

Miniature Messages: The Semiotics and Politics of Latin American Postage Stamps. (Under contract, Duke University Press.).

Introduction to Latin American Literature: a Bilingual Anthology. (with software). Lanham: UPA, 1994.

The Central American Peace Process, 1983-1991: Sheathing Swords, Building Confidence. Boulder: Lynne Rienner, 1992.

Introduction to Spanish Translation (with software). Lanham: UPA, 1992.

Antarctica and South American Geopolitics: Frozen Lebensraum. New York: Praeger, 1988.

Quarrels Among Neighbors: Geopolitics and Conflict in South America. NY: Praeger, 1985.

Unequal Alliance: The Inter-American Military System, Westview, 1980.